White Christian Privilege

White Christian Privilege

THE ILLUSION OF RELIGIOUS EQUALITY IN AMERICA

Khyati Y. Joshi

NEW YORK UNIVERSITY PRESS

New York

NEW YORK UNIVERSITY PRESS
New York
www.nyupress.org

References to Internet websites (URLs) were accurate at the time of writing. Neither the author nor New York University Press is responsible for URLs that may have expired or changed since the manuscript was prepared.

Library of Congress Cataloging-in-Publication Data
Names: Joshi, Khyati Y., 1970– author.
Title: White Christian privilege : the illusion of religious equality in America / Khyati Y. Joshi.
Description: New York : New York University Press, 2020. | Includes bibliographical references and index.
Identifiers: LCCN 2019041467 | ISBN 9781479840236 (cloth) | ISBN 9781479835119 (ebook) | ISBN 9781479836468 (ebook)
Subjects: LCSH: Christianity—United States. | Religious discrimination—United States. | Christianity and other religions—United States.
Classification: LCC BR526 .J67 2020 | DDC 305.6/773—dc23
LC record available at https://lccn.loc.gov/2019041467

New York University Press books are printed on acid-free paper, and their binding materials are chosen for strength and durability. We strive to use environmentally responsible suppliers and materials to the greatest extent possible in publishing our books.

Manufactured in the United States of America

Also available as an ebook

for Kedhar Wallace Bartlett

may this book help us all build
a more perfect union for you

Contents

Introduction

A pervasive *Christian privilege* prevails in the United States today. The United States is recognized as the most religiously diverse country in the world; yet, at the same time, Christianity—particularly Protestantism—has been integral to US national identity. Christian beliefs, norms, and practices, and indeed, a Christian way of looking at the world, infuse our society, enjoying countless legal, structural, and cultural supports whose roots reach back to the arrival of Europeans and the founding of the country. Protestant perspectives have become the "truths" at the bedrock of American society. Christianity dominates by setting the tone and establishing the rules and assumptions about who belongs or does not belong, about what is acceptable and not acceptable in public discourse. It is embedded in our institutions and dictates the structure of our weekend, from Sunday closings for the Christian Sabbath to alcohol sales laws. As a result, the "freedom of religion" enshrined in the pages of the Constitution does not always translate into everyday life. Christian prayer often opens public meetings and graduations all over the US, and the US Congress and state legislatures have always employed chaplains. Christianity has become bound up with US nationalism, with the inscription "In God We Trust" on our currency and our pledge to a nation "under God." This Christian privilege, which undergirds our country's institutions and cultural practices, offers advantages to Christians as they lead their lives, and disadvantages for members of minority religious groups.

This book explains how the effects of this privilege are acted out in our society and provides a historical and contemporary overview of how Christian privilege was created and why it has persisted. It demonstrates that Christian privilege in the United States has always been entangled with notions of White supremacy. Indeed, throughout US history, *Christian, English, free,* and *White* have been superimposed to form mutually supporting advantages based on the co-construction of religion, race, and national origin. These advantages—and corresponding disadvantages, for religious and racial minorities as well as for the nonreligious—persist at both the institutional and individual levels of society, and stand in the way of fulfilment of the promises of equality that were made in the nation's founding documents and more recent laws. Yet, unlike racism, gender discrimination, or homophobia, Christian privilege often flies under the radar. It is so ingrained in our societal dynamics, it continues to be taken as "normal." By shining a light on Christian privilege and its entwinement with White privilege, this book aims to equip readers with tools and ideas regarding how they can recognize it operating in our society and foster a more equitable environment for all.

Today's religious and racial diversity requires that we do far more than just appreciate and embrace it or consider the ways individual experiences shape us. A social justice approach, in which we create change and mitigate bias, requires us first to recognize present circumstances as the product of history—of long and deeply-ingrained patterns and structures of advantage and disadvantage. This book sets out to examine the cultural, institutional, and legal infrastructure on which the experiences of Christians and religious minorities today have been built. Ultimately, it offers a historically informed road map of how Christian privilege developed and has influenced the American experiment from colonial times to the present. Drawing on interviews and personal narratives, it illuminates the impact of White Christian privilege in our workplaces, classrooms, and broader society, and offers strategies to expose and overcome its dynamics.

The book takes a hard look at three specific, related, and mutually supporting phenomena in the US: Christian privilege, Christian normativity, and Christian hegemony. *Christian privilege* is experienced at the individual level, in the everyday; it is manifest in unearned advantages that Christians receive and in the corresponding disadvantages religious minorities, atheists, and agnostics must deal with on an everyday basis. Many people think about bias and discrimination as dynamics that happen between two people. It can be easy to recognize a religious slur like "kike" or "dothead" as bias. We are conditioned to see bias most easily at the individual and interpersonal level, which makes it easy to think that if we all were to treat people with respect and kindness, bias would stop being a problem.

But there's far more to it than individual cruelty. At the level of our society and culture, Christian privilege is structural. It has afforded the Christian majority the historic and contemporary power to shape social norms. This *Christian normativity* makes Christian values intrinsic to our national identity, conveys the status of truth and rightness on Christian culture, and makes Christian language and metaphors and their underlying theology the national standard. Christian normativity imbues Christianity with a unique power, situating it as ordinary and expected. As a result, atheists and religious minorities who embrace different practices, belief systems, and world views are disadvantaged relative to their Christian peers.[1] Very real everyday consequences result from a situation in which the Christian way of doing something comes to be understood as the normal way of living.

Consciously or unconsciously, we may perceive practices outside the Christian norm as exotic or illegitimate. "God," for example, is most often depicted in nonreligious settings, in line with Christian imaginings, as an old White man with a flowing beard. We might also see Christian figures like Jesus and the Virgin Mary representing the divine. Yet it is exceedingly unlikely that in a setting that is not explicitly Hindu, for example, we will encounter a representation of "God" as the Hindu God Krishna, with his blue skin, or as the four-armed Saraswati, Goddess of knowledge, wisdom and learning, or as other Hindu Gods with their colorful clothing and multiarmed bodies. Christianity's images of God are perceived as "normal" images of God because of Christianity's cultural sway. The God images of other faiths may be regarded as idols—"weird" or cultic in comparison.

It is impossible to overestimate the ways Christian normativity influences the dialogue that goes on in America's public square—from the traditional news media to the 24-hour churn of online social media. In fact, it is so pervasive, and often so subtle, that we often may not notice it. While Christianity makes frequent appearances in the media, it appears even more often in the subtext—the impressions implicit in the words and images selected. Consider, for example, the images and associations that come into your mind when you read the word "terrorism." At a meta level, the institutions and legal standards established in the United States over the past 400 years reflect the accretion of Christian privilege and Christian normativity into an infrastructure of Christian hegemony. *Hegemony* refers to a society's unacknowledged and/ or unconscious adherence to a dominant worldview. Hegemonic ideologies are perpetuated through the cultural norms, policies, and practices which set those ideologies up as "business as usual." *Christian hegemony* thus refers to the predominance and endorsement at the national level of Christian observances, beliefs, scriptures, and manners of worship.[2] Christianity is embedded in our national laws, mores, and expectations as "regimes of truth," and endures there with legal and social power that has spanned the length, breadth, and entire history of the country.[3]

Christian Privilege and White Supremacy

Any discussion of religion in the US that does not explore its intersections with race and racism is incomplete. This book takes an *intersectional* approach, not only grappling with Christian privilege as a single phenomenon, but also attending to the way it interacts with other structures of social, economic, and legal privilege. The advantages Christians receive are not experienced in isolation; every Christian, and every religious minority, also holds other social identities. Asian, Black, Hispanic, and Middle-Eastern Christians thus experience Christianity in America differently from the way White Christians do. Their various origins and histories in the US have given these groups different experiences. While they share many of the advantages of being Christian in America, those advantages may be harder to recognize or acknowledge, especially because of the racial discrimination and violence some groups have also faced. In this respect, their Christianity is often "othered," just as racial minorities as such are "othered." They may be targets of violence, a problem that Black churches, for example, have faced throughout history and continue to face. In some cases, it can be difficult for individuals to distinguish religious identity from cultural identity. The identities of Filipino Catholics, Black Protestants, and others, for example, interweave religion and culture in ways that make them virtually impossible to separate. This intimate connection between an advantaged identity (Christian) and a disadvantaged identity (racial minority) can make it difficult for Christians of color to recognize and acknowledge the advantages they do possess.

White Christian supremacy in America is the product of a centuries-long project in which notions of White racial superiority and Christian religious superiority have augmented and magnified each other. White Christian supremacy is an ideology that developed before the European "Age of Discovery" and European colonization of Africa, Arabia, Asia, Oceania, and the Americas. Born from theologies that positioned White Christians at the top of a global social and economic order, White Christian supremacy looked to the Bible for rationales that supported the subjugation and genocide of Indigenous peoples, Black slavery, and a view of Asians as threatening, exotic, and heathen.[4]

These principles coalesced in a series of fifteenth-century Papal Bulls (edicts) that permitted the Portuguese monarchy to seize West Africa by deeming any land not inhabited by Christians as available to be "discovered," claimed, and exploited by Christian rulers, and permitting the enslavement of Muslims, pagans, and other "unbelievers." This "Doctrine of Discovery" became the basis of all European claims in the Americas as well as the foundation for the United States' western expansion.[5] Christianity thus permeated colonial enterprises around the world, both before and after the colonization of North America. In all of these projects, non-Christians were denied the rights to land, sovereignty, and self-determination enjoyed by Christians.

In what would become the United States, White Christian supremacy was developed, rationalized, and spread by theologians, philosophers, and scientists. At the time of the nation's founding, most of its major universities were affiliated with the church, from Puritan Harvard and Calvinist Yale to Anglican Columbia, Presbyterian Princeton, and Baptist Brown. "Scholarship" in these institutions of higher learning helped to create and perpetuate White Christian supremacy. By reproducing and amplifying scientific theories of racial hierarchy and religious destiny, these institutions promoted theologies that rationalized land theft from native non-Christians and enslavement of Black non-Christians.[6] Far from an anomaly in the theological discipline, Whiteness has been a dominant theological outlook by which non-White, non-Christian persons have been assessed along a hierarchy of humanity. The conquest of the US was a colonial endeavor that combined taking land with spreading the gospel of Christ. In the words of Rev. Dr. Martin Luther King, Jr., "Our nation was born in genocide. . . . Moreover, we elevated that tragic experience into a noble crusade."[7]

Over the centuries, Christianity has justified race-based segregation of Whites and Blacks within the same Protestant denominations, be they Baptists or Methodists or Pentecostals. In the present day, Christian normativity perpetuates the societal exclusion of Buddhists, Hindus, Muslims, and Sikhs through public resistance to mosques, synagogues, temples, and gurdwaras being built in their neighborhoods, among other means.[8] The same resistance to sharing space with people of color that characterized segregation is reflected in the rejection of sharing public space with religious minorities. Both are born of the desire not to see, touch, or encounter those who are different. Today's version directs a "NIMBY" (not in my backyard) attitude toward entire religious communities.

The Immigration Reform Act of 1965 opened the nation's doors to immigrants of a variety of faiths who had not been permitted to enter the country for many decades. In the period since then, many members of religious minorities have arrived who trace their heritage to Asia, Africa, and the Arab world. To understand their religious experiences, we must also consider their racial minority status. My experience of growing up Hindu in the South, for example, cannot be separated from my experience of growing up brown.

Examining our history and the present day, we can see legal, historical, and everyday moments that illustrate the persistent connection and conflation of race and religion. For example, ideas of Black inferiority during slavery drew on not only notions of racial hierarchy but also on the idea that as non-Christians, Africans were depraved and barbaric. More recently, religion has become a powerful method of classifying the "enemy" or "other" in national life, in ways that affect primarily non-Christian people of color. Muslims, for example, have become particularly demonized in the US. The vicious acts of a miniscule handful of their co-religionists shaped their image in popular culture long before the events of September 11, 2001. Since that date, narratives around "terrorism" and the "war on terror" continue to associate an entire global religion, Islam, with violent, nihilistic movements. Looking more closely at many incidents, we discover that anti-Muslim bias is manifested racially. When Islam is associated with particular physical characteristics—that is, when it is racialized— South Asian Americans like me find ourselves being "randomly" selected for heightened screening at the airport because we look like we might be Muslim. South Asian American Sikhs, Hindus, and Christians, and even Hispanics have been targets of post-9/11 backlash attacks—suffering injury, and sometimes death, because of their brown skin, beards, clothing, or turbans. Their racial and cultural markers are associated with Islam in the popular mind, even though they are not Muslim.

Critical Conversations

Despite contemporary rhetoric predicting the "decline of White Christian America,"[9] the power of Whiteness and Christianity is deeply dyed in the nation's wool, and omnipresent in American rules and structures. Indeed, those three terms—"White," "Christian," and "American"—have been used interchangeably so often that in many contexts, including in the lexicon of non-White, non-Christian immigrant communities, they remain synonyms for one another. When members of White Christian America react defensively against the nation's growing diversity, it is because they fail to understand the hegemony on which their power is built and to see how normative and privileged their faith and their race still are. They feel they are "losing" and need to fight to preserve their vision of a White Christian America, not realizing how the legal and social deck is still stacked dramatically in their favor. They see existential threats in issues like Sharia law or the "War on Christmas" that are trivial in comparison with the benefits Christians enjoy.

This is not to say that Christian people of faith do not face hostility in certain quarters. There is discrimination against and even hostility toward religion in general from some quarters. Some popular and academic authors have railed against Christianity in particular, and we can find bias against religion more generally in higher education and social justice or progressive circles. Religion is the last topic some of my progressive colleagues in ethnic and Asian American studies want to discuss. While some scholars are comfortable teaching about the sociocultural aspects of religion, they nevertheless keep their distance from matters of faith.[10]

Unfortunately, the bias against religion in ethnic studies is a longstanding tradition.[11] In some cases, it is the product of scholars' own unease with religion; in others it springs from the perception of religion as mere superstition and Karl Marx' influential trivialization of religion as the opiate of the masses. Meanwhile, the study of religion and its role in society and individuals' lives is mostly relegated to departments of religion and seminaries. In those spaces, on the other hand, many of my colleagues are uneasy discussing race and racism. This untenable dichotomy—ethnic studies' unease with religion, and religious studies' unease with race—makes integrative works like this one difficult, but all the more necessary.

Many social justice activists are likewise uncomfortable talking about faith. Some have left organized religion because of its role in the oppression of marginalized communities; others are unable to find congruencies between religious participation and political progressivism. People who are ready to talk about homophobia, classism, or racism are ill at ease including religious discrimination in the conversation. The anti-religious perspective of certain scholars and progressives can—sometimes legitimately—come across as bias against Christianity.[12]

Even if some Christians may have personally faced real obstacles, criticism, or discrimination related to their faith, such experiences do not negate the power of Christian privilege. This book does not deny the existence of anti-Christian bias; rather, it aims to show that White Christian norms nonetheless remain entrenched in our institutions, laws, and civic culture in ways that set up an uneven playing field in everyday public, social, and work life to the disadvantage of many religious minorities. Moreover, none of the strategies presented here to ameliorate this problem aim to diminish Christianity, but rather to ensure equal opportunity for all religious traditions and for those who embrace no religion.

Religious Oppression Today

There are many different types of *religious oppression* in our society, of which the most well-known are probably antisemitism and the anti-Muslim sentiment sometimes referred to as "Islamophobia." Atheists, agnostics, practitioners of Native Americans traditions, Buddhists, Muslims, Hindus, Sikhs, Jains, and others also frequently face religious oppression in various forms. From the Jew whose synagogue was vandalized to the Sikh man killed in a post-9/11 "backlash" attack, to the Muslim woman who doesn't get a job because she wears a hijab, religious oppression is present wherever we find privilege: in legal policies and structures, in social designs and cultural practices, and at the level of individual discrimination.[13]

Long before September 11, 2001, and even more so since then, discussions about terrorism and depictions of terrorists have tended to invoke Islam and Muslim Americans—even though, both in the US and globally, most terrorists are not Muslim.[14] Consider the experience of a young Muslim man growing up in Metro Atlanta in the 1980s and 1990s. Salim was a second-generation Indian American Muslim whose religious identity was a source of conflict for him. In addition to disparaging remarks about Muslims from peers, he dealt with anti-Muslim sentiment— disguised as comedy—from teachers. His ninth grade homeroom teacher "always joked" and said to him: "'You don't have a bomb in that backpack, [do you]?' And he would duck and make a big joke in front of all the other kids. . . . We all kind of laughed and made a big joke out of it but it made me really uncomfortable."[15] For Salim, his teacher's statements and actions legitimized the association of Islam with terrorism in the eyes of an entire classroom; Salim felt vilified by a popular authority figure. His teacher was magnifying a contemporary American cultural perception, of Muslims as terrorists, and placing his own student in that frame in front of all of his peers. Salim's experience took place long before 9/11, in the early 1990s, during the time of the First Gulf War. Unfortunately, even today students who are Muslim or perceived as Muslim (such as South Asian Americans of various religious affiliations) confront harassment, discrimination, and assaults in school, college, and beyond.[16]

The association between terrorism and Islam, and between Islam and Arabs, became the subtext of many other public disputes, like the debate in 2015 and 2016 over the admission of Syrian war refugees to the United States. In the absence of any evidence connecting Syrian refugees with any anti-American terror plot, and in willful ignorance of the 14-step security vetting refugees receive, state governors and presidential candidates nevertheless assumed a connection. The winning candidate in the 2016 presidential contest promised a "Muslim Ban"[17] and ultimately saw the executive order he signed in fulfilment of that promise upheld by the US Supreme Court. By contrast, between 2012 and 2018, White Christian men murdered three Muslim college students in Chapel Hill, North Carolina, shot up a synagogue in Pittsburgh, a gurdwara in Wisconsin, a church in South Carolina, and a concert in Arizona, and yet the words "terrorist" or "terrorism" were rarely used by the media or the politicians to describe these men or their actions.[18] Nor were there many references to the perpetrators' race or religion. By contrast, when the media identifies an act as "terrorist," attention is given to the perpetrators' national and ethnic origins and religion.[19]

A Social Justice Approach

This book takes a social justice approach to religion in American society. This approach sets out to acknowledge, explore, and value religious diversity; to recognize the unequal treatment of specific religions in our society; and to identify solutions that can increase equity and justice for all. Examining the numerous historical moments in which Christianity has been used to establish and maintain political, social and cultural dominance leads us to recognize the long presence of White Christian supremacy in the US. We can use these historical legacies to analyze contemporary religious oppression in our country and show how society often ignores or trivializes the experiences of religious minorities and atheists. This lens enables us to understand how Protestant Christianity interacts with Whiteness and national identity and the ways religious groups are admitted to or denied access to citizenship, housing, schooling, legal protections, and political representation. It also allows us to see how Christianity has been used to maintain, justify, and reproduce patterns of domination and subordination—even as many Christian individuals and communities have been part of the fight against oppression.

Often, topics related to religion are discussed through the lens of *pluralism*, which acknowledges religious diversity in the US and how various faiths are part of the national landscape. A *social justice* approach goes further. It illuminates the systemic inequalities faced by religious minorities and the nonreligious and the underlying White Christian supremacist laws and culture that produced those inequalities. Thus it considers not just diversity, but the structural inequities that generate social hierarchies. White Christians' access to social power, in the form of privilege and normativity, sets them apart from religious minorities and atheists to whom those privileges are denied. Social justice thinking also takes an *intersectional* approach, acknowledging that various religious minority communities are racial minorities also, and taking into account dynamics of class, gender, sexual orientation, and other identities that shape individual and collective experiences. Social justice is a process: it engages in analysis of the contradictions in US history, between aspirations to religious pluralism and the recurring and resurging Christian hegemony that often undermines those aspirations. Social justice is also a goal: we approach and examine legal structures and historical events not just to understand them—though that is an important first step—but to identify the ways in which we can create more just structures to ameliorate historic injustice. Acknowledging how and why religious minorities suffer structural disadvantages helps us to find ways to create a society that takes all kinds of diversities into account and affords opportunities for all kinds of people to lead fulfilling lives.

A social justice approach focuses beyond individual experiences to recognize the structural dynamics of both advantage and disadvantage. More succinctly, examining society with a social justice mindset means acknowledging that for every "down," there must be an "up." To truly understand dynamics of oppression, we have to see the "up": the advantaged group or identity. It took decades for the scholarship and popular dialogue on racism to go beyond looking at how Blacks and others are targeted for racial discrimination, and to focus on Whiteness and White privilege—the "built-in" advantages that members of the nation's historic majority enjoy whether they want them or not. Similarly, in matters of sexism, we have long focused on the challenges women face rather on than the structural advantages men enjoy as a result of history and culture. Along similar lines, to effectively unpack and understand religious bias and discrimination in America, we must understand that the "down"—discrimination against US religious minorities—has a corresponding "up"—the rules of society that have been constructed to benefit Christians.

A social justice approach is also reflective, and looks past easy answers. It asks, for example, why we so rarely recognize the religious facet of oppression against religious minorities who are also people of color. We recognize antisemitism as religious oppression, in part because of its central role in twentieth-century history but also in large part because most American Jews are now considered White; as a result, when they are targeted for discrimination, we see that it is directed at their religious identity. By contrast, headlines about violence against Sikh men, or about the "dotbuster" attacks on New Jersey Hindus in the 1980s, often describe "racial violence." For so many of the reasons described in this book, race is allowed to eclipse what would otherwise be seen as a *religious* attack. Recognizing intersectionality, and situating the disadvantages that racial and religious minorities face in the context of the structural advantages Christians possess, will let us delve into deeper truths.

Contemporary American Religious Diversity

The story of American religious diversity is not a new one. The religions with the longest history on this continent are Native American, but Islam, native African beliefs, and other traditions have coexisted with Christianity on these shores for centuries. The nation grew more diverse with waves of immigration in the nineteenth and early twentieth centuries, which brought Catholics, Jews, Orthodox Christians, and members of other faiths, including Sikhs and Buddhists.

However, demographic changes over the past half century have made it particularly urgent to understand the impact of White

Christian privilege and envision approaches to respond to it. The United States has been experiencing increases in the number and diversity of religious minorities that are unprecedented. Since 1965, when immigration reforms reopened the nation's doors to immigrants from beyond northern Europe, the country has experienced a rapid flourishing of racial, ethnic, and religious diversity. We have had a larger-than-ever influx of followers of the Baha'i faith, Buddhism, Hinduism, Jainism, Islam, Sikhism, Zoroastrianism, and more. These religious groups are building communities and houses of worship in places that have never seen anything like them. Contemporary workplaces, classrooms, and the very "public square" of American social and political dialogue are more religiously diverse than they have ever been, and are growing more so.[20]

How many followers of these faiths are in the US? Answering this question is more difficult than accessing almost any other type of demographic data, such as race, national origin, or gender, because the US Census—the most comprehensive count of American residents—does not collect information on religious self-identification.[21] We therefore rely mostly on non-governmental surveys that collect data on religion based on voluntary responses as well as on self-reporting from organized religious congregations. But since Buddhist, Hindu, Muslim, Sikh, and Native American religious practices are not necessarily congregational or documented by official listings, it becomes all the more difficult to gather demographic data on the numbers of their adherents. Many of these religions' beliefs and practices are individual and highly personal; often, worship will be done at home and through individual actions and choices rather than in a group setting. Thus, individuals may or may not affiliate with houses of worship, and the congregational bias of surveys and scholarship likely results in undercounts of these populations.

TABLE I.1. Current US Religious Affiliation

Group	Pew[22] 327,167,434	PRRI[23] 322,762,018	Other Sources
Unaffiliated, who might identify as Secular, Atheists or Agnostics	26% 85.1 million	24% 77.5 million	
Buddhist	.07%[24] 2.3 million	1% 2.49 million	
Christian	65% 212.7 million	67%[25] 216.3 million	
Hindu	1% 3.3 million	1% 3.2 million	
Jewish	2% 6.6 million	2% 6.4 million	7.5 Million (Steinhardt Social Science Institute, 2019)
Muslim	3.45 million[26]	1% 3.2 million	
Native American spiritualities			
Sikh	200,000[27]		500,000 (Sikh Coalition)[28]

Overall, a substantial majority of Americans today are still Christian, a cohort that includes a growing proportion of Black and Hispanic Christians. At the same time, the Pew Research Forum reported in 2012 that White Protestants are no longer a religious majority in the US, a status they held for more than two centuries. The Pew Research Center in 2015 and the Public Religion Research Institute (PRRI) in 2016 found that 43% of Americans identify as White and Christian, and 30% as White and specifically Protestant. While still the largest single racial/religious cohort by far, this is a substantial change since 1976, when roughly eight in ten (81%) Americans identified as White and Christian, and a clear majority (55%) were White Protestants. The decline in the number of people identifying as Christian is attributable to both the increasing religious diversity in the country and the growing numbers of people who identify as religiously unaffiliated. Minority religions are growing, but still represent fewer than one in ten Americans: Jewish Americans constitute 2% of the public while Muslims, Buddhists, and Hindus each make up about 1% of the US population.[29] Among racial groups, Asian Pacific Americans have a significantly different religious profile and are much more likely to be non-Christians.

When we speak of "religion," we must remember that it is not merely a category—a checkbox on a form, a line of one's personal biography, or an aggregation of thousands or millions of people. Religion has many functions, and is lived by each person in unique and individual ways. Religion is a belief system that helps adherents to make sense of this world and beyond. Religion (including the identity of "nonreligious") crosscuts every other identity category. Sometimes religious groups function like ethnicities, linking people by a common place of origin (real or imagined), or a common language; in other cases, they do not. Either way, religion is a source of personal identity, and of connection to some larger group identity; it may be a vehicle for membership, affiliation, and solidarity. It is a common source of identity and community for immigrant groups. Religion may also be the basis for exclusion, competition, adversarial status, discrimination, or exploitation.

A Hierarchy of Christian Denominations

Members of White Protestant denominations tend to enjoy Christian privilege at its most expansive, while Christian communities of color may enjoy it in different and more constrained ways. Racism has inhibited the social power of African American, Native American, Asian American, and Latinx churches.

In addition to understanding how identities like race, gender, and sexual orientation affect experiences of Christian privilege, it is important to recognize that there are numerous Christian denominations and that a hierarchy or continuum of Christian privilege has been manifest among them. In colonial America and the early United States, for example, discrimination against Christians whose theology was at odds with Protestantism, including Anabaptist Christians (such as the Amish and Mennonites), Mormons (adherents of the Church of Jesus Christ of Latter Day Saints), Quakers, Seventh-Day Adventists, Jehovah's Witnesses, and believers in Christian Science, placed those Christians in a relatively disadvantaged position vis-à-vis the mainstream Protestant majority. Indeed, the question of whether these groups were "Christian" was—and to some degree remains—contested. For other Christian groups, particularly Catholics but also adherents of the many eastern Orthodox traditions, it was their immigration in large numbers and the resulting sense of insecurity among White American Protestants that led to religious discrimination and positioned these non-Protestants as lower in the social hierarchy.

The Path Forward

As long as we treat our foundational ideals of freedom of religion and "all men are created equal" as if they are realities rather than aspirations, the dominance of Protestant Christianity and Whiteness over the political and social institutions of the United States will remain invisible.

The fact that religious freedom is nominally ensconced in the First Amendment, and is applied to the states by the Fourteenth, does not mean that we have religious equality. This book debunks the fallacy of American religious freedom and offers ways to acknowledge the harder truth of White Christian supremacy, in hopes of helping to create a society with institutions and cultural practices in which all can more equitably coexist. It does so by listening to the voices and highlighting the experiences of members of religious minorities in our diverse nation, and by placing early twenty-first-century American politics and society in a long historical context. By considering the changes in thought and approach that could direct us toward a more just coexistence, this book aims to amplify the dialogue on national identity and put forward a social justice approach to religion in the US that may finally unshackle us from the legacies described in the next few chapters.

This book is not an exercise in political correctness. Its aim is to illuminate how Christianity in the US has served the needs of the dominant religious, ethnic, racialized majorities with historically greater access to institutional and cultural power than other groups. This exploration challenges deeply held myths and beliefs about American religious freedom and opportunity. Open and honest conversations are messy and difficult, but they are necessary if we are to advance as a nation. US society is highly segregated, not only by race and religion but also by socioeconomic class and political outlook; most of us socialize with others who not only look like us but also think like us.[30] Casual conversations with those not in our in-group around religion often become contentious, leaving many feeling uncomfortable.

In many parts of our society, difference is seen as a deficit and dialogue as weakness; diversity, even when touted as a benefit, is given mere lip service. But in order to address the inequalities in our midst, we have to get comfortable with being uncomfortable. This conversation will not be easy, but it is essential. This book seeks to offer a guide toward that introspection and to grapple maturely with the challenges and paradoxes of White Christian supremacy in the United States.

1

Christianity and American National Identity

In 2004, the editors of *Khabar*, a South Asian American monthly magazine, asked Georgia's then-Governor Sonny Perdue about his support for displaying the Ten Commandments on government property, and how he would feel about a display of verses from the *Bhagavad Gita* or the Holy *Quran* or other religions' scriptures. Perdue responded: "Well, I think the Ten Commandments transcends its mere religious or historical significance. It's also principle-centered in that way."[1] He continued: "The Ten Commandments form that Judeo-Christian effort that led to the founding of America by the pilgrims on the idea of religious freedom. That has a stronger historical significance from my perspective." When asked specifically whether the presence of the Ten Commandments on government property would be an imposition of Christianity (and therefore unconstitutional), Purdue replied: "I don't think it's trying to impose Christianity. That would be wrong. That's the reason I began my statement saying that the Ten Commandments is a principle-centered basis that guides our moral lives. I don't view it strictly as a spiritual document that you have to adhere to, to be accepted in this country. That's the distinction I make."[2]

The Ten Commandments are literally the beginning verses of the twentieth chapter of the Book of Exodus, regarded as holy Scripture by Christians and Jews. Yet Purdue described them as "transcend[ing] . . . mere religious or historical significance," and denied that the Ten Commandments are a religion-specific scripture rather than "a principle-centered basis that guides our

[American] moral lives." In so doing, he illustrated the powerful effect of *Christian normativity*. Christianity's normative power in US culture reflects the assumption by Christians that their own belief system is universal, or ought to be rendered universal without question or critique. By situating his own religion as a reference point for all, Purdue rationalized government support for the promulgation of Christian teachings as non-discriminatory.

Christian privilege allows Americans to take for granted the elevation of their religion over other faiths. Yet the privilege that American Christians enjoy, notwithstanding popular but unfulfilled ideals like "freedom of religion" and "separation of church and state," results in the oppression of members of religious minorities and atheists. Christianity's normative power is as strong as ever. Moreover, the Christian norm often functions in tandem with the racial normativity of Whiteness to generate structures and ideas of White Christian supremacy, such that Whiteness and Christianity are read as American, while everything else appears foreign.

Norms do not usually "hit you over the head." Their effects are subtle, influencing unexpressed distinctions between usual and unusual, local and foreign, "us" and "them." A norm can be expressed in violence or expressions of prejudice, but more often it exists simply as one group's ideas or characteristics coming to be understood as universal, true, and ordinary. That is what we saw in Governor Purdue's belief that a text from the Bible could be understood not as a religious document but rather as a secular, "principle-centered basis that guides our moral lives."

Christian privilege runs so deep that a Christian does not have to do anything to benefit from its advantages. Christian privilege is possessed by Christians, whether or not they are aware of it. No conscious thought or effort is required. Like Purdue, they can simply *know* that their faith and their worldview are correct. "Business as usual" maintains the privileged status of their beliefs and understandings. Indeed, Christian privilege benefits not only people who identify with Christianity or consider themselves "religious," but even people raised as Christians who might not even label themselves that way today. They enjoy the benefits of Christian privilege, whether they want it or not and whether they know it or not.

Nothing "Civil" About It

Christian privilege is aided and abetted by those who promote the notions of "civil religion" and "secularism." The term *civil religion* was made popular in the 1960s and refers to "a system of established rituals, symbols, values, norms, and allegiances," which gives participants in society "an overarching sense of spiritual unity."[3] Civil religion involves prophets (Washington, Jefferson), rituals (Christian prayer, characterized as non-denominational prayer, at presidential inaugurations, opening sessions of Congress, and even a "National Day of Prayer"), and sacred places (the White House, the Lincoln Memorial), with the goal of understanding the American experience through a universal reality. The construction of civil religion in the United States has been credited with piecing together a diverse nation, and it yet disregards other truths, such as the genocide of Native nations, slavery, Jim Crow, immigration restrictions, and other White Christian supremacist policies. Part of the rationale for civil religion is the idea that, as an industrialized Western nation the US will experience *secularization*—a movement away from participation in religious organizations and a corresponding reduction in those organizations' influence on government and society.

The secularization thesis has been disproven over and over in recent decades, particularly in the United States. Yet the idea of secularization continues to obscure how powerfully Christian hegemony shapes our laws, customs, and habits of thought. Christian values and ideas are manifest, for example, in civil religion's framing of the patriotism all are expected to embrace. The phrase

"Judeo-Christian," which purports to bring Judaism into the mainstream religious fold, is likewise nothing but another fig leaf for Christian normativity. In the United States, civil religion, the false notion of secularization, and the popularity of nominally inclusive religious terminology all operate together to hide Christian norms in plain sight.

Some would argue, for example, that contemporary seasonal celebrations and decorations have nothing to do with religion *per se.* The rationale for this position relies on the premise that images and activities not arising directly from Christian scripture or doctrine—such as the Easter Bunny, Santa Claus, Christmas trees, garlands, wreaths, the colors red and green, Easter egg hunts, and songs like "Here Comes Peter Cottontail," or "Rudolph the Red Nosed Reindeer"—are therefore, somehow, no longer Christian in origin or meaning. Rather, it is argued, these images and activities are merely "seasonal" and, as such, are part of "American culture." On the contrary, such images and activities have clearly religious meanings, symbolisms, and antecedents that are self-evident to non-Christians.[4] Far from being "secular," these images and ideas reinforce an underlying Christian normativity that privileges Christianity above other faiths and traditions.[5]

The danger of the civil religion of American patriotism is not only that it masks Christian normativity, but that it can result in nationalism and ethnocentrism. Indeed, Christianity often becomes an even more visible element of US patriotism during wartime or national crisis, as during the two world wars, when to be a religious pacifist was considered a betrayal of patriotism; during the Cold War of the 1950s, when to be an atheist was to be considered un-American and to be a Jew was suspect; and today, when anyone thought to be Muslim, up to and including the forty-fourth president of the United States, lives under a cloud of suspicion. Treating markers of Christian hegemony as "civil religion" downplays the privileging of Christianity and avoids acknowledging how its social power marginalizes religious minorities and atheists.

Christian normativity also limits our understanding of religiosity. Survey data show an increase in the number of Americans identifying as unaffiliated, a group researchers have begun calling the "nones" because they respond "none" when asked for their religious affiliation in studies and polls. According to the 2018 General Social Survey (GSS), Americans claiming no religion represent about 23.1 percent of the population, up from 21.6 percent in 2016.[6] But as Russell Jeung and his colleagues point out in their writing on Chinese Americans, a rise in "nones" is not the same as an increase in nonbelief or nonbelonging. Jeung warns that "non-religiousness cannot be conflated with . . . secularism," particularly in those faiths where religion is not carried out through prayer and congregational practice. Chinese Americans, for example, "do not believe in religion as much as they *do* religion."[7]

In other words, the very theory of "nones" is itself influenced by Christian normativity. It assumes a norm of religiosity defined by congregational activity and worship. Yet an increase in "nones" does not indicate a net decrease in religiosity, as Jeung points out. Nor does it indicate that "religion" is giving way to "secularism" in any sense that changes the foundational role of Christianity in US law, society, and culture. Christianity remains embedded in US legal and social structures. The world is as modern as it has ever been; still, both in the US and abroad, religious and tribal identities are as strong and divisive as they have been in a century or more. Focusing on the decrease in the proportion of Americans who identify with a Christian faith also ignores the continuing increase in the number of adherents of other faiths, largely due to immigration. Moreover, "nones" of Christian origin continue to benefit from Christian privilege, and "nones" of other faiths do not.[8]

An Optical Illusion

As we have discussed, Christian privilege is often not apparent to those who benefit from it. The idea that there is equal religious freedom for all in the United States is an *optical illusion*. Optical illusions do two things: they prevent you from seeing what is right in front of you, and/or they distort the thing you are looking at so it appears to be something else. The optical illusion of American religious freedom begins with the idea that just writing it down makes it real. Since religious freedom is enshrined in the First Amendment of the Constitution, people assume that religious discrimination does not exist. The illusion is fed by the one of the United States' grand narratives: that the nation was founded as a haven for those fleeing religious persecution, where all can worship freely and equally. The facts behind the illusion are very different. The Puritans created a society where Protestant Christianity was the norm, and where religious affiliation, like race, became a basis for exclusion and discrimination.[9]

One of the most powerful ways the optical illusion of religious freedom is perpetuated is through constant use of the phrase "separation of church and state." This phrase is invoked in public debates about issues like prayer at government meetings or Nativity scenes on public property. It is often brought up as a way to push back against members of religious minorities who assert their First Amendment rights in public spaces—because Christians do not see the omnipresence of Christianity in those very same spaces. Many Americans erroneously believe that the words "separation of church and state" are found in the Constitution and/or the Declaration of Independence. The phrase actually comes from a letter President Thomas Jefferson wrote to a Baptist religious committee in Danbury, Connecticut, in 1802. Jefferson was responding to the Danbury Baptists' concern about the possible establishment of Puritanism as the official religion of the new republic. Jefferson wrote that the religious protection clauses of the First Amendment represent an "act of the whole American people" in "building a wall of separation between Church & State." Jefferson's letter then went largely unremarked-upon for almost a century, until the US Supreme Court's 1878 decision in *Reynolds v. United States*. In that case, the Court quoted another passage in Jefferson's letter to articulate a distinction between religious belief and practice. The Court referenced Jefferson's "wall of separation between church and state" in the majority opinion in *Everson v. Board of Education of Ewing* in 1947,[10] a case involving the state reimbursing families for the cost of busing their children to religious schools. Since *Everson*, the phrase has often been quoted in court decisions and has entered the popular culture as an articulation of what most Americans think is the legal line between religion and government.

In reality, the separation of religion from civic life at local, state, and federal levels in the US has always been an optical illusion. The phrase "separation of church and state" represents the idea of a desired Constitutional principle—namely, that in a pluralistic democracy, religious ("church") and governmental ("state") authorities do not intersect or interact. Yet, in the past as today, encounters and intersections of piety and policy have generated intense political controversy and legal contests. Interactions between democratic civic life and diverse religious cultures have inevitably led to conflicts over issues like prayer in public schools, Christmas or Easter symbols on government property, and religious expression in supposedly neutral spaces like workplaces, the military, and prisons. Rather than a reality, the "separation of church and state" serves either as an aspiration, for those who believe that personal freedom resides in the separation of religion from civic life, or as an obstacle, for those who would use the powers of the government to impose their religious beliefs on others.

The First Amendment states: "Congress shall make no law respecting the establishment of religion or prohibiting the free exercise thereof." The first part of this directive, known as the *Establishment Clause*—"Congress shall make no law respecting an establishment of religion."—prohibits the federal government from supporting any single religion or religious denomination or sect—the concern the Danbury Baptists expressed to President Jefferson, resulting in his 1802 letter, described above. The second part of this Constitutional guarantee, known as the *Free Exercise Clause,* bars Congress from making any law "prohibiting the free exercise" of religion. Among the topics in the Bill of Rights,[11] religion is in a category by itself. The Bill of Rights does not protect people from institutional discrimination based on race, class, gender, or any attribute other than religion. Racial protections, like the extension of US Constitutional restrictions to the states, did not exist until the passage of Thirteenth and Fourteenth Amendments after the Civil War. Religion is also the only attribute with explicit and absolute constitutional protection: "Congress shall make **no law** . . ." All other protections in the Bill of Rights are adjective-modified and thus limited ("unreasonable searches," "speedy . . . trial," "cruel and unusual punishment").[12] The interpretation of these clauses is left to judges who are themselves products of existing cultural traditions and social hierarchies.

Some see the religion clauses as a grand gesture conveying broad freedoms to all. However, the First Amendment was really designed to be a religious "mutual assurance pact"[13] agreed upon by the major competing Protestant denominations in the original thirteen colonies to prevent any one of them from becoming a federally established church supported by federal taxes or from being eradicated through restrictions on the freedom to practice or believe. (Official *state* churches were funded by state taxes until the mid-nineteenth century.[14]) The motivations behind the First Amendment would thus be better summed up with the words: "If I can't have it my way, you can't have it your way."

To be clear, the optical illusion here is the idea that the Constitution demands a separation between church and state, and that such a separation actually exists as a result. Most Americans believe that government is not involved with religion and *vice versa*; this idea of separation helps to maintain the myth that all religions are welcomed and can be practiced freely. In fact, both clauses, but particularly the free exercise clause, have been subject to numerous interpretations by the US Supreme Court. These Supreme Court decisions have often functioned to support free religious practice claims brought by Christian groups, and to restrict free religious practice of non-Christians.[15] The principle of church/state separation has sometimes been ignored entirely, such as when the federal government funded Christian missionaries as part of its campaign to corral and control Native American populations in the nineteenth century. As we will see below, the cumulative effect of these rulings and policies has been to permit Christians to follow their beliefs even when they are in violation of some civil laws, but frequently to allow restriction of religious minorities' ability to practice their beliefs and atheists' ability to avoid religion in public spaces.

Remember the other function of an optical illusion: It distorts our view of what is right in front of us. In this case, the optical illusion of religious neutrality functions like "color-blind racism." Color-blind racism is a form of modern racism exemplified by the statement, "I only see you—I don't see the color of your skin." By its very logic, color-blind racism requires that individuals pretend a person of color is socially raceless.[16] Usually ignorant and naïve rather than malicious, such a stance functions to sustain the White racial dominance by ignoring the continuing effects of historical prejudice and the racially different life experiences of people of color in America today. It is based on the principle that "all people are equal"; while valid, this principle ignores continuing systemic racial inequality. It results in the marginalization and oppression of people of color by failing to acknowledge and respond to their needs, experiences, and identity. It avoids confronting racism and thereby safeguards existing structures of White privilege, which reinforces and maintains White supremacy.

In the same way, pretending that US society is religiously neutral can result in the marginalization of, discrimination against, or even violence toward religious minority communities. It prevents us from addressing genuine inequities and injustices in the lives of religious minorities and from seeing how the design of society and its laws maintains White Christian supremacy. Believing that the *reality* of religious freedom matches our Constitutional *aspirations* obscures the Christian privilege and religious oppression encountered by religious minorities. It hides the fact that privilege and oppression are the product of centuries of law, policy, and cultural practices that are still supported by today's institutional structures. Even in the current century, new laws and leaders continue to reinforce and perpetuate these practices and structures. Christian hegemony remains invisible to people born and socialized into these traditions, assumptions and values, largely because of the optical illusion of American "religious freedom." Christianity has been rendered invisible, or less visible, because race and racial difference came to replace religion as the nominal reason why freedom and opportunity were extended to some groups and not to others.

Myths and Realities

The American creation myth insists that the Puritans sought religious freedom. Indeed they did, but only for themselves.[17] In reality, the colonial period in the Americas was complex, with various groups in search of religious refuge caught in economic as well as religious conflict with each other. The mutual ill will and religious competition among different Protestant Christian faith traditions led the people of New Netherland to cleanse their colony of Lutherans and Quakers, and to try the same with Jews. Name any religious group, and there has been a moment when its members discovered that American "religious freedom" is enjoyed disproportionately or exclusively by Protestant Christians—or, as in New Netherland, by an even more narrowly defined group like the Dutch Reformed Church.

The Puritan presence in New England set the tone and is the basis for the Protestant Christian norms that characterize mainstream White American culture today. Even in the absence of a legally established religion, Protestant mores and ways became the "normal" manner in which things were done in civic America. Most colonial settlers were affiliated with one of a few Protestant faiths, from Puritans in New England to Anglicans, Congregationalists, Lutherans, and others, but there were also others, including Quakers and anabaptists whose "Christianity" was more contested in the eyes of the majority.

The White Protestant Christian ethos of contemporary US life is rooted in this religious competition over a homogeneous religious identity, community control, wealth, and land. Christian norms dictated the rules of political life, from mandatory Church attendance to tax-supported religious institutions. Christianity was regarded as superior to the oral religious traditions of the Native Americans; to the Islamic, animist, or other traditions of enslaved Africans and free Africans; and to the beliefs of immigrants from Jewish and other religious traditions. Even Bible-based religions outside the Protestant norm encountered hostility in government and society.

Throughout the later part of the eighteenth century and well into the nineteenth century, litigation was rarely brought under the religious protection clauses of the First Amendment, either because

Protestant hegemony remained unopposed or because oppressed religious minorities, such as slaves and Native Americans, lacked Constitutional protection. Also, it was not until the adoption of the Fourteenth Amendment, after the Civil War, that the Bill of Rights' reach was extended to protect individuals from the acts of the state governments. Christmas became the only separately recognized federal holiday with a religious basis in 1870. Sunday, the Christian Sabbath, has been recognized as a national day of rest from colonial times; Saturday only joined Sunday as the legally recognized weekend in 1938—and that in response to the demands of organized labor, not religious minorities. From 1793 until at least 1868, the US Capitol building was used as a Christian church, which most of the elected officials attended.[18]

All the while, religious minorities in most cases did not challenge these policies. Even into the early decades of the twentieth century, Jews were arrested for working on the Sunday Sabbath[19] and Jewish children were ostracized and harassed and their parents' businesses boycotted if they protested public school Christian prayer or Bible readings.[20] Overt "No Jews Here" policies in hotels or business clubs, quotas at elite colleges and professional schools—none of these antisemitic practices were constitutionally challenged until the mid-twentieth century.[21]

Christian Hegemony and the Law

Religion was never meant to be entirely absent from public life. Rather, the Constitutional protections of the First Amendment were meant to prevent the federal government from putting its power behind any specific religion. While successful in preventing the legislative or executive establishment of an *officially* mandated national religion, such as characterized church and state in the early colonies, Protestant Christianity's culture and mores have defined US history. Even Jefferson's Christian-centric word "church" in the phrase "church and state" proves this point. The Protestant norm has shaped laws and court decisions on religious freedom.[22]

Christian privilege is built into the edifice of American law. Across time and topic, we find the normative power of Christianity, particularly Protestant Christianity, shaping the Courts' decisions on whether and when the First Amendment protects religion. We see this, for example, in court rulings that rely on the distinction between belief and action. This distinction is an enduring theme connecting Free Exercise cases across numerous decades.[23] Protestant religious practice is primarily about holding particular beliefs rather than taking religiously mandated actions, such as wearing a religious head covering, growing one's hair, or engaging in the consumption or veneration of nature. Of course, there are things that Protestants "do," such as attending church and participating in the Sacraments, but Protestantism's religious mandates are more about belief than action. This has shaped, in many ways, what the courts will or will not allow when it comes to religion.

The Supreme Court articulated this action/belief divide in *Reynolds v. US* (1879) after Congress banned polygamy in 1862. The Court rejected the claims of George Reynolds, a Mormon, that that ban violated the First Amendment. In support of his right to plural marriage, Reynolds had argued that the anti-polygamy statute violated the Free Exercise clause. The high court disagreed, upholding the law by ruling that polygamy was an "action" not a "belief," that only beliefs are protected by the Constitution, and that polygamy should be restricted for the good of society.[24] In other words, Reynolds was free to *believe* in plural marriage—just not to engage in it.

The *Reynolds* case is important because the Court defined "free exercise" narrowly, in a way that restricted religious *practices* that violated political and cultural norms, without limiting religious *belief.* Consider for a moment the deep power of Protestant normativity in the *Reynolds* case. In a host of societies and times in history, including times described in the Bible, plural marriage was common or accepted. In nineteenth-century America, however, "marriage" had a definition—singular and heterosexual—grounded in Protestant Christian beliefs, and that was enough to put Reynolds' religious practice beyond the protection of the First Amendment.

Reynolds is part of a continuity of cases in which the belief/action distinction has been applied in ways that protect Christianity and its norms and not the religious activities associated with Native American and Caribbean spiritualities, Judaism, Islam, or Sikhism, for example; these are less likely to receive protection in the Courts. For example, most Christian sects do not require men to cover their heads. Judaism does, and in 1986 a suit filed by a Jewish officer in the US Air Force, Dr. S. Simcha Goldman, seeking to overturn the Air Force's uniform policy as it related to religious headgear, reached the US Supreme Court as *Goldman v. Weinberger*. Goldman sought a Free Exercise exemption that would allow him to wear his yarmulke while on duty in the on-base hospital where he served as a psychiatrist. A denial of Goldman's rights would leave him in a difficult position: he owed the Air Force three years' service in exchange for scholarship funding already received, so he would either have had to violate his religious obligation or face court martial. Goldman lost. The Supreme Court's majority opinion mischaracterized wearing a yarmulke as a personal preference rather than a religious obligation,[25] and gave priority to the military's stated need for standardized uniforms that did not allow religious head covering.

Shortly after *Goldman* was decided, Congress added an amendment to a military appropriation bill to allow servicemembers to wear religious head coverings. Yet, twenty years later, we can hear echoes of Goldman's experience in the cases of multiple Sikh physicians who also sought exemptions from the military's uniform policies to wear uncut hair (including beards) and turbans. Sikh servicemen had to fight for their rights as if theirs was a new dilemma—without the benefit of Congress' legislative reversal of *Goldman*. Likewise, in 2018, US Secret Service Agent Anshdeep

Singh Bhatia was asked to remove his turban and shave his beard in order to become the first Sikh in the president's security detail; it took filing a lawsuit for the Secret Service to relent and allow him to be himself on the job.[26] It seems that each new non-Christian group that comes along has to "reinvent the wheel." And they have to do so repeatedly: Sikhs, for example, had to advocate anew for the right to wear the *dastaar* (turban) while serving in the military, the Secret Service, and the New York Police Department.

By giving legal meaning to the distinction between "faith" and "action," the courts have also disadvantaged Native American and Caribbean faiths. For example, the Supreme Court has upheld governmental actions that restrict the religious use of peyote, a hallucinogen consumed as part of certain Native religious practices. In *Employment Div., Dept. of Human Resources of Ore. v. Smith* (1990), two men who "ingested peyote for sacramental purposes at a ceremony of the Native American Church" were denied unemployment benefits after losing their jobs for using "illegal drugs." Upholding the denial of benefits, the court reasoned that when the government prohibits an activity—in this case, drug use while on unemployment—a person cannot avoid that rule by saying they were engaged in a religious obligation.[27] Likewise, in *Church of the Lukumi Babalu Aye, Inc. v. Hialeah* (1993), the United State Supreme Court upheld a ban on the Santeria religious practice of sacrificing small animals as a violation of public health standards.

The Court has also refused to recognize that reverence for and preservation of nature and land are part of spiritual belief for many. In *Lyng v. Northwest Indian Cemetery Protective Association* (1988), the Supreme Court allowed the US Forest Service to build a paved road through six miles of wilderness that the government's own study had found was "significant as an integral and indispensable part of [American] Indian religious conceptualization and practice." The study concluded that constructing a road along any of the available routes "would cause serious and irreparable damage to the sacred areas that are an integral and necessary part of the belief systems and lifeway of Northwest California Indian peoples," because essential to the peoples' religious use of the area were "certain qualities of the physical environment, the most important of which are privacy, silence, and an undisturbed natural setting." Even as it acknowledged that the road would threaten "the efficacy of at least some religious practices" in a way that would be "extremely grave," the Court refused to compel the government to protect citizens' religious practices. Road construction through sacred land was deemed constitutionally permissible under the free exercise clause.

Across all of these cases, one can argue that the Court was upholding the outcome that appears to affect everyone equally: military uniformity, a ban on using illegal drugs, a non-recognition of religious traditions that would protect a particular geographic location or topographic feature. But if we are going to call these laws "facially neutral," as courts often do, we must recognize Christianity as the "face" against which other traditions are being compared. If Christian practice included devotional head covering, Dr. Goldman and Sikh soldiers would not have had to fight those fights. If Christians used peyote in their religious practice, it would never have been declared an illegal drug in the first place. If Christianity recognized the notion of sacred lands and called for spiritually important natural spaces to be undisturbed, the logging operations in *Lyng* would never have commenced. Thus, Christians will never experience a "facially neutral" ban on their practices, and the burden of government regulation will continue to fall only on religious minorities.

Indeed, when Christians find themselves at odds with a "facially neutral" law, they tend to win rather than lose. In *Yoder v. Wisconsin* (1972), the Court allowed Amish[28] residents to withdraw their children from public schooling after eighth grade despite a state law requiring all children to attend school until the age of sixteen. The Court went to great lengths to convey its respect for the Amish religious belief, and ultimately permitted the Amish to withdraw their children from school two years before the law allowed. The Amish succeeded, in part, by appealing to the justices' nostalgia for a mythic American past—the simple Christian America of horses and buggies and life on the farm. This national past, however romanticized, was one most of the justices could readily understand: Of the seven justices who participated in *Yoder*, six were Protestant and one, William J. Brennan, was Catholic. So, whereas in 1986 the Supreme Court would call Goldman's yarmulke a "personal preference" which the Air Force could "subordinat[e] . . . in favor of the overall group mission," in 1971 the *Yoder* Court wrote: "the traditional way of life of the Amish is not merely a matter of personal preference, but one of deep religious conviction."[29] In the Court's own words, the Amish were aided in their appeal "by a history of three centuries as an identifiable religious sect and a long history as a successful and self-sufficient segment of American society."[30] If access to religious liberty is most available to groups who have been here a long time and are familiar to the justices, can we really expect "equal justice under law" for immigrant religious minorities?

Even more recently, in *Burwell v. Hobby Lobby* (2014), the Supreme Court applied the Free Exercise clause and the Religious Freedom Restoration Act of 1993 (RFRA) to protect corporations whose individual owners were Christians with "religious objections to abortion." Hobby Lobby sought to avoid providing its employees with a health plan that included family planning coverage, despite the Affordable Care Act's requirements that health plans include reproductive health care for women. The Court ruled that Christian-owned businesses can avoid complying with the Affordable Care Act's coverage requirements based on "the sincerely held religious beliefs of the companies' owners."

The *Hobby Lobby* ruling shows that Christians may be able to use Christianity's normative social power to upend First Amendment jurisprudence. In cases brought by religious minorities, like

Goldman and *Lyng*, the "free exercise" of religious observances outside the Christian norm were not protected by the Constitution. Rather, the Court concluded that a standard applicable to everyone is religiously neutral, even when it prevents everyone but Christians from practicing their faith. Based on that reasoning, the Court perpetuated legal discrimination against religious minorities. But in *Hobby Lobby*, the Court treated the Affordable Care Act—a health insurance mandate—as if it were *not* religiously neutral. According to the majority opinion, individual evangelical claims of free religious exercise can supersede a federal law about health insurance, so that a business could avoid providing the coverage the law requires. Clearly, the notion of "neutrality" is shaped by the deep effects of Christian normativity on the Christian-majority Court. The collective message of the Court's free exercise cases is that a burden on Christian practice offends the Constitution, while a burden on non-Christian practice does not.

Because most Supreme Court justices are themselves born, raised, socialized, and educated within the symbols and structures of White American society, with its deep Christian normativity, they tend to reach decisions that reflect this influence. The power of social norms, particularly those shaped by centuries of Christian hegemony, shapes "the law of the land."[31] Indeed, as we will see in the next chapter, an earlier generation of Supreme Court justices stripped a Sikh immigrant of his citizenship because "the common man knows perfectly well" that a Sikh is a "brown Hindu" and not a "white person" entitled to US citizenship.[32]

Litigation and debates over the Establishment Clause ("Congress shall make no law regarding the establishment of religion") also show the strong influence of Protestant norms, and a bias in favor of behavior that is clearly Christian. In 2014, for example, the Supreme Court ruled that beginning a public meeting with prayer from a "volunteer chaplain" does not violate the Establishment Clause. The plaintiffs in Greece, New York, were not even trying to eliminate prayer from public meetings—only asking the Court to instruct the town that prayers should be "inclusive and ecumenical" and addressed "to a 'generic God.'" Greece's practice was to have chaplains offer only Christian sectarian prayers—"prayers steeped in only one faith," to quote Justice Kagan's dissent. The town had never invited non-Christian clergy to deliver the prayers. A lower court concluded that these practices affiliated the town with Christianity, excluded other faiths, and therefore violated the Establishment Clause.[33] But the Supreme Court found no problems with how Greece conducted its public meetings. The majority opinion looked to jurisdictions across the country and throughout US history, including the First Congress of the United States in 1789, and concluded that employing clergy to open legislative meetings with prayer is a "tradition long followed in Congress and the state legislatures." As long as Greece's policy "fits within tradition"—that is, as long as Greece followed traditions established in colonial times, when the Puritan ethos reigned and all legislators were Christian—its policy of opening every meeting with Christian prayer would not violate the Constitution.[34] The Court rejected the plaintiffs' theory "that the constitutionality of legislative prayer turns on the neutrality of its content," because a representative government should not appear to favor one faith over another. In fact, the Supreme Court ruled that telling clergy to constrain their prayers to "generic" or neutral references to the divine would violate the Constitution because it would amount to government censorship of Christian clerics.

Like *Yoder* in the Free Exercise context, the Supreme Court in *Greece* relied on the fact that legislative prayer was a long-standing practice at all levels of American government. Because it was traditional, the Court reasoned, it could not be unconstitutional. Five of the Court's six Catholics joined the majority opinion; only Sonia Sotomayor joined the Court's three Jewish justices in dissent. Here again is the deep power of Christian normativity: under the *Greece* precedent, Christian prayer to convene a public meeting is literally subsumed within the definition of the American way of life. Even government chaplains, ordained by religious authorities and paid for by taxpayers, do not constitute an "establishment of religion" because—like Legislative opening prayers—the Supreme Court has ruled that such publicly employed chaplains were part of tradition in state and federal legislatures throughout American history. But what kinds of clergy were selected to these roles over the years? Not rabbis, imams, or pandits. If a government meeting opened with prayers from a Hindu priest, an imam, or a rabbi, would it be similarly received? The answer is no. And all this still fails to address the millions of Americans who do not believe in prayer at all, but who nonetheless, when attending public meetings, as is their right, promptly hear the words, "Let us pray."

Even if Galloway and her co-plaintiff had gotten the "generic," "nonsectarian" prayers they asked for, those prayers would still promote Christian norms. A chaplain who carefully omits references to Jesus will still be speaking a prayer in English, likely using words like "thee" and "thy" and a vernacular and cadence familiar to Christians, and concluding with an "Amen." Any veneer of religious neutrality accomplished by omitting references to "Your Son our Savior," or the words "in Jesus' name," is just that: a veneer. The chaplain's words will still sound like a Christian prayer to everyone in the room—especially the religious minorities.

This is not to say that the Establishment Clause's protections from coercive state-sponsored religious activities are never applied to Christianity. For example, the Establishment Clause was held in two major Supreme Court decisions, *Engel v. Vitale* (1962) and *Abington Township School District v. Schempp* (1963), to prohibit schools from requiring students to participate in devotional prayer and mandatory Bible reading. Sadly, the tragedy here is not that *Engel* or *Schempp* did not go far enough, but that the Christian majority saw this as an attack on Christians and schools and was

successful in perpetuating the idea that government is "taking religion out of schools." The goal was never to remove religion, but
to remove compelled prayer and forced religious practice: school
rules and traditions that obligated children to pray Christian prayers
under the supervision of their teachers and coaches. School admin-
istrators and policy makers have often taken these rulings much too
far—treating them as a virtual ban on the discussion of religion in
schools, as if schools must exist as "religion-free zones."[35]

Treating religion as a barred topic in school discourages students
from expressing important elements of their identity. Like "color-
blind racism," it perpetuates the "optical illusion" of freedom of
religion because it allows educators to deny the reality that religion is in schools every day—specifically one religion, Christianity.
Christianity is there, from the calendar to the culture to the history books. Pretending otherwise results in curricula that ignore
religion's role in history and society, and allows educators to ignore religion-based conflicts and bullying when the right thing to
do is to talk openly about the issue. I think of a seventh-grader I
encountered years ago. An Indian American Hindu immigrant, he
was held down in the lunchroom and force-fed a hot dog by several
classmates who thought it would be funny to make the religiously
vegetarian boy eat beef. How does pretending religion doesn't exist
help that child articulate what happened to him? How does it help
educators properly punish the perpetrators, or provide restorative
justice to the victim?

In fact, the Supreme Court in *Schempp* wrote that the study of
religions in the nation's public schools is both legal and desirable:

> It might well be said that one's education is not complete without
> a study of comparative religions or the history of religion and its
> relationship to the advancement of civilization. It certainly may be
> said that the Bible is worthy of study for its literary and historical
> qualities. Nothing we have said here indicates that such study of the

Bible or of religion, where presented objectively as part of a secular program of education, may not be effected consistent with the First Amendment.[36]

In other words, the Establishment Clause does not prohibit the study of religion, or even the reading of sacred Scriptures in school as part of a course of study. Schools and teachers are forbidden only from crossing the line between academic presentation and religious advocacy—between "teaching" and "preaching."[37] Schools should promote awareness of religion and expose students to the diversity of religious worldviews; they are prohibited only from encouraging students to accept religion, and from endorsing or denigrating any particular religion or belief. Schools need to acknowledge the role of various religions in shaping world and US history and religions' influence in society today, and nothing in *Engel* or *Schempp* prevents that.

Understanding the roles Christianity plays in the development of American law and society—and even of how laws and public perceptions define who is or may become "American"—allows us to see through the optical illusion of "religious freedom," and to understand how Whiteness and Christianity have coexisted and mutually supported each other. That edifice of privilege for certain Americans, and the corresponding struggles and disadvantages faced particularly by non-White non-Christians, are fundamental to the ways the US has fallen short of the "more perfect union" it could be and should be.

Judging Devotion

In New Jersey, students pursuing a teaching career must complete an internship in the schools. Each student intern is paired with a mentor teacher who has been identified as a role model. One fall semester, around the time of the Jewish "High Holy Days" of

Rosh Hashanah and Yom Kippur, two interns who had taken my Multicultural Education class described a conversation between their mentor teachers. The topic was several students' absence for the Jewish holidays. One teacher remarked, and the other agreed: "I don't know why they keep the kids home on these days; they're not really that Jewish."

This statement illustrates the judgments and attitudes of people who have spent a lifetime internalizing their dominant status as Christians in America, to the point that they feel at ease to pass judgment on their Jewish students based on their Christian interpretation of what makes a person "that Jewish." My interns were troubled by the exchange because they could see how their mentor teachers were deciding how others should behave religiously. It is not appropriate—particularly for religious outsiders, as these teachers were vis-à-vis their Jewish students—to critique how others express their faith or celebrate religious holidays. As my students correctly recognized, their teachers' remarks exemplified several facets of Christian privilege.

Let us unpack the situation a bit more. First of all, are the Jewish students really free to observe the Jewish holidays? Many school districts across the country have policies that treat religious holidays as "excused absences." While appearing progressive, these policies still create a structural bias against students who are not Christian. The notion of an excused absence for Christmas or Easter is moot, as the school year is designed around the Christian calendar. Christian students never have to be absent (excused or otherwise) to observe their major holidays, while religious minority students and their families face the conundrum of observing their religion or going to school.

Second, the teachers are casting judgment on what it means to be "that Jewish," or Jewish enough to observe the holidays. In doing so, they are applying Christian standards of what religiosity looks like. Too many people's understanding of other religions is limited to what I call "Wikipedia knowledge"—a general understanding, at best, that boils down to rudimentary knowledge that "Jews do X" or "Buddhists believe Y." This monolithic approach ignores how religions are actually lived. Christians may be selective about belief and practice, choosing to believe only certain passages of Scripture, or to abide by some religious prohibitions and not others. Yet this idea—that a person can agree with or observe only certain tenets of their faith, such as going to temple on the High Holy Days even if they do not keep kosher or wear a yarmulke—is not always extended to how we think about members of other religions. To really understand another person's religious identity, and the way they experience lived religion, we have to ask a slightly different question. Instead of asking, "How Jewish is she?" we need to ask, "How is she Jewish?"

Policies cannot police attitudes. For example, when students are absent from school for observing a religious holiday, they still have to complete assignments. This can result in more work for teachers. The words and tone of these mentor teachers displayed resentment over giving up their own time to help students whom they felt should have just come to school on their holidays because they are "not that Jewish." The feeling of entitlement to say that their students are not Jewish enough illustrates an attitudinal dimension of Christian privilege[38]: the perceived authority to judge and opine on others' religiosity, and to generate opinions based on *one's own* understanding of *someone else's* faith. White Christians' way of life is reinforced and reflected in everyday culture, which provides an additional sense of entitlement to judge, categorize, or condemn members of minority faiths. The fact that those public school teachers could make those judgments, and share them aloud, shows the power of Christian normativity. Such attitudes may be reflected in their interactions with the students and their families. Whether in schools, or workplaces, or the public square, the judgments and reactions my interns identified are carried out thousands of times in thousands of places in America every day.

The Racialization of Religion

As an obstetrician and gynecologist with a medical practice in Cobb County, Georgia, my dad has delivered thousands of babies and had patients from all walks of life. His right hand in the practice was a bright and talented office manager who worked for him for twenty-eight years. Vicki is a White woman of great faith, very involved in her Southern Baptist church community. Soon after she started, members of her church started criticizing her for working for my father because he is not a Christian. Although he was a healer, my father was a foreigner and not a church goer, so the message to Vicki from the church community was that he could not be trusted. Thankfully, Vicki believed more in God's message than in the community's slanders and she continued to work for my dad. She and her family defended my father's character, telling everyone at the church that he was a good man. In the end, Vicki prevailed. In fact, after a few years, a new minister joined the church and his wife also came to work for my dad.

Vicki's fellow congregants—White folks—did not know my Dad was Hindu, and may not have really understood what that meant. They may or may not have realized he was Indian; more likely, they recognized him as part of an undifferentiated racial "other." They knew he was not White and not Christian, which made it unacceptable for Vicki to work for him. Were they trying to protect Vicki from being tainted by contact with my father, or to deny an unwelcome foreigner the help of a good Christian lady? It does not matter. Whatever it was, my father's religious and racial identity made him foreign, different, not normal, and therefore untrustworthy.

Vicki's fellow White Christians in the 1980s were exhibiting the feelings later captured in Robert Jones' 2017 book *The End of White Christian America*: "While the country's shifting racial demographics alone are certainly a source of apprehension for many White Americans, it is the disappearance of White Christian America that is driving their strong, sometimes apocalyptic reactions."[39] Suspicion of the dark-skinned religious minority is symptomatic of White Christian communities' concern about growing racial and religious diversity in the US today. "The American religious landscape is being remade, most notably by the decline of the White Protestant majority and the rise of the religiously unaffiliated" (the "nones" we discussed earlier).[40]

With the recognition of diverse religious voices, and the increasing visibility of religious minorities who are racially non-White, the White Christian majority[41] perceives their religion as being lost or supplanted in the very land that popular American history had said would be theirs. Parts of White Christian America view the move toward social equality as discrimination against them. Nothing feels so imbalanced as a level playing field, when for as long as you can remember the field has been tilted in your favor. But of course, the playing field is still far from level. It is still tilted against religious and racial minorities. White Christian Americans often do not see the structural benefits they continue to benefit from—built up over centuries of law, policy, and tradition. Nor do they see how those privileges are part of White Christian supremacist foundation of this country.

At the intersection of racial and religious bias, where the notion of Americanness (nationalism) sweeps together Whiteness, Christianity, and native-born status, both non-White communities and "foreign" faith traditions are denigrated and seen as suspect and un-American. White Christian supremacist projects are rooted in entrenched racial and religious privilege, along with racialized notions of who belongs within the national community. The *racialization of religion* is a process in which particular religions are associated with certain physical appearances and human differences come to be treated as absolute, fundamental, and heritable, like race. Modern antisemitism, for example, echoes the centuries-old conflation of religion with racial difference as a way of isolating and delegitimizing the Jew as "other." In the United States, Christianity has been racialized as White in a way that establishes it both as virtuous and superior, while the religions of African, Asian, and Native peoples are racialized by association with phenotypical (racial) features that are seen as markers of savage, uncivilized, exotic, and inferior peoples. The racialization of religion also results in the religious dimension of discrimination becoming obscured or disappearing entirely.[42]

The racialization of religion occurs in a specific social and historical context. Centuries of European domination over such racially different groups as Asian Buddhists and Hindus, African Muslims and animists, and others has resulted in an entwinement of religious and racial meanings. Those meanings position a variety of faiths together in the colonialist mind as an undifferentiated, racially and religiously inferior group of "heathens." Racialization thereby leads to essentialism—it reduces individuals to one aspect of their identity and presents a homogeneous, undifferentiated, and static view of migrant religious communities. It can result in religions being conflated with one another, or treated as similar, because of shared racial associations; it can also produce situations of "mistaken identity," in which the perception that they are members of a given racial group leads to the assumption that they are members of a given religion when they are not.

The most conspicuous example of the racialization of religion today is the association of brown skin with Islam. From the oil shock of 1973 and the Iran Hostage Crisis of 1979 through the Gulf Wars and the post-9/11 "Global War on Terror," the West has been confronting "enemies" whose ideology is expressed and explained by reference to their interpretations of Islam. This ideology is racialized via its association with Islam: "Arab" and "Muslim" are used interchangeably and the politics and tactics of terrorist movements are described as "Islamic" by the popular media.[43] Edward Said argued that Islam had been turned into the West's "post-Soviet devil," replacing "godless Communism" as its sinister global enemy.[44] Note that both of these perceived enemies, Communism and Islam, are positioned as the opposite of Christian. More recently, legal scholar Neil Gotanda has argued for making "Muslim" a racial category when examining the law because "[e]qual protection categories in constitutional law are inadequate to describe the racial nature of the Muslim terrorist."[45] In addition to endangering brown Muslims and non-Muslims alike, the racialization of Islam also diminishes it as a global religion, ignoring Muslims who are African American, East and Southeast Asian, and White.

Racialization can create false assumptions about theological similarity among faiths because they are associated with a particular racial group, such as the association of Hinduism, Islam, Jainism, and Sikhism with South Asian Americans. Aggravated by most Americans' lack of knowledge about these faiths, this conflation of geographic identity and religious theology generates assumptions that religions with divergent practices, beliefs, and scriptures, are theologically similar due to the racial commonality of their adherents. Sikhism, for example, has been treated as theologically similar to Islam or Hinduism—words such as "offshoot" and "sect" are often used—when it is in fact a revealed religion with its own scripture and historic line of *gurus* (religious authorities).

The racialization of religion can also produce situations of "mistaken identity," in which membership in a racial group causes members of one religion to be assumed to be members of another. When this occurs, social trends like Islamophobia can have effects not just on Muslim Americans but also on those mistaken for them because of race. South Asians and others, regardless of their actual religious affiliation, have faced attacks because their race connotes a religious identity that the American public imagines to be disloyal and unpatriotic.[46] Sometimes even a "foreign" name is enough to create a target. In the 1970s and 1980s, some Indian Americans with the last name Shah faced harassment as a result of the Iran Hostage

Crisis. Shah is a common family name in parts of India. Daily news reporting had made the phase "the Shah of Iran" ubiquitous in US culture; even though the Shah was a US ally, and "Shah" was a title and not a name, the phrase and the name became associated with Iran as a foreign enemy of the US. I have a friend whose family—the Shahs of Shaker Heights, Ohio—received so many telephone calls with death threats that they decided to change and delist their telephone number.

In the months after 9/11, media images of Osama Bin Laden and Afghan Taliban leaders, Muslims who wear a type of turban, customary in parts of Afghan culture, produced the belief that Sikh men were followers of an Islamic sect. Balbar Singh Sodhi, a gas station attendant killed in a "9/11 backlash" attack in Arizona, was a victim of "mistaken identity"—murdered not for being Sikh, but for being mistaken as Muslim.[47] In the years since 9/11, Sikh Americans continue to be profiled and targeted for violence as a result of the erroneous association of turbans with Islam. Sikh American scholar Jaideep Singh has identified a new American racial classification, "Apparently Muslim,"[48] which involves state action like humiliating searches of turbans performed by airport security and private discrimination in restaurants and other accommodations.[49] Whether we diagnose these incidents as symptoms of a lack of information or a disregard for accuracy, the experiences that Sikhs and others, including myself, have had during police stops and airport searches arise from a theological misunderstanding of our brown skin.

The racialization of religion reinforces and exacerbates the marginalization and devaluation of minority religious groups.[50] When a belief system is rendered illegitimate, the ideas, images, and items associated with that religion may no longer appear to hold religious value in the eyes of those in power and can be appropriated for a variety of uses. Western appropriation of Hindu terms such as *karma* and *guru* can reflect distortions and decontextualizations of the theological meaning of those terms.[51] The commodification of religious images and ideas allows the sale of Native American "dream catchers," statues of the Buddha as home decor, and the replication of religious imagery for secular use—such as placing Hindu god and goddess images on candles, perfume, and clothing. Reducing Hinduism's vibrant anthropomorphic representation of gods and goddesses to a consumer product permits them to be seen as cartoonish and theologically invalid—"false gods," in the words of some government officials.[52] Scholar Jane Naomi Iwamura reminds us that the "the change in Americans' perceptions of Asian religions from 'heathen' cultures to romanticized traditions should not necessarily be taken as a sign of social progress. . . . These viewpoints are also shaped by how we have come to know the spiritual East—namely, through mass media representations and channels of consumption. There is much at work in our pursuit of Asian religions, far beyond the noble desire for universal understanding and world peace."[53]

One irony in the treatment of these faiths as new and foreign is that some, such as Asian American faith traditions, are of more ancient origin than Christianity. Yet they are perceived as new—even grouped with "new age" beliefs—in mainstream American society. This perception exists precisely because for centuries federal law excluded Asians by favoring Protestant Christianity and Whiteness (and thus immigrants of northern European origins) and by expressly barring Asians from immigration and citizenship.[54]

The terrorist attacks on September 11, 2001 gave renewed sanction to the White Christian supremacist movement. Even before then, but more so since, virtually every national discussion involving Islam has been framed around questions of national security. Faced with a particular set of political movements around the world, which invoke Islam to rally support for or opposition to various regimes and ideas, the US response has been to reimagine the entire religion as a foreign enemy. The Global War on Terror was also being waged within our borders. In the decade after 9/11, perhaps one of the biggest concerns of Muslim Americans was their experience of large-scale arrests across the nation. Hundreds of immigrants were rounded up in the months after the terrorist attacks, often on flimsy evidence or simply on the basis of national origin. It is estimated that more than 5,000 individuals were arrested, the vast majority of them non-citizens who were deported after spending months in detention.[55]

During the same time period, an entire "War on Terror" public relations industry and culture developed, fueled and funded by a few charitable organizations. A network of organizations, right-wing think tanks, "scholars," and activists generated and circulated propaganda to rally support for the detention and surveillance of American Muslims and for military actions abroad. These "disinformation experts" produced and disseminated books, policy reports, blogs, websites, and lectures designed to stoke fears of Islam and Muslims. Between 2001 and 2009, a small number of charitable organizations provided $42.6 million to produce information spreading hate and fear.[56] The culture of the War on Terror means that Muslims and Islam are only seen through a post-9/11 lens, never on their own terms.[57]

In 2010, this anti-Muslim complex seized on a proposed expansion of the Park 51 Islamic Cultural Center in lower Manhattan to imagine and popularize what became known as the "Ground Zero mosque" controversy. The Park 51 expansion project was designed as a community center that was to include far more elements than an Islamic prayer space alone. Two blocks away from the World Trade Center site, it was designed to include a memorial to the victims of the 9/11 attacks. Its opponents, however, peddled the idea that Park 51 was a mosque to be built on Ground Zero, the former site of the World Trade Center. They raged that "the Muslims" were trying to take over the site and Park 51 would be their "victory mosque" in celebration of the Twin Towers' destruction. The controversy reached its zenith that summer, and became a talking point for Republican elected officials and candidates up and down the ballot in advance of the 2010 federal midterm elections. To hear the media report on it, a mosque in lower Manhattan sounded like a new, unprecedented development. In fact, Muslim American communities had been present in Lower Manhattan long before 2010. At least two mosques existed near the World Trade Center, and several designated Muslim prayer rooms had existed within the World Trade Center buildings themselves before 2001.[58]

The Park 51 mosque controversy roiled the nation. CNN and FOX News polls showed about two-thirds[59] of Americans opposed the building of the mosque. 9/11 survivors and victims' families could be found on both sides of the debate, with some calling the plan offensive or insensitive because the perpetrators of the attacks had acted in the name of Islam. A number said that it was not an issue of freedom of religion, property rights, or racism, but rather that locating the center so close to Ground Zero was insensitive to the families of those killed.[60] Commentators invoked a combination of American nationalism and anti-Muslim rhetoric. Former Speaker of the House of Representatives Newt Gingrich declared: "There should be no mosque near Ground Zero in New York so long as there are no churches or synagogues in Saudi Arabia."[61]

Voices like Gingrich's, particularly among political conservatives, said they were just looking out for the country. Yet, on the contrary, they were weaponizing political, cultural, and racial differences between "Muslims" and "Americans" and, in doing so, defining the latter by implication as solely Christian. Gingrich and others like him were redefining "Muslim" aggression and "conquest" to include not just violence like the 9/11 attacks but any efforts by Muslims to assert themselves in US politics, law, and culture. After 9/11, this set of ideas became a central element in contemporary right-wing nationalism in both Europe and North America.

Whether it was about "sensitivity" or nationalist territorialism, these speakers had a particular version of America in mind—one that excluded Muslims. The "hallowed ground" where the World Trade Towers had once stood was now American sacred space. And even though that "hallowed ground" also held the remains of numerous Muslim American victims of the attack, there was no place there for their faith. The entire framing of the debate—"American" sacred space on one side, "Muslims" on the other—reified the idea that Muslims cannot be American, and that Muslim worship or Muslim grief is not American worship or American grief. It also placed American Muslims in a position of being called on repeatedly to denounce violence when it was undertaken in the name of their religion. Christians are never asked to do the same, despite the fact that far more terrorist violence in the US is perpetrated by right-wing White Christian nationalists than by Muslims.[62]

Belief in a Christian Nation

Christian supremacy has continued to thrive in White America. "[N]early sixty percent of White Tea Party movement identifiers believe America 'has been and is now a Christian nation,'" a belief that spurs them to target minorities in hopes of maintaining their White Christian majority.[63] Most press coverage about the "Tea Party" movement that emerged in 2010 described it as an uprising against taxes and "big government," but paranoia about Islam was also prominent in the movement's rhetoric and policy agendas.[64] The movement gave a platform for mainstream politicians like Gingrich and many others to spout bigoted language and conspiracy theories from the fevered fringes of the political right. Islamic law, or *Shari'a*, was presented as a looming threat to the American way of life, leading legislators in states like Tennessee and Oklahoma to enact bans on the (non-existent) use of Shari'a in the state court system.

One state lawmaker in Oklahoma refused to meet with Muslim constituents unless they replied to a questionnaire asking whether they beat their wives. Elsewhere, both before and since the "Tea Party Summer" of 2010, elected officials shared hate-filled social media posts urging violence against Muslims. In 2016 alone, Arkansas state Senator Jason Rapert wrote on Facebook that Muslims "wait for every opportunity to convert Americans to Islam or kill the infidels—that is what their holy book the Koran instructs them to do"; New Hampshire lawmaker Kenneth Weyler said giving public benefits to "any person or family that practices Islam is aiding and abetting the enemy"; and Florida lawmaker Tom Goodson asked a witness representing the Council on American Islamic Relations (CAIR), a civil rights organization, whether it was safe for him to ride in the Capitol elevator with her. Others, in local office, used subtler, loaded language to smear Islam as they opposed local mosque-building projects. These and other lawmakers' comments play on popular bigoted tropes about Islam, which paint the religion as inherently violent and incompatible with life in the United States.[65]

A huge swath of White Christian America perceives the presence of religious diversity, particularly in public and civic life, as a threat to its existence. Political scientist Janelle Wong's research, for example, shows that almost 80% of White evangelicals believe that "discrimination against Christians is now as big a problem as discrimination against other groups in America."[66] Like the imagined threat of "Shari'a law," the perceived need to protect White Christian dominance in public space has been a continuing source of conflict. As the Supreme Court noted and endorsed in *Greece v. Galloway*, Christian prayer is recited in public spaces, such as state legislatures and the US Capitol, all the time. But when minority religious faiths' prayers are allowed into those same places, it can spark outrage. In 2007, then Senate Majority Leader Harry Reid invited Rajan Zed, a Hindu priest from Reno, Nevada, to offer Hindu prayers in place of the usual Christian invocation at the opening of the US Senate. As the *pandit* was about to begin, Christian extremists in the Senate gallery disrupted the Senate proceedings by loudly asking for God's forgiveness for the "abomination" of allowing "a prayer of the wicked," of a Hindu, in the Senate chamber.[67] The organization behind the protest later wrote: "The Senate was opened with a Hindu prayer placing the false god of Hinduism on a level playing field with the One True God, Jesus Christ. . . . This would never have been allowed by our Founding Fathers."[68]

Eight years later, in 2015, the same *pandit* was invited to deliver the daily invocation for the Idaho State Senate. Three Republican lawmakers refused even to attend the prayer. Senator Sheryl Nuxoll did not attend "because she believes the United States is a Christian nation." She added: "Hindu [sic] is a false faith with false gods. . . . I think it's great that Hindu people can practice their religion but since we're the Senate, we're setting an example of what we, Idaho, believe." Her colleague Senator Steve Vick asserted that a Hindu prayer should not be allowed because the United States was "built on the Judeo-Christian not only religion but work ethic, and I don't want to see that undermined. I'm very supportive of the way this country was built, and I don't want us to move away from it."[69]

The message of the Capitol protestors and Idaho Senators was clear: Hindus, and indeed anyone not Christian, do not belong in "American" sacred spaces. Hinduism "undermines" American values, and handing the legislature's microphone to a Hindu, even for a moment, is an unacceptable departure from the government's constant and full-throated support for Christianity. As we will see in the chapter ahead, these beliefs emerge from historical antecedents that have consistently positioned Asian Americans as "forever foreigners,"[70] whose physical characteristics, cultural traditions, and religious beliefs don't fit within America. Like the resistance to Park 51, this thinking construes "others" as unwelcome in American public space because they dilute and pollute what is genuinely American: Whiteness and Christianity. In a patriotic nation, what is "American" is what is good; by implication, the nation's goodness and light will dim if Hindus offer prayers in the Capitol building or Muslims gather to worship in lower Manhattan.

As this hysteria is amplified, false beliefs about history are created: The words "under God" are assumed to be original to the Pledge of Allegiance, when in fact they were added in 1954. Alabama's Ten Commandments monument is assumed to be historical, when in fact it was erected in 2001 by then-Chief Justice (and later failed US Senate candidate) Roy S. Moore. The Eleventh Circuit Court of Appeals, ruling against the monument, compared Moore to "those Southern governors who attempted to defy federal court orders during an earlier era" of racial segregation.[71] Like desegregation and voting rights, which Southern governors had opposed in their time, growing racial and religious diversity led to a resistance that claimed the monument as a symbol of their apprehensions and resentments, and a longing for the days when Christianity had a stranglehold on all public sacrality. What would otherwise have been an obscure, local incident involving an eccentric judge was magnified into a national movement of Christian Americans who suddenly felt besieged in the heart of the Bible belt. If a three-ton monument that quotes the Bible, placed in a State Court rotunda, is an illegal "establishment of religion," how then would Christians mark their territory? Many Christians in Alabama and around the nation took the ruling that a Christian monument in civic space was unconstitutional as an attack on their faith, and on what they viewed as its right to occupy any US space they wished to claim as their own.

Often, the ways in which government continues to promote and protect Christianity to the exclusion of other faiths pass unseen and unacknowledged. This is part of our "optical illusion." Legislators who resist "Shari'a law," or city council members who try to stop construction of a mosque or gurdwara in their neighborhood, tend not to see that for 400 years Christianity has benefited from, and continues to benefit from, *de facto* and often *de jure* state sanction in virtually every aspect of society. When other religious communities and neighbors rise in solidarity to expose the specious arguments of the opposition, though they may oppose the discrimination, even they may not recognize its systemic roots.

The simultaneous weight and invisibility of this history explains why a level playing field feels so off balance to White Christians in America. The angry and virulent reaction to religious minorities, who are only seeking recognition of their faith traditions within the public religious sphere, reflects the manufactured idea that White Christianity is under assault. These activists' and lawmakers' efforts are palpably supremacist, given that their explicit goal is not social equity, but the return of Christianity to a place of unquestioned primacy in public and private society. In short, they "want their country back"—they want it as theirs, and theirs alone.

The Roots of Twenty-First-Century White Supremacy

While the dynamics of White Christian privilege have been in play for a long time, xenophobia and racist rhetoric experienced a new resurgence during and after the 2016 presidential campaign. Little of the rhetoric was new, but it had not been spoken by such prominent figures—including a US presidential candidate and then president, along with his political allies—in at least half a century. The stakes go up, and the very real physical and emotional risk to religious minorities is magnified, when elected officials—not schoolyard bullies or racist neighbors—use their position of authority to vilify a group. There is a causal connection between Trump's emboldening of his anti-Muslim, anti-immigrant base and the increase in hate speech and hate crimes. Data correlating anti-Muslim rhetoric in time with terrorist attacks show barely a blip after the Boston Marathon bombing in 2013 or the *Charlie Hebdo* attack in in France in January 2015, in which journalists and cartoonists were killed by two Muslim men upset by cartoon depictions of the Prophet Muhammad. By contrast, when then-candidate Trump barnstormed the nation making xenophobic speeches in 2015, data show a dramatic jump in anti-Muslim rhetoric.[72] Hostile political rhetoric increases the frequency of hate crimes targeting immigrants of all religious backgrounds, particularly Muslims.[73] By contrast, when former president George W. Bush publicly defended Islam in the immediate aftermath of 9/11, hate crimes dropped.[74]

One of the most visible and violent manifestations of these trends took place in August of 2017. I was preparing for my fall semester classes, beginning at the end of the month. Toggling over to my social media feeds, I could hardly believe the images: White supremacists and neo-Nazis in a torchlit procession and rally in Charlottesville, Virginia. The *New York Times* headline read "White Nationalists March on University of Virginia."[75] The chants included the Nazi slogan "blood and soil" and "Jew (You) will not replace us." The scenes evoked memories of the Hitler Youth and the Ku Klux Klan, both paramilitary organizations that were formed to protect not just White people, but specifically White Christians.

The catalyzing event was a "Unite the Right" rally, organized by members of the "alt-right," a loose coalition of political conservatives and White supremacist organizations, to protest the removal of a statue of Confederate General Robert E. Lee from a public park. They marched across the University of Virginia grounds, carrying tiki torches, swastikas, and semi-automatic rifles and chanting slogans. The rally and march turned violent when a group of counter-protestors also showed up. Incidents continued over the weekend; protesters and counter-protesters could be seen fighting until the crowds were dispersed by the police.[76] On its second day the encounter turned deadly, when a White supremacist drove into a crowd of counter-protesters, killing thirty-two-year-old Heather Heyer and injuring many more. Charlottesville would later be acknowledged as the largest White supremacist gathering in a generation.[77]

The public discussion of these events, and their meaning, was vigorous, in particular after the president stated a moral equivalency between the neo-Nazi ralliers and their opponents: "You had a group on one side that was bad. You had a group on the other side that was also very violent."[78] This remark, and a later comment in which the president referred to "very fine people on both sides," signaled the president's support of White nationalists. The president's statements contributed to the normalization of White Christian supremacist rhetoric across the country.

But the debate and the news coverage omitted a key element of how we must think about, talk about, and understand the events in Charlottesville and the twenty-first-century American "alt-right" movement. Many different words were used to describe the rally, including "White nationalist" and "Neo-Nazis." These terms are silent on the religious dimensions of alt-right belief. Based on the chants alone, people of color were not the only targets: so were Jews. It is clear that this was not just White supremacy but White *Christian* supremacy in action. We need to call it what it is. In *Antisemitism Here and Now*, historian and noted Holocaust scholar Deborah Lipstadt writes:

> we must forthrightly acknowledge those on the right who say they are merely trying to protect "European culture" as the antisemites and racists that they are. It was not by chance that those who gathered in Charlottesville in 2017 to protest the removal of a statue of Robert E. Lee also chanted "Jews will not replace us," or that when Richard Spencer ended a speech at an alt-right conference in Washington, D.C., shortly after the 2016 presidential election with the cry "Hail Trump, hail our people, hail victory," some of those in attendance responded with the Nazi salute.[79]

So, how did we get from Vicki's fellow Southern Baptists, who did not like her working with my father, to the deadly violence at Charlottesville? Part of the answer is the political rhetoric of recent years. But we must recognize that Vicki's congregation and the men in Charlottesville exist on the same spectrum of thought and approaches comprising the philosophy of White Christian supremacy. Treating supremacy as a violent project—as something the Klan does, but "kind" White Christians do not, recognizes only its extremes.

The attitudes of White Christians who would never pick up a tiki torch or fly the Confederate flag nevertheless give license to those who would. Institutions are made up of people. The problem is not limited to the elected officials who engage in explicit anti-Muslim or anti-Hindu rhetoric; it is also those officials who are less interested in the concerns of their religious minority constituents. Movements to preserve certain Confederate monuments or the Confederate flag in the name of "tradition," resistance to diverse prayer in legislatures, and the way people look down on their religious-minority neighbors are all part of the same phenomenon. We need to acknowledge White Christian supremacy in all the places it exists, and we specifically need to see that Christianity is virtually always there alongside White supremacist thought in xenophobic movements. Finding these supremacist attitudes and rules wherever they exist in the crevasses of everyday life is the essential first step in addressing these problems.

Conclusion

This chapter has provided examples of Christian normativity and privilege as individuals experience it. It is perhaps the least invisible part of the larger superstructure of White Christian supremacy. Christians' social power to define what is normal excludes, degrades, and harms religious minorities. The preeminence of

European and Protestant influences in US culture is not just a vestige of colonialism. It is the product of centuries of social policy since then, all influenced by shifting notions of Whiteness and Christian identity. Enduring cultural norms have affected US immigration and naturalization policy since the First Congress convened in Washington. Muslims, for example, were not the first minority religious or racial group to face the kind of bias described above: Native Americans and Japanese Americans, among others, were earlier targets. Their differing appearance and beliefs implied that they were dangerous and they were rounded up, excluded, interned, or killed as a result.

Now that we have begun to see through the optical illusion of "religious freedom" in the United States, and to understand that Whiteness and Christianity coexist and mutually support each other, we will explore the social and legal history that got us here. Understanding that history will enable us to better understand the situation today. This begins with seeing the path from the European origins and American manifestations of the dichotomy between Christian and heathen through the nineteenth-century experiences of Catholic, Jewish, and Orthodox immigrants. It continues with a ride on the twentieth century's legal roller-coaster from banning Asian immigration and stripping some Asians of their US citizenship in the roaring twenties, through to the emergence of the most diverse wave of American immigration yet after 1965. We will then see how all these developments created a twenty-first-century social and political environment in which unprecedented diversity has led to a new backlash that is redefining Americanness yet again.

2

Christianity and the Construction of White Supremacy

In 2018, *National Geographic* looked back over its 130-year history and issued an exceptional apology under the headline: "For Decades, Our Coverage Was Racist."[1] In an extensive, introspective article, the magazine set out "to rise above our past" by acknowledging how it perpetuated and contributed to colonialist and racist notions of civilization and barbarism. It recognized that its coverage had encouraged "seeing the cultures and religions of Asia, Africa, Oceana and Central and South America as exotic things to be consumed," including by offering images of barely clothed aboriginals, "black people . . . doing exotic dances," and villagers wearing ritual garb or engaging in unfamiliar spiritual practices. In its text, images, and selection of subjects, the magazine had perpetuated a dichotomy between the moral, civilized West and the depraved, uncivilized other with its "savage" and "exotic" rituals.

"How we present race matters," *National Geographic*'s editors concluded. But the flaws and failures in the magazine's White supremacist writing and photography were not just about race. For more than a century, the magazine had offered numerous depictions of religious rituals beyond the Christian realm, including both world religions and unique regional faith practices. Rituals and traditions of South America, Asia, Africa, and Oceania particularly tended to be presented as a collection of superstitions, delusions, and curiosities. *National Geographic* had helped to produce and promote not only notions of racial others and a dynamic of racial superiority and inferiority, but also notions of backward, idolatrous, religious others and the inherent superiority of Christianity over them.

By defining its shortfalls as merely racist, *National Geographic* ignored the specific ways it misrepresented and mistreated non-Christian peoples. *National Geographic*'s self-critical analysis still divided the world into White and "other," without recognizing how numerous factors, including religious practices and beliefs, interacted to form both Whiteness and "otherness." Whiteness is a not a free-standing idea; its shifting definition is given contour by other factors such as culture, geography, *and* religion. Nor is it uniquely American. The concept of race as it operates in our society today emerged in the fifteenth century,[2] as the product of even earlier encounters between Europeans and people from North Africa, sub-Saharan Africa, and Asia whose physical appearance was very different from theirs. The intimate embrace of Whiteness and Christianity (specifically, Protestant Christianity) in the United States contains roots in the repression of Jews and Muslims in the Iberian Peninsula, the transatlantic slave trade,[3] the Orientalist gaze on Arabia and Asia that accompanied European colonialism, and European Enlightenment thought as it shaped colonial projects in the Americas. Through all of these eras the Bible was, in the European, and later the American colonial settler mind,[4] "the world's constitution,"[5] and differences that came to be seen as racial first emerged from religious differences.

Exploring Christian privilege in the United States requires an understanding of the symbiosis between race and religion. Christian privilege and Christian normativity are part of the larger construct of *White* Christian supremacy. In the US, as in Europe before it, religion has been central to the construction of race.[6] From the first colonist/settler encounters with Native Americans and the arrival of slave ships to the debates over the status of Asian immigrants and the political framing of America's global rivals and allies, religion and religious identity have been inextricably bound up with notions of racial difference, assimilability, and American identity. In tandem with White social and economic power, Christian theologies of racial difference have helped to codify advantage for those who are perceived as "White." It takes an understanding of Whiteness's role in US history and its collusion with Christianity in the construction of American identity for us to trace how laws, court decisions, public policies, and social movements perpetuate White Christian privilege despite the optical illusion of religious freedom for all.

The European Roots of Whiteness and Christian Hegemony

To understand the interaction of race and religion and specifically to follow the ties connecting Whiteness and Christianity, we must go back to the fifteenth century. During this time, Spain was "the first great colonizing nation and a seedbed for Western attitudes toward race."[7] Throughout Europe, Jews had been demonized, vilified, expelled, or segregated in ghettos, mainly on religious grounds. While outcast from Christian European society because they did not accept Christ and were blamed for the Crucifixion, Jews were at one time absorbed into Christian culture if they converted to Christianity. These *"Conversos"* (Jewish converts to Christianity) needed to adopt Christian cultural conventions, such as grooming, style of dress, and bodily comportment, as proof of their genuine worthiness of the privileges only Christians enjoyed. Almost a century later, the *"Moriscos"* ("Little Moors"[8]), Muslim converts to Christianity, also faced expulsion. Thus, the term "Moor" was originally a religious identifier; its meaning shifted over time to include racial connotations of brownish skin color.[9] For the converts, tests of religious purity conflated ideas of blood lineage and biology with religious faith and cultural notions of kinship.[10]

Ultimately, conversion was not enough and as early as the fifteenth century, Spain required that Christians show "certificates of birth" to attest to their blood purity (*limpieza de sangre*). Spanish society became preoccupied with determining who was a "crypto-Muslim" or "crypto-Jew" even after conversion, thus beginning a conceptual connection between religion and blood. That connection led easily to the conflation of the idea of a "religion" and of a "race." In effect, Catholic Spain constructed its Jewish and Muslim minorities as infidels in relation to Christianity. In doing so, it connected the notion of *raza* (race) with the religious opposition of Christianity. The notion of blood purity led to the emergence of a caste system, *sistema de castas*, in which those with "pure" Spanish Catholic genealogies were held above those with mixed, impure heritage.[11] Mixed heritage was often, but not exclusively, associated with skin color and physical characteristics and with religious difference.[12] We can see echoes of this thinking in later US racial notions like the "one-drop rule," which imagined anyone with even one drop of African blood (racial heritage) to be inferior.[13]

In European Christians' demonizing of Jews and Muslims we detect the precursors of colonial racism in the Americas. In particular, we see how race gradually replaced religion (and, in particular contexts, race and religion remained interchangeable) as a way to distinguish among different peoples. In the European political context of the time, Muslims and Jews were the early categories of religious and racial others. Later, the European patterns of thought about and treatment of those religious others were brought across the Atlantic and applied to enslaved and indigenous groups in the Americas, whose theologies included animism and ancestor veneration.[14] Notions of race, nation, and religion were conflated and consolidated in these interactions. By beginning with religious difference, and reconceptualizing the Christian/non-Christian rivalry in biological or "natural" terms, European Enlightenment thought replaced religion with race as the defining distinction between superior and inferior peoples. As European society continued to encounter different "others," including during precolonial and colonial times in the United States, race was foregrounded as the basis for distinguishing peoples who were also religiously different.

European colonialism was a worldwide enterprise that involved not only economic exploitation but also the perpetuation and enforcement of ideas of White Christian superiority over the uncultured heathen masses through displacement, genocide, and missionary work.[15] Through colonization, religious conceptions were transposed or reinvented as racial conceptions in a process of *racial othering*. In this way, the church "became the handmaiden of European world domination."[16] There has always been a religious dimension to colonialism's economic and territorial agendas. In addition to providing a religious "purpose" for an economic and territorial subjugation of others, the church, as it sought to convert non-Christians, used the Gospel message to encourage indigenous populations' obedience to European colonial powers.[17] European powers sent missionaries to participate in these imperial efforts—acts in which we can see the origins of America's ideology and ambition of *Manifest Destiny*, in which the superior Anglo-Saxons would bring Christianity to the lands of the West, to claim America from sea to shining sea.

The idea of spreading Christianity motivated Prince Henry of Portugal (1394–1460), later called "the Navigator," to put in motion Europe's aggressive and ruthless expeditions to Africa. Henry viewed conversion and enslavement as interchangeable and used Christianity as a "civilizing" agent in service to the transatlantic slave trade.[18] In the eyes of Henry and others, however, conversion did not result in release from bondage: the European masters of the trade relied on observable phenotypical human differences, not professed faith, to define "slave" and "free."[19] Portuguese, Spanish, and English explorers carried with them an essentialized idea of religious superiority—which, because it was conceptualized as "blood-based," could be conflated with, and could mutually reinforce, racial domination. This equivalence provided a rationale for European colonialism based on a self-serving history in which "the West" constructed "the East" as extremely different and inferior, and therefore in need of Western intervention.[20] The British emerged as an overseas colonial power a century after Spain did, and absorbed aspects of the Spanish racial caste system into its colonialist rationalizations, particularly with regard to African slavery. Whereas the Spaniards were Catholics, the British operated within the context of Protestantism, which imagined a chosen people founding and raising a New Jerusalem in the New World—a Protestant nation, built with God's blessing on a new continent.[21]

Fifteenth and sixteenth-century Europeans not only colonized most of the world, they colonized information about the world. The way the West gazed on the East is encapsulated in the term *orientalism*, a worldview described by scholar Edward Said that imagines, exaggerates, and distorts the ways Arab and Asian peoples and cultures differ from Europeans. "Orientalism was ultimately a political vision of reality whose structure promoted the difference between the familiar (Europe, West, 'us') and the strange (the Orient, the East, 'them')."[22] Colonial encounters produced distortions, stereotypes, and patterns of misrepresentation about the multiple "others." Orientalism reinforced Christian supremacy by providing a way of looking at Christian peoples, cultures, and religions as collectively superior or to all others. Scholar Ricky Lee Allen argues that "European thought produced White supremacy by constructing perceptions of humans along a measuring stick, informed by Christianity's vocabularies of difference, that read "'civilized' on one white end and 'uncivilized' on the darkened other."[23] The colonial and orientalist mindset believed that Christians were superior to Muslims, Jews, and followers of indigenous religions native to Africa and the Americas, and that Europeans were superior to all others.

Orientalist and Christian supremacist thought provided a veneer of religious justification for this worldwide enterprise involving the expropriation of lands, minerals, and peoples in Africa, Asia, the Arabian subcontinent, and the Americas. Military conquest and economic exploitation were conducted "in God's name," with the idea that the uncivilized, heathen peoples would benefit by the imposition of the presumed gifts of a superior White Christian culture and the "good news" of the one true Gospel. This mindset enabled European colonialists to rationalize, to themselves and those peoples they were colonizing, how the different and inferior "East" would benefit from "rescue" by the benevolent West. Inevitably, these self-serving narratives reinforced the colonial enterprise.

These ideas were even formalized as "science." One instructive example is British scholars' development of the Aryan Invasion Theory (AIT) in the late nineteenth and early twentieth century.[24] This now-debunked, Orientalist theory held that the South Asian subcontinent had historically been populated by Dravidians—a dark-skinned, short-statured people—but that in about 1500 BCE the Aryans, fair-skinned and blue-eyed, invaded the subcontinent.[25] "Aryans" were considered to be from Central Asia, Scandinavia, Germany, Hungary, and/or Ukraine. Derived from the pseudoscience of the time, now known as *scientific racism,* the AIT was designed to support European colonial projects in Asia by casting the Western invader as part of a historic continuity and as a savior.[26] The AIT served to provide the British with a rationale, perhaps better described as political or diplomatic "cover," for colonizing present-day India, Pakistan, Nepal, and Bangladesh. If it was accepted as "science" that the Aryans invaded and occupied the same region millennia ago, this theory provided the rationale for the British occupiers to be there in modern times; as imagined, the British presence merely continued the region's "Aryan" cultural origins and was not a hostile or foreign occupation. British scholars thus rewrote history to suit their purpose of lowering resistance from their colonial subjects and rationalizing British claims to South Asia.

The work of the British Indologists diminished the legitimacy of local faiths by applying Christian normative lenses to them. This scholarship delegitimized the myriad forms of beliefs, rituals, and traditions that became known as Hinduism. For example, by emphasizing the idea of a single textual authority (the Bible) and clergy as its interpreters and gatekeepers,[27] scholars could regard the individual devotion and rituals (e.g., in-home worship) as mere superstition and cultural novelty. The White supremacist thought of the European Enlightenment period was deployed to justify Europeans' brutal treatment of people of color, the seizure of land and other resources of South Asian civilizations, and similar colonial ventures in Africa and elsewhere. Indeed, the AIT and other Orientalist approaches to Africa, Asia, and the global South drew heavily on the theories of scientific racism, which advocated the pseudoscientific idea that race was biological and that there were inherent, genetic differences that resulted in the intellectual and moral superiority of "Caucasians," the White race, and the inferiority of all other groups: Arabs, East and Southeast Asians (the "Mongoloid" race), Oceanians, and at the very bottom, Africans (the "Negroid" race).[28]

Religious difference became "biologized" so as to justify the idea that racial difference reflected a hierarchy of social evolution and to support the idea of the binary of civilization and "barbarity."[29] In scientific racist schools of thought, religious meanings were replaced in favor of identifying differences of a secular kind—in particular, phenotype, the observable physical characteristics. In reality, religion continued to be a key component of race and the practice of racism in the modern era.[30] Scientific racism was propagated in service of other colonial or racist projects, including the treatment of Native Americans, the perpetuation of slavery, and Jim Crow segregation in the United States. Scientific racism was the precursor to eugenics and even Nazi ideology.[31]

During colonialist expansion and settlement in the Americas, we see all of these phenomena play out: the colonial enterprise encountered people who were simultaneously racially and religiously different, including Native Americans and enslaved Africans. Whiteness and Christianity coexisted as the superior origin and theology, but the more visually conspicuous of the two—race—was emphasized. This emphasis resulted in the normalization of Christianity and its conflation with Whiteness in American national identity; rendering religion invisible, and foregrounding race as the nexus of difference and social privilege, makes possible the optical illusion of American religious freedom. By the late eighteenth century, when the framers were writing the Constitution and the first laws of the newly independent United States, race was front and center. The Constitution's "We, the People"[32] included the enumeration of enslaved Blacks as three-fifths of a human being and completely excluded "Indians not taxed,"[33] while the Naturalization Act of 1790 extended the right to citizenship only to "free white" men who exhibited "good moral character." By contrast, with the religious freedom guarantees in the Bill of Rights, religion seemed placed in a privileged position but also de-emphasized as a source of social hierarchy. The truth, of course, was far more complex.

Christianity and Whiteness in American History

Christianity remained at the center of life in the American colonies, reflected in European colonial encounters with both Native Americans and enslaved Blacks, like their forbears' encounters with racial and religious others in Europe. These interactions resulted in Whiteness emerging as a common identity across other lines like class and (European) national origin.[34] Whiteness, as a social construction, entered American history in the seventeenth century, when the colonists began to identify themselves as "white" in contrast with the Indians whose land they were appropriating and Africans who were regarded as property, or nearly so. Muslims first arrived in the Americas in the early 1500s, before the rise of the

Atlantic slave trade, and there is far more to the story of sub-Saharan Africans, and the American indigenous peoples than enslavement, exclusion, and involuntary labor.[35] The settler colonists, who were White Protestant Christians, regarded themselves alone as the chosen people and ordained by God to rule the land: superior, natural masters, hereditarily pure, glorious, and free citizens.

These settlers were living in a land they saw as the "New Israel," a reference to the story of the people of the Tanakh (Jewish scripture), to whom God promised the land of Israel as place of perpetual prosperity and peace.[36] Controlling these territorial lands and exploiting their natural resources, these colonists believed, would result in the establishment of God's kingdom on earth. Here we note the emergence of White Christian supremacy as an underlying principle of the American colonial endeavor. This stance cast people of African descent, Native Americans, and later Asians and Mexicans as holding subordinate status: inherently defective, depraved, and inferior. The result was a theologically justified racial conquest, harking back in some ways to the treatment of Muslims during the Crusades but remade in the "New Israel" of the American frontier.

Christianity, imperialism, and expansion came together in the doctrine of *Manifest Destiny*, which envisioned the end result of the colonial enterprise to be the spread of Christian civilization and the gospel across the United States. The need to spread the Protestant gospel to the uncivilized and savage provided the racial and religious justification for the persistent westward economic expansion of fur traders, settlers, ranchers, miners, railroad builders, federal marshals, and soldiers into territories that had been Native American, French (Louisiana), and Mexican (Texas and California, New Mexico and Nevada, parts of Arizona, Colorado, Utah). The doctrine of Manifest Destiny "embraced a belief in American Anglo-Saxon superiority" in a continent "intended by Providence as a vast theatre on which to work out the grand experiment of

Republican government, under the auspices of the Anglo-Saxon race" where "the inferior must give way before the superior race."[37] Living out Manifest Destiny meant that "the more heathens saved prior to the second coming of Christ, the more one could rest assured of their right to the tree of eternal life."[38] Native Americans' reception of this knowledge was their path to civilization and salvation.

Native Americans/Indigenous Peoples

The dehumanization, conquest, and genocide of the hundreds of indigenous nations is central to the White Christian supremacist project.[39] The Doctrine of Discovery, laid out in a number of papal documents, authorized any Christian monarch "who locates or discovers non-Christian lands and territories . . . to claim a superior and paramount title to these lands, territories, and resources. The Doctrine of Discovery states that non-Christian lands are considered to belong to no one because no Christians are living there and no Christian monarch or lord has yet claimed dominion."[40]

These papal papers supplied legal justification for White Christian supremacy and fueled settler colonialism endeavors, offering religious sanction for military, racial, and cultural domination. They thus enabled colonists to perceive divine purposes behind their appropriation of Native American lands, villages, and farmlands by conflating *religion* (Christian versus barbarous and heathen) with *civilization* (civilized versus primitive and savage), and conflating both with *race*.[41] Christian settlers imagined divine purposes behind the epidemics that wiped out Native populations and allowed colonial theft and exploitation of Native American villages and farmlands. The ensuing tribal displacements and cultural genocide were justified by belief in the inevitable victory of Christianity over heathens, and Western civilization over primitive indigenous cultures.

The erasure of Native peoples from the accounting of the new nation was ensconced in the Constitution, which provided that the census should count all residents to a greater or lesser degree, "excluding Indians not taxed." Even when the Fourteenth Amendment promoted former slaves to fully counted people in 1868, nullifying the original "three-fifths" provision, "Indians not taxed" were still excluded from the national accounting of who was in the country and worthy of representation. In effect, Indians were not considered to exist by federal or state authorities unless they paid taxes. Indians who paid taxes had integrated themselves into White communities economically, socially, and probably religiously. Any other indigenous peoples were not considered worthy of Constitutional protection, as they were not "civilized"—that is, not Christian.[42] In a parallel to orientalism, Native traditions were seen as impediments to progress and civilization.

The impact of Christianity is emblematic in the federal government's invocation of religious themes and the way it coordinated with religious figures in an ongoing effort to "civilize" Native Americans while also dispossessing them of their lands. In 1819, Congress established the Civilization Fund, which encouraged missionaries to aid in the "civilization process." The legislation supported mission schools that taught White culture and Euro-American trades, and employed the Bible to teach English. Ultimately, this law led to the creation of the boarding schools where clergy and teachers frequently cut the hair of Native children and dressed them in Western clothes. By removing Native American children from their home environments and imposing Christianity as a key component of instruction, they also discouraged continuity of native religious practices and language. By emphasizing the skills and tools of success in the Anglo-American way of life, schools became a way to force Protestant Christian values on Native American children. To "save the man," it was said, one must "kill the Indian."[43]

For a population whose connections to a higher power were intimately connected to place and nature, the Indian Removal Act of 1830 was not just the beginning of a forced migration now known as the Trail of Tears, but a policy that separated Native peoples from places with deep spiritual meaning. To understand the spiritual relevance of the Trail of Tears and of contemporary disputes involving Native American claims and access to particular lands, we must recognize that in Native American spiritualities, nature is not an abstraction but a concrete reality of conscious beings with spirit and power that must be treated with respect and care.[44] For North America's indigenous peoples, religion is based on where one lives and one's place of origin. Land represents not just a place to reside, cultivate, or hunt, but the locus of the people's creation or emergence from the earth of their ancient ancestors. Place is irreplaceable, because it is the source of identity and divine power. The very reverence of Native peoples for the land was twisted into a rationale for their removal.

As late as 1823, a US Supreme Court decision endorsed the White Christian supremacist effort to take Native American lands. In *Johnson v. McIntosh*, the Court ruled that the United States, to the exclusion of other tribes or private individuals, had the sole right to buy lands from Indian tribal governments. The Court referred to the Doctrine of Discovery, and stated that the federal government had inherited the right of England and other European countries—those who "discovered" America—to purchase, appropriate, and occupy the land.[45] Under President Ulysses Grant, the US government appointed Christian missionaries to oversee day-to-day operations on Indian reservations and enforce the terms of peace treaties with Native Americans.[46] In 1884, Congress passed the Religious Crimes Code to ban traditional Native American religious practices on reservations. This ban consisted of a systematic attempt to eradicate "heathenish" activities.[47]

As the discouragement of religious and folk knowledge and the prohibitions on nature-focused rituals were enforced by the Bureau of Indian Affairs in the late nineteenth century, Native Americans were forced to adopt subterfuges just to continue their religious life. Many Native communities adopted Christian practices, combining them with centuries-old indigenous rituals. Groups such as the Indian Shaker Church, a religious movement founded by Squaxin shaman John Slocum and his wife, encountered problems when trying to incorporate as a religious entity under US law. Apparently, government authorities only recognized "churches" as entitled to the benefits of religious institutions, such as non-taxation. Although the Shakers engaged in various Native rituals, combining them with references to Protestant and Catholic ideas, only when the group listed the Bible as the source of their faith on the government incorporation documentations did government officials allow their incorporation as a "church" in 1907.[48]

African Americans

We can also see the symbiosis between race and religion in the invention of American White supremacy in the enslavement of millions of Africans brought to the United States to accumulate wealth and fuel the colonial enterprise. Social justifications for slavery drew on the notion that Africans brought to the United States were heathens, not Christians.[49] The distinction between slave and free preceded the distinction between Black and White. It is estimated that a third of the enslaved population were Muslim; others practiced indigenous rituals specific to various regions of Africa. As in Europe, the rationalization of slaves' inferiority underwent a transition where race emerged to the foreground and religion's role was deemphasized. As this change occurred, the justification for Black servitude morphed from religious status to something approaching "race."[50] Race, religion, and the idea of White Christian superiority neatly excluded the multiple non-Christian "others" in the New World. Colonists could identify themselves as "White" in contrast to both the Indians whose land they were appropriating and the Blacks they were enslaving.

By the Revolutionary era, "race" had come to denote broad divisions of humankind, marked by physiological difference. Whiteness and Christianity became not so much conflated as coexistent, like two sides of a wide ribbon. As the ribbon twists through American history, we sometimes see the "religion side" (Christian superiority) while at other times we see the "race side" (White superiority). Yet, whichever side we see, the other side is still there, too.[51] Racism colluded with Christian supremacy: Africans were "beings apart," inferior to the point of being less than fully human, because they "were not merely black, they were black *and* heathen."[52] Non-Christian Africans' "depraved condition"—a condition their enslavement both rescued them from and condemned them to—was applied to all enslaved Blacks to explain their place in society as slaves. Colony by colony, new laws made slavery permanent and heritable for Black people, and for the first time the word "White," rather than "Christian" or "Englishman," began appearing in colonial statutes. Racism was instituted to justify slavery, not vice versa. As it had been for Spanish *Conversos* and *Moriscos*, even conversion to Christianity solved nothing for Black slaves. They were still considered heathens—not because they were actual heathens, but because it was believed that they had heathen ancestry that justified their continuing servitude.[53]

When White Protestant missionaries arrived in the plantation colonies intending to convert enslaved Africans to Christianity in the 1670s, they were met by slave owners who opposed slave conversion. Many slaveholders believed slaves were incapable of understanding Christianity. This belief stemmed from a prevailing idea that there was an "ordering of religions [that] mapped African religions," Islam and heathenism, as "the most fundamental, base manifestation of evil."[54] Further, slaveholders feared that allowing for Christian baptism would convince the enslaved of their equality to Whites—and, indeed, slaveholders blamed the evangelizing newcomers for slave rebellions.

Missionaries in favor of conversion articulated a vision of "Christian slavery," arguing that Christianity would make slaves hardworking and loyal.[55] They stressed not liberation and equality but racial hierarchy as God's will. Deploying the biblical story of Noah's curse on Ham, which European colonialists interpreted as a tale of blackness and servitude, a worldview was promoted in which bondage was God's will for people of African descent. According to the book of Genesis, after the flood Ham disrespected his father Noah. Noah cursed Ham's son Canaan and his descendants for Ham's transgression, declaring that they would be "servants unto servants."[56] Translating Ham as "dark" or "black" allowed the other characters in the story to become implied as White. This identification of "black skins with servile status" meant Black bodies could be bought and sold using biblical interpretation as justification.[57] The "Curse of Ham" provided a divine justification for the European and American slave trade, in which White citizens legalized slavery in America in the seventeenth century with the Curse as a biblical justification.[58]

The evangelical revivals of the Great Awakening beginning in the 1740s instigated widespread conversion of enslaved African Americans and supplied theological resources for the development of African American Christianity. The ranks of the evangelical White Baptists and Methodists grew, motivated by a commitment to sharing the Gospel with all and by doubts about the moral grounds of slavery. Those followers opposed slavery and believed that its continuation would prevent Black Americans from accessing the benefits of civilization and Christianity.[59] Ultimately, due to opposition to abolition by most southern White Christian slaveholders, these denominations retreated from their antislavery positions. However, Baptists and Methodists supported the development of Black Christianity, even as political, cultural, and racial discourses within these White Protestant denominations continued to rationalize race-based segregation between White and Black congregations within the church.[60]

The revivals of the Second Great Awakening of the late eighteenth and early nineteenth centuries extended the geographic reach of evangelicalism as the country expanded into new territory and also drew increasing numbers of African Americans to Christianity. White-governed churches nevertheless perpetuated society's racial hierarchy, with Blacks forced to sit in rear pews or in "nigger heaven" (church balconies, often with separate entrances) rather than in the company of their White brethren. Notwithstanding Christian theology that could be interpreted as racially egalitarian, "a racial tribalism [among Whites] . . . militated against sharing a common experience with Blacks as equals under any circumstances, religious or otherwise."[61]

In response, the Black Church developed on its own. The phrase *Black Church* is used as a "sociological and theological shorthand reference to the pluralism of Black Christian churches in the United States," particularly those independent, Black-governed denominations such as African Methodist Episcopal Church, the African Methodist Episcopal Zion Church, and the National Baptist Convention. These churches and denominations emerged after the formation in 1787 of the Free African Society, an interdenominational congregation of free Blacks in Philadelphia.[62] They became significant arenas for spiritual support, educational opportunity, economic development, and political activism for Black Americans in the resistance against White Christian America.[63] In the 1950s and 1960s, these churches and others became a spiritual home for the Civil Rights Movement; religion and its role as an inspiration and organizing center for African American communities was an important component of the struggle for freedom. As a physical and social venue to gather, churches were a locus of the movement. They also became a target for anti-civil rights violence; numerous

Black churches were bombed in the mid-twentieth century, killing many, including children.

Throughout this era, civil rights activists and leaders were being surveilled by the US government, particularly the FBI. The FBI began the monitoring during the 1955 Montgomery Bus Boycott. FBI Director J. Edgar Hoover believed Dr. Martin Luther King Jr. was influenced by communist ideologies and Soviet agents in the West. Hoover ultimately came to believe that King, with his agenda of racial and economic justice, was a member of the Communist Party. The goal of the FBI's monitoring effort was to discredit King and other movement leaders. In 1967, the Bureau labeled the Southern Christian Leadership Conference a "black nationalist hate group." As a Senate Select Committee found years later, after King's assassination, "Rather than trying to discredit the alleged Communists it believed were attempting to influence Dr. King, the Bureau adopted the curious tactic of trying to discredit the supposed target of Communist Party interest—Dr. King himself."[64]

While the White majority, as represented by the FBI, thought of Black Christians as "communists," Africans American Muslims were considered even more different and dangerous. The same year it began surveilling Civil Rights groups, the FBI began targeting the Nation Of Islam, publishing a training manual called "The Muslim Cult of Islam."[65] It contained misleading information about African Americans, negatively profiled leaders of the Nation Of Islam, and attempted to point out the differences between traditional Islam and this "cult." The FBI advocated that the "true religion of these Black subjects, in other words, was not an acquired religion of Islam as practiced in the Middle East but an essentially limbic religion of primitivism that stemmed from the racial constitution of Blacks."[66] As people both Black and Muslim, NOI's members were even more suspect than the Black Christians Hoover imagined as communists. Even during World War II, Hoover stated of NOI: "This Negro cult showed strong evidence of Japanese influence." Hoover was taking exception to the Muslim adherents' refusal to comply with military service obligation because of "their Mohammedan religion"—and doing so by tying them to another racial/religious enemy of the time. Nation Of Islam and other Black Muslim groups were thus positioned as an enemy even more suspect than the Black Church, and we see the emergence of the imagined rivalry between White Christianity and the Islam practiced in communities of color emerging decades before the Middle East became the United States' primary imagined enemy.

Protestant Power

While this chapter has concentrated on the symbiosis and conflation of Whiteness and Christianity in the United States, it must be acknowledged that it has most often been *Protestant* Christianity in that active role. Other Christian groups, or groups that would describe themselves as "Christian" if that designation is contested, have not always been similarly situated. Until at least the mid-1800s in most of the United States, to be White meant to be not merely Christian, but specifically to be a member of one of a few sects of Northern European or European American origin, such as Baptist, Episcopalian, Methodist, or Lutheran. In addition to the *racial* exclusion of Christian communities of color from White churches, there was often also a *religious* exclusion of minority *White* religious sects from this mainstream. This includes the anti-Catholicism we will discuss in the next chapter.

The link between Whiteness and specifically Protestant Christianity is particularly evident in the treatment of the Church of Jesus Christ of Latter-Day Saints (the Mormons), Seventh-Day Adventists, and Jehovah's Witnesses. The violence experienced by these groups in the nineteenth century was harshly similar to the colonial expulsions of so-called heretics who threatened the established religious/political order, from the Salem Witch Trials to the expulsion of Roger Williams and his followers from the Massachusetts Bay Colony. Although Mormons, Jehovah's Witnesses, and Seventh Day Adventists could plausibly claim to be Christian, their theological claims, political separatism, and aspirations toward autonomy placed them outside of Christianity as it was generally understood. The clashes that pitted police and armed mobs against Mormons or Jehovah's Witnesses ended only with the withdrawal of these religious sects into relatively autonomous geographical spaces and/or the relinquishment of their sectarian claims to political autonomy.[67] Their fraught relationship with mainstream Christianity did not preclude these groups' participation in the broader colonial and racial projects of the United States. For example, Mormon "expulsion" into the Utah Territory in the nineteenth century served US goals of westward expansion and the dispossession of Native Americans. Meanwhile, these faiths themselves had complex relationships with race and racism: Mormons, for example, did not recognize Blacks' rights to equal religious participation, including priesthood, until 1978, and did not renounce religious doctrines of Black inferiority until 2013.[68]

Despite these and other complexities within the American experience of race and religion even in the eighteenth and early nineteenth centuries, American society was developing two key binary categories of race. The first of these categories contrasted the "heathen" state of the native population with Whites, who represented not only a civilization worthy of spiritual and cultural greatness but also a civilizing force setting out to conquer the natives' wilderness home. The second was a contrast of a "Blackness" identified with chattel slavery and a "Whiteness" that served to mobilize poor and non-slaveholding Whites on the side of wealthy planters and slaveholders. Both of these binaries encompassed elements of religion, in that Blacks were heathen or descended from heathens. Even Black Christians occupied different physical space and performed religious practice differently from the White Christians who defined the norm. Likewise, the native population was both brown and heathen—visibly different, White Christians could imagine, from God as well as man.

Conclusion

The social structures created over centuries carry forward into modern formulations that perpetuate both racial notions of religious difference and the idea of religion as a rationale for the marginalization of minority communities. In the eighteenth century, land owners and poor Whites could agree on the notion that abolitionism violated their religious freedom. They imagined a First Amendment right to believe and engage in slavery. When twentieth-century White Christian congregations mobilized to restrict African Americans and Latinos from purchasing homes in their neighborhoods, or White Christian employers viewed the 1941 Federal Fair Employment Act as a threat to their religious freedom, they perpetuated these same patterns: invoking an expressly racist version of religion that protected White Christians at the expense of non-White, including non-Christian, others.[69]

These movements share a theological common ground with those twenty-first-century religious figures who oppose the gay rights movement as an affront to their Christian freedoms. For those whose faith tells them that Blacks should be enslaved, or that LGBTQ people are evil, legally enforced equality is imagined as an infringement on a religious freedom to engage in biblically sanctioned discrimination. For those who imagine an American "blood purity" that interweaves Christianity and Whiteness, current immigration trends represent not just demographic change but a loss of national identity. Likewise, the resistance to tribal arguments regarding the environmental protection of spiritually significant sites[70] perpetuates religious and racial biases of colonial origin. As we will see in the chapters ahead, all of these historical legacies have profound real-world effects on US religious minorities even today.

3

Immigration, Citizenship, and White Christian Supremacy

"When will minorities be the majority?" blared a *Boston Globe* headline in 2016. The article, one of many at the time, described how the changing racial and religious demographics of the United States are approaching a tipping point: "By mid-century, it looks as if the United States may become a majority-minority nation, a place where whites make up less than half the population." A few years earlier, the Associated Press (AP) newswire carried a story, published in papers across the nation, warning of "historic change in a nation in which non-Hispanic Whites will lose their majority in the next generation, somewhere around the year 2043."[1]

Especially when presented so hyperbolically, demographic trends tend to worry and concern White Christians, particularly those who view these trends as proof that their race, their religion, or the nation's identity is under attack. The resulting anxiety is why they frequently see themselves as victims of discrimination rather than its systemic beneficiaries. As a result, they often "giv[e] power to politicians who implicitly or explicitly stoke that fear."[2] For many, America is *supposed* to be White and Christian: that represents those who founded the country, and that is who remains in the majority, at least for now. Changing demographics cause segments of the White Christian population to perceive a loss of their dominant status, what Janelle Wong calls "perceived in-group embattlement" and to believe that the "American way of life needs protection."[3] In other words, something that is "ours" is being "taken away" by people who are different. It is going to become "theirs." But it was "ours" in the first place.

Yet while demographic changes are indeed happening, White Christian America is not actually losing its power, even when it may become a numerical minority. Why? Because 275 years of embedded advantages in our laws and public policies are not going to disappear overnight. Let us unpack this situation. Alongside these racial trends, the Pew Research Forum in 2015 reported that Protestants are no longer a religious majority in the United States.[4] As we saw earlier, 43% of Americans identify as White and Christian, and 30% specifically as White and Protestant.[5] While still the largest single racial/religious cohort by far, this is a substantial change since 1976, when roughly eight in ten (81%) Americans identified as White and Christian, and a majority (55%) were White Protestants. Overall, a substantial majority of Americans today remain Christian, a cohort that includes a growing proportion of Asian, Black, and Hispanic Christians. While much of the decline in the White Protestant majority can be traced to immigration, as we saw discussed earlier, at least as much is likely accounted for by religious disaffiliation: about a third (34%) of Americans now identify as religiously unaffiliated.[6] Jewish Americans constitute 2% of the public while Muslims, Buddhists, and Hindus each make up about 1% of the US population. All other religious minority groups together constitute an additional 1%. Among racial groups, Asian and Pacific Islander Americans are significantly more likely to be religious minorities.

For White Christian Americans who perceive these demographic trends as threatening, and need someone to blame, racial and religious minority communities become targets. They are blamed for everything from being public health nuisances to undermining our nation's moral fiber. Ignoring the longer trends behind the change, the conservative Christian Broadcasting Network (CBN) framed the news in politically loaded terms in 2016, implying a connection between religious change and the election of a Black president: "In the time since President Barack Obama was elected, the nation has experienced a dramatic shift and . . . white Christians are increasingly becoming the minority."[7]

In the words of another 2017 headline, "White fear of demographic change is a powerful psychological force."[8] Reporting like the *Globe*'s and CBN's, sensationalistic and with a tone of alarm, is framed to stoke fear and resentment in a growing segment of White Christian America. As we have seen, the privileges afforded Whites and Christians in America are largely invisible to their beneficiaries. After eight years of the Black president whom CBN implicitly blamed for the nation's changing racial and religious complexion, White evangelicals in overwhelming numbers voted for Donald Trump, who repeatedly promised to protect the religious liberty of Christians.[9] Among other pledges, candidate Trump in 2015 promised voters "a total and complete shutdown of Muslims entering the United States until our country's representatives can figure out what the hell is going on."[10]

The resulting Executive Order 13769, commonly known as the "Muslim Ban," which aimed to limit Muslims coming to the United States, harkened back almost exactly a century to the Immigration Act of 1917, which restricted Asian immigration. After the executive order was signed in January 2017, its opponents on television news and social media lamented: "This is not who we are as a nation." On the contrary, this is exactly who we have always been. Although treated as astonishing, the Muslim Ban was consistent with how the federal government has conducted immigration and naturalization policy for much of US history: as a political response to popular fears of dark-skinned non-Christian people.[11]

Americans on all sides of the debates over immigration, naturalization, and the nation's growing diversity are products of history. The United States' racial and religious hierarchy is not a result of coincidence. The demographics of every era, whether in the idealized 1950s or the present day, are a consequence of public policies, intentionally adopted and implemented by government officials and approved by the courts over the course of centuries. The normative power of Whiteness and Christianity in the US did not just emerge out of thin air. It is the product neither of happenstance nor of the moral superiority of White Christians, but of their legal and social power to define the parameters of "us" and "them," which has lasted since European settlement. In other words, the majority (soon the plurality) status of Whites and Christians is the product of centuries of socially engineering the country's demographic makeup through domestic, foreign, and immigration policy.

Our laws bear enduring legacies for our social realities. The association between Whiteness, Christianity, and American national identity has been established and reproduced through naturalization and immigration policies since the time the First Congress convened in New York. By restricting citizenship to "free white" men, the First Congress in 1790 formulated a racial definition of "American." (Birthright citizenship was still a thing of the future, established by the passage of the Fourteenth Amendment after the Civil War.) The American idea of Whiteness, in turn, encompassed Christian religious identity. The 1790 Act did not establish an explicitly religious test, but Europe was the geographic home of Christianity and had been since before the Crusades. In tandem with the attempted eradication of Native Americans and the enslavement of Africans, US law established and maintained a definition of "American" that encompassed racial and religious elements.

As for immigration, the United States' famous tag line—"a nation of immigrants"—perpetuates the popular belief that everyone from anywhere in the world has been allowed to enter the United States, at all points in history. Yet similar to the "optical illusion" in which the idea of "religious freedom for all" has concealed Protestantism's dominant influence in US law and culture, America's self-proclaimed image as a nation of immigrants obscures a reality in which restrictions with religious and racial roots have always determined who can migrate to the United States. Examining both immigration and nationalization policy is essential to understanding who we are as a country today, how America's twenty-first century population came to look (and pray) the way it does, and why the current national furor over demographic change misses the point.

Immigration

Our nation has always maintained a love-hate relationship with immigration. Seventeenth and eighteenth-century European immigration established the nation and its identity, including its design as a democratic republic based on European Enlightenment thought. The tide of immigration debates has ebbed and flowed, but has never disappeared from the halls of Congress, US workplaces and the popular news media. Today's raging immigration debates, both in our communities and at the national level, echo sentiments and statements from the 1840s through the 1920s. Many who identify as deeply patriotic equate patriotism with defending and preserving America's heritage as White, Protestant, and English-speaking— conflating those identities with Americanness itself.

How did we become a nation that is 76.5% White[12] and 70.6% Christian?[13] In order to answer this question, we have to understand the critical impact of immigration policy. First, the backdrop. At the establishment of the nation, the republic was largely populated by Western and Northern European people and their offspring. This profile shaped early notions of who was "native" to the US and extended that definition to people descended from the White population present at the founding, a group that was overwhelmingly Anglo-Saxon and Protestant. From this "native stock"—not Native Americans, but those in power at the time of the founding—was distinguished "foreign stock," or immigrants.[14] The White Anglo-Saxon Protestant population developed negative views of these immigrant communities, a stance that became known as *nativism*. Nativism, then and now, is a combination of *xenophobia*, the express hatred or fear of others, and *ethnocentrism*, the preference for one's own group. Nativism emerged almost as soon as European immigrants, particularly Jewish, Catholic, and Orthodox immigrants, began arriving in material numbers in the mid-nineteenth century.

Pushed by famine in Ireland, political instability in southern Europe, and pogroms in the east, large numbers of Italians, Irish, Slavs, and others began arriving to the eastern United States beginning in the 1840s. They brought with them Catholicism, Judaism, and the Russian and other Eastern Orthodox denominations.[15] A steady increase of immigrants in the subsequent decades resulted in the proportion of US residents who were foreign-born reaching its historic peak in 1890,[16] when the census showed that 14.8 percent of residents were born abroad. With continued immigration, that figure still stood at 14.7% in 1910. (For comparison, 13.3% of US residents were foreign-born in 2010.)[17]

European Jewish and Catholic immigrants in the late nineteenth and early twentieth centuries experienced exclusion and discrimination in employment, housing, and elsewhere in society. The combination of their non-Protestant religious identities and their darker complexion, as compared to the northern European majority of the time, made them targets for discrimination by the White Protestant majority. The Immigration Restriction League and the "Know-Nothing" Party were among several national organizations that propagated nativism and lobbied government officials to restrict immigration. The agenda of these organizations and others like them reflected the sentiment of the "native stock," and included anti-immigration, racism, anti-Catholicism, antisemitism, and pro-eugenics beliefs. The Know-Nothing Party's nativist political ideology became a national movement in the 1850s. The adherents believed some immigrants to be political agents of the Roman church, and successfully organized to restrict Irish immigration and bar immigrants from holding public office and, in some cases, from voting.

Many mainstream American Protestants viewed Catholic schools not simply as educational institutions but as producers of "papal converts." They wanted to remove the children of Irish Catholic immigrants from parochial schools to educate them in "proper" Protestant environments. "[T]he loudest voices in the organized nativism of the 1840s and 1850s harped on matters of Catholicism and economics, not race," writes Matthew Frye Jacobson, although in the stereotypes, for example of "Papists," "religion was sometimes seen as a function of race."[18] European Catholic immigrants remained apart, often living in ethnic enclaves and retaining their own habits and customs, many of which were repugnant to Protestant observers. Catholic immigrants were disparaged for not assimilating—though, in fact, many WASPs (White Anglo-Saxon Protestants) did not even want them to assimilate.

Jewish immigration from Europe started as a trickle in the 1830s and developed into a flood by the 1850s. The American Jewish population of about 4,500 in 1830 rose to approximately 40,000 in 1845 and leapt to 150,000 by the time of the Civil War. Despite their acceptance as citizens in the United States, the Jew was "everywhere an alien."[19] Christian culture permeated America so that even those who did not attend church still picked up on the bigotry and antisemitic attitudes. Jews were referred to as "mysterious," "cursed," and "wanderers," and attacks on synagogues, Jewish cemeteries, and Jewish individuals and families occurred across the United States throughout this period.

During the Civil War, General (later President) Ulysses Grant enacted General Order number 11, which expelled all Jews from Tennessee and parts of Kentucky in December of 1862. The rationale for this policy was the need to control Jewish peddlers, but the directive was directed at all Jews, no matter their vocation, sex, or age, including families with children. President Abraham Lincoln quickly rescinded the order, but not before several families were displaced.[20] Throughout the 1800s, Jews faced discrimination in society and education, up to and including exclusion from literary and social circles in college and adult social clubs and other posh venues. In 1877, for example, German-Jewish immigrant Joseph Seligman, a prominent banker, was barred from registering as a guest at the Grand Union Hotel in Saratoga Springs, New York, though Seligman was a banker of great prominence and a friend of the late Abraham Lincoln.[21]

Antisemitic tropes emerged that still circulate today, as mainstream Americans voiced concern about the influence of Jews over the American economy, and banks in particular. In 1896, Democratic presidential candidate William Jennings Bryan stoked nativist worries about economic instability by invoking biblical imagery in a screed against US banks: "You shall not press down upon the brow of labor this crown of thorns, you shall not crucify mankind upon a cross of gold."[22] The antisemitism evoked by the metaphor of the crucifixion was powerful and appealed to rural Protestants in the South and the West. A minister in Detroit proclaimed that "Jews constituted a greater threat to the United States than the 'yellow peril,'" evoking fears that the new Jewish immigrants would destroy America's grand Christian civilization.[23] Henry Ford, the founder of the Ford Motor Company, became a strong believer in the antisemitic idea of a global conspiracy of Jews attempting to control the world's financial resources. He bought a newspaper, the *Dearborn Independent,* a copy of which was distributed to every person who bought a Ford automobile. The newspaper trafficked in antisemitic stories, including by promoting the Protocols of the Elders of Zion—a spurious tract that purported to be the Jewish blueprint for world financial domination, but was actually fiction. This antisemitic idea of a Jewish conspiracy to control of global finance continues to be repeated today.

Today we see the nineteenth-century Know-Nothings' ideological descendants in the contemporary White Nationalist movement associated with supremacist groups like the Aryan Nation and the

Church of Jesus Christ Christian. While often spoken of primarily as White supremacist, neo-Nazi, or "racial" hate groups, many of these organizations in fact inhabit the same crossroads of White and Protestant identity as their predecessors.[24] Their ideology combines racism with a pseudo-biblical and religious mythology and considers Whites to be the true "lost tribes," Jews to be the children of Satan, and non-Jewish non-Whites to be descended from pre-Adamic "mud peoples." In 2018, a White Protestant man entered a Pittsburgh synagogue armed with an AR-15 rifle and murdered eleven people; after he was captured, he explained his actions to a SWAT officer this way: "They're committing genocide to my people. I just want to kill Jews." Further investigation revealed that the man's prolific online history included rants against Jews, refugees, and African Americans. Studying White nationalist movements and the motivations of violent actors like the Pittsburgh shooter reveals that they often view themselves as heroes and saviors of an originalist idea of America for White Christians only.[25]

Asian Immigration to the United States

As Europeans were arriving on the East Coast in the nineteenth century, an influx of Asian immigration was changing narratives of race and religion in the South and West. Asian immigration in the nineteenth century included Filipinos entering New Orleans via the Caribbean and the arrival of numerous Chinese, Japanese, Koreans, and South Asians on the West Coast.[26] These Asian ethnic groups brought with them Buddhism, Confucianism, Hinduism, Islam, Sikhism, and Shintoism as well as many syncretic sects and localized folk traditions.

Major economic developments in the West functioned to draw Asian immigrants to American shores during this time period: the California Gold Rush, the construction of the Transcontinental Railroad, and the development of agriculture in the newly acquired western states. Construction of the western portion of the Transcontinental Railroad, the most massive industrial undertaking of its time, employed thousands of Chinese workers beginning in 1862. In 1869, the railroad was completed when the tracks laid by the Central Pacific Railroad company met those laid by the Union Pacific in Utah.[27]

While Asians were valued as cheap labor, they quickly became targets because they were considered to be different and deviant. In addition to visual markers of difference, their faiths were "foreign" to Protestant eyes. Chinese and South Asian laborers were called "coolies," a pejorative term used to describe poor and indentured Asian laborers, and a colonial construct influenced by religious difference.[28] Although Asians were recognized as good workers, there was fear about the "importation of heathen coolies"[29] and the term encompassed both Asians' racial difference and the distinction, perceived by Whites, between Asians' less "civilized" religions and the Christianity Whites regarded as their own. The prevailing sentiment at the time was while coolies were industrious it would be difficult to convert them to Christianity; indeed, one common view was that the "immorality" of these races made them difficult to convert.[30]

The South Asian immigrants at the time were Sikhs from the Punjab region, who were exploited as farm laborers. In addition to their brown skin, those Sikhs kept the turban, unshorn hair, and other religious elements of dress and comportment would stand out as visibly different to White observers. Despite their religion but due to their origins on the subcontinent, they were often referred to as "Hindoos," while the Chinese were called "heathens" and "devil-worshippers."[31] In the social and economic hierarchy, Christianity and Whiteness were associated together as moral and cultural attributes deemed a necessary part of the American experiment.

East Asians in the United States—already a visible "other" due to their physical appearance—were increasingly perceived through a cloud of entangled religious and racial meanings that justified White domination over them. Particularly as job competition between Asians and working-class Whites increased social friction, the mainstream public dialogue referred to "hordes of Chinese," the "Yellow Peril," and "heathen coolies"[32]—tropes that wove together notions of foreignness, racial and cultural inferiority, and religious difference. The implied threat this "horde" of "heathens" represented to White Protestant society fed discrimination and sometimes violence against Asian individuals and communities.

Mainstream America's simultaneous attention to religious and racial difference was evident in comparisons between the Chinese and enslaved Blacks that appeared in newspapers. In 1853, newspapers reported Chinese to be "morally a far worse class to have among us than the Negro . . . they are not of our people, and never will be." The fact that the Chinese were not Christian, along with being considered racially inferior, made them subject to suspicion. Some politicians cited their differing religious beliefs as a justification for exclusion. "How long, sir, will it be before a million of Pagans, with their disgusting idolatries, will claim the privilege of voting for American Christians, or against American Christians?" asked an Alabama congressman in 1855. Such beliefs regarding religious competition helped to strengthen White supremacist attitudes and feelings of distrust toward the Chinese.[33] Just a few years after the Civil War had ended slavery and Constitutional amendments had extended citizenship (and therefore, at least theoretically, the vote) to Blacks, Reverend S. V. Blakeslee, a White advocate of restrictions on Chinese immigration, advised the US Senate:

> But now observe the practical superiority of slavery over Chinese immigration, as an impelling force for good. Slavery compelled the heathen to give up idolatry, and they did it. The Chinese have no such compulsion and they do not do it . . . Slavery compelled the adoption of Christian forms of worship, resulting in universal

Christianization. . . . Slavery took the heathens and by force made them Americans in feeling, tastes, habits, language, sympathy, religion and spirit; *first* fitting them for citizenship, and then giving them the vote. The Chinese feel no such force, but remaining in character and life the same as they were in Old China, unprepared for citizenship and adverse in spirit to our institutions.

By 1882, growing hostility against the Chinese resulted in Congress' adoption of the Chinese Exclusion Act. The Act, passed in part as a result of loud demands from organized labor, was a watershed in US immigration history: it was the first time that the United States barred an entire group of people from immigrating based on national origin.[34] Initially written as only a ten-year ban on Chinese immigration, the law was later extended indefinitely and made permanent in 1902.

Similar in tone was increased opposition to South Asian laborers and farmers. The Asiatic Exclusion League, founded in San Francisco in 1905, asked what would become of the nation "if this horde of fanatics should be received in our midst?"[35] The League argued that immigrants from India, China, and Japan would "substitute the semi-barbarous heathen civilization of Shintoism and Brahma, Buddha, and Confucius, for our Christian civilization" as well as "outnumber and dominate our present population."[36] An article in a 1910 issue of *Collier's Weekly* described a "Hindu Invasion." In this article, the Asiatic Exclusion League promoted the sensationalistic notion that "Hindus in California numbered 10,000" and that their presence is an "unmitigated nuisance."[37] In reality, the 1900 Census had reported that 2,050 residents had been born in India.[38] We can find this practice of inflating or simply inventing numbers to make the "problem" appear larger than it is still in use in the racist, xenophobic rhetoric of today.

While immigration continued to both coasts, two other events engendered major demographic changes for the US population.

First, the United States emerged victorious in the Mexican–American War. The war, motivated by the doctrine of Manifest Destiny, ended in 1848 with the signing of the Treaty of Guadalupe Hidalgo. Under this treaty, the United States acquired from Mexico the land that constitutes the present day southwestern United States, and residents of these former Mexican lands could become US citizens. Then, in 1868, African Americans were granted freedom and citizenship with the passage of the Thirteenth and Fourteenth Amendments. Together with immigration, these changes in the demographics and social power structures of the country were frightening for many in the WASP majority. As geography, law, and immigration expanded US citizenship, the fabric of White Protestant national identity seemed to be stretching thin. The result was a xenophobic and sometimes violent backlash and the implementation of anti-immigrant policies that would put the brakes on the nation's growing diversity for generations.

From 1882 to 1924, an emboldened and increasingly successful political and social movement of nativist and xenophobic WASPs against immigration patterns generated some of the most restrictive immigration policies in US history. Repeated amendments and extensions of the Chinese Exclusion Act in the last two decades of the nineteenth century were just the beginning. Immigration restrictions increased again in 1917 with the Barred Zone Act. Signed by President Woodrow Wilson, an avowed segregationist and advocate of preserving the nation's WASP Protestant "purity," the 1917 legislation recognized an Asiatic Barred Zone, banning immigration of "inhabitants of most of China, all of India, Burma (Myanmar), Siam (Thailand), and the Malay states, part of Russia, all of Arabia and Afghanistan, most of the Polynesian Islands, and all of the East Indian Islands." This represented approximately one fifth of the world's land area, with an estimated population of 500 million people. As Chinese and Japanese immigration had already been excluded by separate laws and diplomatic agreements, South Asian immigrants were the clear targets of the law.[39] The Barred Zone Act contains no references to religion, but when we apply our "optical illusion" lens, it is clear that the Act had the effect of restricting immigration of non-Protestant populations. The geographic regions "barred" by the 1917 Act were home to most of the world's Buddhists, Confucians, Hindus, Sikhs, and many Muslims; these religious groups were effectively shut out of the United States.[40]

At the same time, in addition to the Asiatic Exclusion League, groups like the Immigration Restriction League (IRL) were ascendant, as were the Ku Klux Klan and new Christian Identity groups that added anti-Catholicism and antisemitism to their racist agendas.[41] Launched in Boston by three Harvard alumni in 1894, the IRL attempted to maintain America's Anglo-Saxon heritage and traditions. Its members believed the nation could not endure, nor could its values be sustained, without restricting "the scum of Europe" from American shores. According to the IRL, the latest immigrants consisted not of sturdy Anglo-Saxons with a proud heritage, but of people "of objectionable races" from parts of Europe Americans had never visited; the habits, values, and behavior of these "undesirables" were at odds with everything that "real" Americans cherished. They feared that eventually the foreigners would undermine American culture and impose their own culture throughout the land.[42] Madison Grant, a vice president of the Immigration Restriction League and an officer of the American Eugenics Society who traced his ancestry to colonial America, wrote *The Passing of the Great Race* (1916), a widely referenced publication that popularized the idea of a racial hierarchy. He doubted that a "man, deeply tanned by the tropical sun, and denied the blessings of Christianity and civilization" could have any place in American society.[43] Congress and the courts relied on the text, and on Grant's testimony, to support racist immigration and naturalization policies.

Nativists like Grant were further emboldened by their success in passing the Barred Zone Act. The original Ku Klux Klan, founded after the Civil War as an anti-Black, anti-Republican militia, had withered during Reconstruction under federal antiterrorist prosecution. The isolationist hysteria of the World War I era, however, drove new supporters to the Klan. Re-launched at Stone Mountain, Georgia, in 1915, the second Ku Klux Klan articulated hate more broadly, no longer limiting its attacks to Blacks with political ambitions. In the 1920s, boasting five million members nationwide, the Klan assailed "Katholics, Kikes, and Koloreds"—that is, Catholics, Jews, Black people—as well as foreigners and organized labor.[44]

Riding the momentum of 1917, economic insecurity resulting from a postwar recession, and enduring WASP anger and unease at the influx of Catholic, Orthodox, and Jewish immigrants from Europe, anti-immigrant Congressmen succeeded in passing a pair of restrictive immigration acts in 1921 and 1924. Both aimed to drastically reduce the entry of southern and eastern Europeans, who were deemed inferior "breeds." The National Origins Act of 1924 (an amendment to the Immigration Act of 1921) also known as the Johnson-Reed Act, accomplished this goal by indexing foreign countries' immigration quotas to the number of Americans of that national origin as reported in the 1890 census. Specifically, the law capped new immigration at two percent of the number, reduced from three percent in the 1921 law, of a particular nationality already in the United States at that time, with the aim of preserving the nation's demographic profile of 1890. Relying on more recent Census counts would allow more immigration of Catholics and Jews. Instead, Congress blatantly set out to socially engineer the nation's demographic profile by indexing post-1924 immigration quotas to the *1890* Census. Referring back more than thirty years would yield an immigration scheme to replicate an earlier America. One effect of the 1924 Act, for example, was to reduce English immigration by only 19% but Italian immigration by 90%.

The countries from which immigration was most curtailed by the 1924 Act included Italy, Poland,[45] Czechoslovakia, the Soviet

Union, Greece, Lithuania, and Latvia. "America of the Melting Pot comes to End" crowed a 1924 opinion headline in the *New York Times*. The author, Republican US Senator David A. Reed of Pennsylvania (the "Reed" of "Johnson-Reed"), pledged that strict new immigration quotas would "preserve racial type as it exists here today." Consider the countries that were targeted with this immigration act. Consider the religious backgrounds of the majority of the people coming from these countries. They are Catholic, Jewish, and Eastern Orthodox. They are not Protestant Christians.[46] Here, again, we see the substitution of "racial" imagery for religion—our optical illusion. The Johnson-Reed Act also cemented the exclusion of Asian immigrants on the grounds that they were racially ineligible for citizenship.[47]

If Congress could not get rid of the Catholics, Jews, and other "undesirables" who had arrived during the intervening thirty-four years since 1890, it could at least set out to make America Protestant again—or bend the demographic curve in that direction. The 1921 and 1924 acts constituted the nation's first comprehensive effort at immigration restriction, specifically designed to remap a demographically evolving nation—to rewind the clock and restore White Protestantism's flagging demographic advantage. Not merely barring particular groups, as it had done from 1882 to 1917, the immigration reforms of the 1920s articulated Congress' vision of the only desirable breed of American population growth: northern European Protestants. This restrictive immigration quota system remained in place for more than forty years, with only a few small exceptions.[48] The European Protestant bias put in place by the acts of 1917, 1921, and 1924 shaped and constrained immigration for generations. By 1960, barely one in twenty Americans was an immigrant, and 84% of the US immigrant population was of European or Canadian descent.[49]

With the influx of non-Protestants staunched, mid-twentieth century America was a time when ethnic difference among Whites "melted" away. Class mobility, and the post-WWII segregation between Whites (who could buy homes in the suburbs with help from the GI Bill) and Blacks (who were confined to the cities by redlining and racial restrictions in many suburban neighborhoods), created a new imagined reality in which Catholicism, Judaism, and Protestant faiths were reimagined as the three "pillars of democracy." The social effects of World War II on American soldiers, many of whom left their respective enclaves and encountered different sorts of White Americans for the first time, helped create the optical illusion that Protestantism, Catholicism, and Judaism were viewed as equally acceptable forms of American religion.[50] In fact, the Catholicism of John F. Kennedy—still today, the nation's only Catholic president—prompted great public hand-wringing about his possible loyalty to the Pope over the American people. Nor was antisemitism a thing of the past; Jewish people continued to face discrimination in education and employment during this time. In sum, the United States' mid-twentieth century White and Christian majority, shown in the idealized suburban lives of a thousand sitcom families, was the end product of deliberate social engineering efforts by early twentieth century Congresses carrying out an explicitly racist and religiously discriminatory agenda.

It was not until the Immigration Reform Act of 1965 that Asians, Africans, and Arabs could enter the United States again in large numbers. This time immigrants were attracted by the United States' need for physicians to supplement a medical work force stretched thin by the Vietnam War and for engineers to bolster American efforts to wage an arms and space race against the Soviet Union. Later, the technology boom of the 1990s provided a major economic draw for educated young immigrants, particularly from East and South Asia.[51] Immigration from Southeast Asia was expanded further by the Indochina Migration and Refugee Act of 1975, which established a program of domestic resettlement assistance for refugees from Cambodia and Vietnam. The post-1965 wave of immigration, particularly from former "barred zones" in Asia, is the reason for the increased religious diversity in the country today.

The 1965 Act was as profound an opening of the doors as 1882–1924 had been a closing. The annual inflow of approximately 650,000 newcomers from Latin America and Asia since 1965 surpasses the pace of the last great immigration wave of a century ago. According to a 2015 Pew Research Center projection, immigrants will make up a record 18% of the US population in 2065, compared with 14% today and 5% in 1965. Immigrants and their children—that is, first and second generation Americans—will represent 36% of the US population in 2065, which equals or surpasses the peak levels last seen around the turn of the twentieth century. That share will represent a doubling since 1965 (18%) and a notable rise even from today's 26%.[52]

Immigration policy, reflecting who may enter the United States, is only part of the story of understanding the entwinement of Whiteness and Christianity. Another facet of the story is citizenship. Who is allowed to become an American? As with immigration, the evolution of American laws on citizenship illustrates the strong relationship of Whiteness and Christianity in national identity and legal interpretations of who we *are* and who we *aren't*.

Citizenship, Race, and Religion

While citizenship had been restricted to free white men since 1790, in 1952 the racial restriction was finally lifted, making members of all races and religions eligible for citizenship. More than half a century after this federal legislation, however, we began to see new public debates over who should be a citizen. The question of birthright citizenship—the automatic citizenship of any child born on US territory, guaranteed by the Fourteenth Amendment—is now being debated again.

Alone among his forty-four fellow presidents, Barack Obama, our only Black president, faced constant and vigorous questions about his citizenship. Even in a presidential contest in which his opponent was an individual literally not born on American soil—Senator John McCain was born in the Panama Canal Zone[53]—it was Hawaii-born Barack Obama whose citizenship and presidency was called into question because he did not fit the White Protestant Christian archetype of president of the United States.

Unlike any president before or since, President Obama faced a "birther" movement that questioned his patriotism, his fitness to be president of the United States, and his legal hold on the office. These "birther" attacks were based on the fact that Obama's father was Kenyan (his mother was a White US citizen) and were combined with conspiracy theories that he was a secret Muslim based solely on his middle name, Hussein, though in fact he is Christian. Questions regarding his loyalty to the office of the Presidency were raised, from alleged photographic "proof" that he had bowed to a Saudi prince, to his having once worn Kenyan tribal garb, to his allegedly having failed to place his hand over his heart for the Pledge of Allegiance at a campaign stop in the Midwest in 2008. Of the attributes that distinguished Obama from his forty-three predecessors, four in particular can help us to think about popular notions of national identity that stretch back to the founding of the Republic.

First, as noted above, Obama's father was a foreigner, a Kenyan without US citizenship. In that respect, he was different not only from the White American majority but even from most African Americans, whose legacy is not of immigration but of ancestors enslaved and forcibly brought to the United States, including conversion to Christianity. Despite the senior Obama's absence from his son's life, this father narrative led the media "back" to Kenya, where they would film segments with his half-brother or cousin or grandmother, sitting next to a mud hut. The imagery was meant to convey Obama's close connection to a culture still seen in America as savage, backwards, and uncivilized.

Second, attention was called to Obama's middle name, Hussein. Perhaps the most recognizably Muslim name besides Mohammed, Hussein was the last name of the Iraqi dictator against whom the United States had fought two wars within recent memory. The president's full name, including "Hussein," was often deployed by Obama's political opponents to confuse voters that Obama was not an American, or at least was an unfamiliar (and implicitly unwelcome) sort of American—and to suggest that he might be Muslim. This political gambit evoked the European hunt for the "crypto Muslim" and the notion of blood purity, and draws on deep notions of Americanness as being exclusively White and Christian.

Third, Obama had spent a significant portion of his childhood not in the United States but in Southeast Asia—precisely Indonesia, where his mother lived with her second husband. Thus, in addition to being the son of an African immigrant, Obama has a half-sister whose father was Asian. Obama's Asian connections invoke the notion of Asians as perpetual foreigners, seen before in nineteenth century discussions of the "Yellow Peril," in the internment of Japanese Americans, and in the fact that today even third-, fourth-, and later-generation Asian Americans are often assumed to be foreigners.[54]

Finally, although candidate Obama consistently described himself as a Christian, even that description was questioned because Obama was, more specifically, a member of an *African American* church congregation in Chicago. With their unique history, theology, and cadence, Black churches remain culturally unfamiliar and visually different in the eyes of White Christian audiences. Obama found himself having to defend the pastor of his church, Jeremiah Wright, and distance himself from him after Wright was criticized for delivering what became known as the "God damn America" sermon, in which he charged that the deep ingrained racism in American culture is the reason for so many troubles in the lives of African Americans. Wright's sermon, drawn from long traditions of liberation theology in the Black church, had done what numerous Black clergy do, vividly invoke biblical themes to explain the Black American experience. Yet the unfamiliar practices of the Black church were put under a microscope by the mainstream media, and due to their departures from normative notions of Christian belief and practice—that is, from the White Church—they became another source of the characterization of Obama as different, as outside the norm as most White Americans understand it. Obama emphasized that "I don't agree with everything he says." But Wright's preaching led many White Christian listeners to wonder if Obama could be trusted. Could someone who sat every Sunday through the fire-and-brimstone of Wright's sermons be a true patriot?

Any one of these factors would have distinguished Obama from his predecessors. All of them together made it impossible for him ever to fully shake the "birther" attacks, or to be seen as a fully legitimate American president by all Americans. The birther movement had legs because on multiple vectors of what is really considered American—what we find in the history of the laws surrounding immigration and citizenship—Obama does not fit the "American" mold. Can a man whose middle name is Hussein, and whose father was Muslim, really not be Muslim? Despite the Christian belief in salvation or conversion, even people who might have preached about their own moment of being "born again" could not believe that Barack Obama really meant it when he called himself Christian. The challenge of proving his religious authenticity echoed the dilemma of the converted slave: he may have found God, but his legacy is still heathen, and as such, he is less than fully "one of us."

In the eighteenth century, the question of who could be American, and the role of identity in that question, was one of the first things the newly formed national government had to address. After certifying the election of President George Washington, establishing the departments of government, and forming the American judiciary, one of the earliest major acts of the First Congress was to adopt a law saying who could become a citizen of the new nation. Congressman (later President) James Madison of Virginia described whom he hoped to attract to become American citizens:

> When we are considering the advantages that may result from an easy mode of naturalization, we ought also to consider the cautions necessary to guard against abuse. . . . Those who acquire the rights of citizenship, without adding to the strength or wealth of the community are not the people we are in want of.[55]

Madison's guidelines for the sort of Americans the new republic sought were, of course, self-fulfilling when we see the language that was selected for the first naturalization law, because all the opportunities to become wealthy and strong were then reserved for free White men—as was citizenship.

And so it was that the Naturalization Act of 1790, as amended in 1795, provided legal sanctions for race's preeminent role in US society for centuries to come. It stated that "any alien being a free white person . . . may be admitted to become a citizen" of the United States, provided that "he has behaved as a man of a good moral character, attached to the principles of the constitution of the United States, and well disposed to the good order and happiness of the same," pledged an oath, and had resided in the United States for two years before applying for citizenship by naturalization. The language foregrounds race over religion, but as we have noted repeatedly, Europe is, and was then, regarded as the geographic home of Christianity. To speak of a White man "of good moral character" was to speak of a northern European Protestant Christian.

Thus, while the nation's first naturalization law appears to have been about race, it was also about religion. There was no express prohibition on the ability of immigrant Catholics, Jews, or members of other non-Protestant faiths to become citizens of the United

States. Indeed, when immigration from Europe began to swell in the 1840s, many WASPs looked back at the 1790 Act and regarded it as excessively inclusive in relation to their own Protestant, northern European image of Americanness. Catholic and Jewish immigrants, as Europeans, were sufficiently "White" to become citizens.[56] For other immigrants, however, the right to be naturalized hung on the ability to prove that they were "White" as a matter of law. Religion was part of what determined whether someone was White or not. As Ian Haney-López has described it, "To be unfit for naturalization—that is, to be non-White—implied a certain degeneracy of intellect, morals, self-restraint, and political values; to be suited for citizenship—to be White—suggested moral maturity, self-assurance, personal independence, and political sophistication."[57] Christianity could elevate one's status among people of color, but only to a point.[58]

In matters concerning naturalization and citizenship, religion has thus not been an isolated factor—indeed, an express ban on the entry of particular religious groups into the United States would violate the First Amendment, as the Supreme Court repeatedly ruled in response to Trump's multiple attempts at a "Muslim Ban." At the same time, however, religion is never entirely absent from the equation. Throughout US history, Christianity has interacted with culture and racism to foreclose or restrict opportunities for ethnic and religious minorities—that is, non-White non-Christians—to become citizens.[59]

Due to Christianity's role and the fluid nature of how US law and society understood the term "White" and gave it legal meaning, nineteenth- and twentieth-century courtrooms were the field of battle for the continuing American dispute over to whom the privileges of citizenship would be extended. Could any immigrant to the United States become an American citizen? Federal courts wrestled with these questions in trials over the racial identity of national groups including Armenians, Syrians, Japanese, Mexicans, and South Asians. Meanwhile, federal statutes on citizenship preserved the essential elements of the 1790 Act (limiting naturalization to "free white persons" of "good character") while extending citizenship to other racial groups in response to specific historic events. Citizenship became available to people of "African nativity" in 1866, after the Civil War; to the "Five Civilized Tribes" of Native Americans in 1901, then to all Native Americans in 1924[60]; and to the *Chinese* in 1943.[61] The racial restriction of citizenship to "free white men" was not eliminated from federal law until the McCarran-Walter Act in 1952.

While on the surface the McCarran-Walter Act seems to suggest that boundaries of citizenship were widening, in practice, it was interpreted then—and is remembered now—as a form of forced assimilation, in which citizenship was extended in name only.[62] The Act created an "Asia-Pacific triangle" to which a restrictive global race quota of one hundred individuals per country applied. Persons of Asian descent born or residing anywhere in the world could immigrate only under the Asia-Pacific quotas of one hundred per country of racial origin (e.g., China, Korea). This scheme continued to severely constrain Asian immigration into the United States. The law preserved non-quota immigration from countries in the Western hemisphere, but imposed quotas on the former British colonies in the Caribbean, a move designed to limit the immigration of Caribbean Blacks. This combination of restrictions thus still limited the immigration of religious minorities, from Asian Muslims, Sikhs, Buddhists, and Hindus, to Caribbean practitioners of Vodou, Santeria, and other traditions.

Even though the 1952 legislation preserved most of 1924's racial quotas, the law's sponsors stated that there was no claim to "any theory of Nordic superiority" but rather only a "concern for . . . similarity of cultural background."[63] The retention of the national origins quota reflected the logic that cast the native born as the most loyal Americans, especially whites of British and Northern

European descent, and the foreign-born as subversives, especially when it came to Jews (who were imagined as Bolsheviks) and Italians (who were viewed as anarchists). So, in the end, while the racial restriction for naturalization was lifted, there were other limits, especially on communities of color, many of whom were also coming from non-Christian majority countries.[64]

Christianity—The Fulcrum for Citizenship

For over 160 years, between the 1790 Act's extension of citizenship rights to "free white men" and the elimination of the express racial quota in 1952, courts made *ad hoc* determinations of whether an immigrant applying for United States citizenship was White. From the beginning, both naturalization and immigration law "reflected, reinforced and reproduced racial hierarchy," thus producing racial distinctions that excluded or restricted immigration and citizenship of any group not considered White.[65] In this context, being Christian, and specifically Protestant, provided an advantage; combined with a racial identity that was adequately White, it could position one as "civilized" in comparison to non-Christians. By contrast, Asian Buddhists, Hindus, Muslims, or Sikhs, and Native Americans believers in indigenous spiritualities, as well as Catholic Mexicans who were involuntarily annexed by the 1848 Treaty of Guadalupe Hidalgo, and Blacks prior to the passage of the Fourteenth Amendment, were considered *not* "civilized" because they were neither Protestant nor White.

The use of the word "White" as the standard for citizenship did not cause race to supplant religion as the relevant question; rather, it positioned Christianity to have a preeminent role in constructing Whiteness. As we have seen, even in the absence of an explicit religious requirement for citizenship, Christianity played a role in determining who was White or who could be considered civilized enough to be afforded the right to US citizenship. Christianity alone did not result in religious freedom, but the hegemonic presence of Christianity, together with Whiteness, bestowed superior moral and cultural attributes that became the foundation for American naturalization and citizenship. The courts' decisions on Takao Ozawa, Bhagat Singh Thind, and Syrian applicants for US citizenship, all discussed below, provide illustrative examples of this phenomenon.

The racial status of Mexicans, and their eligibility for citizenship, was a highly contested issue for nearly a century. In the nation's evolving answer to the question of Mexican racial status and the rights of Mexicans to naturalize, we can again find that Christianity played a powerful role in constructing Whiteness. The 1836 Constitution of the Republic of Texas extended the rights of citizenship to free Whites and to Mexicans who were not Black or Indian. When Texas was annexed to the United States in 1845, these citizenship clauses were upheld. Just three years later, most of the American southwest was annexed from Mexico under the Treaty of Guadalupe Hidalgo. The Treaty gave residents of the annexed territory the right to become American citizens. However, this did not indicate that Mexicans' status as legally White was clear or uncontested.[66] "By law, Mexicans were eligible for naturalization," as Cybelle Fox and Irene Bloemraad describe the situation. "But unlike European immigrants, their eligibility was a product of foreign relations and treaties rather than any 'scientific' or common acceptance of their Whiteness."[67] They attended segregated schools, lived in marginalized neighborhoods, and labored in dead-end jobs in a market stratified by race, all of which significantly affected their ability to accumulate resources and live a life without social or cultural restrictions. So, "even though Mexicans were white by law," their "non-white social status significantly decreased Mexicans' likelihood of naturalization."[68]

The Treaty of Guadalupe Hidalgo emerged in a context in which most Mexicans—even if descended from indigenous ancestors who

followed non-Christian traditions before the European arrival—
were Catholics by the time of the annexation. The Catholicism of
most Mexicans positioned them closer to citizenship than indigenous populations of the region who had not adopted the colo-
nizers' religion. Alongside the Mexicans living in the territory that
became part of the present-day southwestern United States, there
were indigenous peoples ("Indians") for whom the issue of citizenship was more questionable. The policy of the governments of
Spain and Mexico had been to transform the indigenous peoples
into subjects and later citizens of the state with a common religion
and national culture. Among this native population, "Christianized
Indians" were identified by the US government separately from
"emancipated Indians," who were in a different category.

Evidence of the linkage of Whiteness[69] and Protestant
Christianity can be found in the Texas State Supreme Court's decisions in *McMullen v. Hodge and Others* (1849), in which Christian
Indians theoretically became eligible to become US citizens.
Specifically, *McMullen* provided that eligibility for US citizenship
could be had by Indians who could prove that they and their ancestors: (1) held no tribal affiliation, (2) had been Spanish subjects or
practicing Mexican citizens (e.g., voted, ran for office, practiced
the holy Catholic sacraments), (3) spoke Spanish, and (4) if they
were former mission Indians, had passed a two-year secularization probationary period where they were observed to have practiced Mexican traditions, which meant relinquishing indigenous
tribal rituals.[70] Even as policies liberalized toward "Christianized
Indians," naturalization policy grew more restrictive toward
Mexican immigrants from beyond the annexed territories.[71]

As with Mexicans, Christianity had an important but little-
noticed role in naturalization being extended to African Americans
after the Civil War. At the time of the emancipation amendments,
the Supreme Court had recently declared in the notorious *Dred
Scott* decision that people of African descent born in the United

States, whether free or slave, could not be considered citizens. The right to become a citizen, as established in law by the 1790 Naturalization Act, was available to Whites only. It took the Union victory in the Civil War, and the adoption of the Thirteenth and Fourteenth Amendments to the Constitution, to extend birthright citizenship and the right of naturalization to Black Americans. The Fourteenth Amendment's deceptively simple language was in fact revolutionary in its effect. The pertinent part of the Fourteenth Amendment reads: "All persons born or naturalized in the United States and subject to the jurisdiction thereof." This clause attempted to offer African Americans an ironclad citizenship guarantee and deny future courts the ability to do what the Taney Court had done in *Dred Scott* in 1857—to strip any native-born American people of their citizenship.

The Fourteenth Amendment established birthright citizenship and the Fifteenth ensured African American men the right to vote. In the debates leading up to their passage, it is apparent that Christianity provided an advantage that differentiated African American men, most of whom were Christian, from Asian immigrants and Native American men, most of whom were not. So, while the Fourteenth Amendment established certain new rights for both Christians and non-Christians, including birthright citizenship, only Christians were considered civilized enough to be naturalized through the Fifteenth Amendment and could thus gain voting rights in the United States.

Californians' position on the Reconstruction amendments illustrates the social and political ramifications of the debate. In California at the time, less than 1% of the state's population was African American, but Chinese were almost 8% and Native Americans about 5%. Many believed that if Chinese and Native Americans received the right to vote, it would result in the degradation of the White race and the demise of the government.[72] Chinese and other members of the "Mongoloid" race were viewed both as racially inferior *and* as spiritually misguided. Their religions, including Buddhism, Confucianism, and folk traditions like ancestor veneration, were regarded as superstitions and idolatrous.[73] While Congress debated the Fifteenth Amendment, California legislators, church leaders, and others expressed concern over extending voting rights to freed slaves. The concern was less about the merits of Black suffrage than about the possibility that adopting the Fifteenth Amendment could be a step toward granting the same rights to Native Americans and Chinese.

Thus, Reconstruction opened the door for generally Christianized African American men to become citizens, while continuing to shut out Asian immigrants and Native American men.[74] From this point onward, the right to vote did not rest on Whiteness, as it had before, but on the distinction between Christianity and "heathenism," which rendered a man unfit for suffrage. African American men's status as Christians rendered them superior to pagan non-Whites.[75] So, while emancipated Blacks had citizenship extended to them, the "heathen races" did not, and were thus kept at arm's length from political power.

In translating these ideas to legislation, our optical illusion surfaces again: Christianity's influence is pervasive, and manifests as race. Even if they could not transform the United States into an entirely Protestant nation, as some openly desired to do, those officials writing the laws could marginalize those groups they considered the most depraved, uncivilized, and Godless.[76] So, the postwar amendments and related legislation singled out the races regarded as pagan and heathen—categories that encompassed much of the world's population, and in the United States separated Native Americans and Asian immigrants from African Americans, excluding the former from citizenship while extending it to the latter. The rejection of Native Americans and Chinese immigrants as citizens was not a matter of race "trumping" religion or vice-versa. Rather, the division was simultaneously racial and religious—the distinction between the mostly Christian Blacks and the mostly non-Christian Asians—and its application was further abetted by the nativist immigration reforms of the time. In both the immigration and citizenship, a preference for Christians was used to the detriment of all others.[77]

Who is White?

The extension of citizenship only to African Americans after the Civil War, combined with the shifting meaning of the word "White" in the heyday of nineteenth-century immigration, led to an increase in efforts by Asian and Arab immigrants, many of whom were not Christian, to gain their citizenship. Between 1878 and 1952, fifty-two court cases, including two heard by the Supreme Court, were argued to determine who would be considered "White" under the 1790 Act.[78] Christianity restricted naturalization by shaping conceptions of Whiteness under the law. An applicant who was neither White nor Christian was less likely to prevail before the government and the Courts. Yet Christianity alone was insufficient to claim Whiteness. Whiteness alone could be acceptable, but the shifting nature of Whiteness made it unavailable even to a litigant who had "science" on his side.

These *racial prerequisite cases* worked to set racial parameters for citizenship and illustrate the role of religion in the construction of Whiteness. In all but one of the racial prerequisite cases, the litigant sought naturalization by trying to prove that he was White. The petitioners for citizenship were of many different nationalities: Syrian, Filipino, Indian, Mexican, Chinese, and Japanese. As Bruce Baum has put it, "The fact that so diverse a group of petitioners laid claim to whiteness at this historical juncture indicates that whiteness had been defined primarily in opposition to Blackness and still lacked geographical specificity or clarity."[79] Most immigrants whose petitions reached the courts came from groups that could were considered racially ambiguous at the time: not Black, White, or "Mongoloid" (East Asian), based on a visual inspection. These applicants were also fighting an uphill battle against the perception that their religions and cultures were unassimilable and even "fundamentally at odds" with the American way of life.[80]

Phenotype, including skin color, geography, and the question of "Congressional intent"—how did the First Congress define a "free white man"?—were all factors that determined the granting of citizenship. Whiteness and Christianity played a mutually supporting role in the legal arguments over which immigrants could be considered "assimilable" and which could not. Together, they defined the perceived ideal. Jews and Catholics of European origin were sufficiently White to be naturalized, despite enduring anti-Catholic and antisemitic sentiment. For all the other would-be citizens, making the case for their eligibility and their assimilability often meant invoking religion as well as race. For example, to convince government officials and the courts that they were White, Arabs who identified as Christian pointed to their religious status as evidence that they were sufficiently White to become American. Some Arab applicants for citizenship argued that they were Semites, and were therefore like the Jews and worthy of citizenship as a result.

Most of the people we call "Arab Americans" today were identified as "Syrians" a century ago. Syrians who had applied for citizenship prior to 1909 had been granted citizenship, without much deliberation or debate. This changed with a change in the Census from 1900 and 1910. For the 1900 Census, Syrians and Palestinians were identified as White and in the 1910 Census, they were classified as Asiatic.[81] This reclassification reflected the overall desire of many in the federal government at that time to limit immigration. A group of cases involving Arab applicants, sometimes referred to collectively as the "Syrian cases," illustrates how the courts vacillated over the racial status of these individuals and how the intersection of religious identity and skin color often determined the outcome. Consider the contrasting experiences of two applicants for US citizenship: Syrian-born Costa Najour and Ahmed Hassan of Yemen. In 1909, Costa Najour, fair-skinned and Christian, was granted citizenship. His initial application had been denied, but Najour appealed that ruling. The judge was adamant that his decision not rest on the issue of "color," but on "science." He rejected the idea that the statute referred to skin color – making a statement that would be repeated in other rulings that "race" was not to be determined by "ocular inspection alone."[82] Sarah Gualtieri argues: "In other words, color did not necessarily matter if it could be determined by some other rationale that the applicant was white and possessed the personal qualifications deemed necessary for naturalization." (P.34) Here personal qualifications could include, religion or perceived religion (Najour was Christian), as well as "a democratic mind" and "assimability" – two value-laden measures. While Najour's judge ultimately affirmed Syrians as members of the "white race" and ruled him eligible for US citizenship, it was not before the district attorney made a distinction between those fit for citizenship and those unfit for the American polity. The attorney expressed this concern by asking rhetorically whether "subject of the Muslim Ottoman Sultan was incapable of understanding American Institutions and government."[83]

Contrast Najour's case with the 1942 case of dark-skinned Ahmed Hassan, a Yemeni Muslim. Hassan was denied citizenship on the grounds that "a wide gulf separates [Mohammedan] culture from that of the predominantly Christian peoples of Europe."[84] While the judge mentioned he was dark brown in color and that was a relevant factor in determining race, Hassan's application was rejected on the basis of geographical and cultural distance between Yemen and Europe and between Islam, his religion, and Christianity, religion of Europe. Religion was a disqualifying criterion. Religion impacted the way Syrian immigrants were identified racially for the naturalization process. Christian Syrians faced fewer difficulties, as compared to Muslim Syrians, in gaining US citizenship. Their main advantage according to Gualtieri was "an emphasis on the Syrian connection to the Holy Land and Christianity."[85]

The intimate, complex relationship between Christianity and Whiteness in determining citizenship is best illustrated by the pair of racial prerequisite cases that went all the way to the US Supreme Court. In the first case, plaintiff Takao Ozawa was born in Japan, moved to the territory of Hawaii, and later lived in California. Altogether he had lived in the United States continuously for twenty years when applying for citizenship in 1914. In the briefs filed on his behalf in *Ozawa v. United States*, he mentioned that he and his family attended American churches and spoke English at home. Nevertheless, the government opposed his application to become a citizen on the grounds that he was not "white." Eight years after his application was filed, the US Supreme Court ruled that Ozawa was not eligible to become a citizen. The Court's 1922 decision emphasized that Ozawa was from the Orient, a land that was not part of Christendom, and "science" of the time marked him as "Mongoloid" (East Asian) rather than "Caucasoid" (White). Specifically, the Court held that the Japanese emigrant petitioner was not of the type "popularly known as the Caucasian race." Ozawa's Christian identity was insufficient to overcome the "science" of race.

Ozawa's case was watched closely by many immigrants, including the lawyers for Bhagat Singh Thind, whose case offers a fascinating window into the interaction of religion and race in America. Thind was a Punjab-born Sikh and a US army veteran. The US Immigration Commission's *1911 Dictionary of Races or Peoples* defined an *East Indian* as any native of the East Indies, which included peoples ranging from the inhabitants of the Philippines to the "Aryans" of India. Consistent with long-standing US practice of describing emigrants from the subcontinent as "Hindoos" regardless of their actual religious affiliation, the Commission decreed that any native of India was to be called "Hindoo." The term was a misnomer for the majority of nineteenth-century Indian emigrants, who were Sikh farmers and laborers, including Thind.[86] The question of citizenship for "Hindoos" was actually a topic of some debate in the early twentieth century. On one hand, the tripartite scientific racist theory of human origins divided humanity into the categories "Caucasoid," "Mongoloid," and "Negroid," and categorized "Hindoos" as Whites because they were considered to be "Aryan" and thus of European ancestry. On the other hand, Indians were swarthy and their forebears had been "enslaved, effeminate, caste-ridden and degraded"[87]—a set of terms laden with religious meaning, as of course was the word "Hindoo" itself.

Against this backdrop, and with other racial prerequisite cases roiling the lower federal courts across the country, Thind petitioned for citizenship in US District Court of Washington on the same day in July 1918 when he enlisted in the US Army. The court granted Thind's citizenship application on December 9, 1918, but it was voided by the Bureau of Naturalization just four days later. In early 1919, with World War I hostilities over, Thind was honorably discharged from the US Army and he petitioned again for citizenship, this time in Oregon. The US District Court of Oregon granted Thind's application the following year in 1920, which prompted the federal government to appeal the case to the Ninth Circuit Court of Appeals,[88] arguing that Hinduism was "an alienating and barbaric social and religious system, one that rendered 'Hindus' utterly unfit for membership in the 'civilization of White men.'"[89] The Ninth Circuit requested instruction from the Supreme Court of the United States on the following question: "Is a high caste Hindu of full Indian blood, born at Amritsar, Punjab, India, a white person within the meaning of [the 1790 Naturalization Act]?"

In 1922, as Thind and his lawyers were preparing to appear before the Supreme Court, the Court issued its ruling in Ozawa, that the Japanese American applicant was not Caucasian based on "scientific" evidence, and therefore he was not legally White. Thind's lawyers therefore also decided to rely on science to guide their legal strategy. They applied a popular Orientalist theory of the time, which has since been debunked: the Aryan Invasion Theory. As noted earlier, the AIT posited that the people of northern India and Pakistan were racially descended from Caucasian (European) stock, and thus were "Aryan." Thind's lawyers described him as a "hindoo," a "high-caste Brahmin," and an "Aryan"; as such, they argued, he was Caucasian and, unlike Ozawa, was a "white man" eligible for US citizenship. The Supreme Court, however, found a place where the "science" they had relied on a year earlier had to give way to raw prejudice. Encountering a man with a turban and a long beard, visual cues that surely helped them to reach the conclusion that he was unassimilable, the nation's highest court wrote in 1923,

> It may be true that the blond Scandinavian and the brown Hindu have a common ancestor in the dim reaches of antiquity, but the average man knows perfectly well that there are unmistakable and profound differences between them today. . . . [The law] does not employ the word "Caucasian" but the words "white person." . . . [The intention of the founding fathers was only to] confer the privilege of citizenship upon that class of persons [regarded as "white."]

In so ruling, the Supreme Court further codified the role of Christianity in the construction of Whiteness. A "blond Scandinavian" was Protestant; a "Hindu" manifestly was not. Perhaps Thind's lawyers' description of him as a "high-caste Brahmin" reminded the Court of casteism, which it would surely have regarded as a backward and un-Christian element of Indian culture. Finally, whatever "science" and the Aryan Invasion Theory might have said about Thind's European biological origins, the Court applied the prejudices of "the average man" in 1923—the height of anti-immigrant furor.

Juxtaposing *Ozawa* with *Thind* provides a fascinating look at the social construction of race, as court decisions about who would be

deemed White ricocheted between relying on "scientific" definitions of race popular at the time and invoking the prejudices of "the
average man," using both to justify restricting citizenship to those
who fit the twin American norms of Whiteness and Christianity.
For Ozawa, being a Christian and going to church was not enough,
because "science" told the Court he was neither Black nor White.
For Thind, being "scientifically" White—that is, Aryan—was not
enough because as a Sikh and a "hindoo" he was an unassimilable
heathen.

In truth, both definitions continued to construct Whiteness by
reinforcing White Christian prejudices and reifying them in law. In
neither decision did the Supreme Court specifically identify what
made an individual White. Instead, faced with various individuals
who claimed Whiteness based on faith or science, the court offered various explanations of how and why the petitioners were *not*
White. This pair of cases demonstrates the uncertain and shifting
nature of racial status, and its dependency on prejudice and social
norms that said to a succession of religions and racial minorities, in
essence, "whoever *we* are, we know *you* are not one of us."

The *Thind* case, together with *Ozawa*, the Syrian cases, and
other so-called "racial prerequisite" decisions, reveal a multitude
of ways in which religion and race together shaped legal decisions
and popular understandings of who could and could not become
American. The most obvious equation, of course, is "White +
Christian = Eligible for Citizenship." European immigrants, even
if Catholic or Orthodox, were generally granted citizenship. For
individuals who were *either* White *or* Christian, but not both,
eligibility was sometimes extended but often subject to limits or
other social forces. For example, Blacks received citizenship via the
Fourteenth Amendment in the late 1860s, by which time most were
Christian, and generations removed from their Muslim or animist
ancestors who were brought from Africa by force. Likewise, Native
Americans were subjected to religious indoctrination (along with

dispossession and other harms), only after which the rights of citizenship were extended first to the five "civilized tribes" in 1901 and then to all native peoples in 1924. The citizenship granted to Native Americans was contested; many nations did not want it. As for populations that were White but not Christian, European Jewish immigrants were eligible for citizenship. By contrast, Christian immigrants from Asia like Ozawa were not.

To be neither White nor Christian generally meant that one was ineligible for the privileges of citizenship. This ineligibility was expressed using various rationales. These excuses included scientific racism, such as the Supreme Court applied to Ozawa. Where science did not provide a clear enough answer, as with "high-caste . . . Aryan" Bhagat Singh Thind, the Courts would apply popular prejudice to establish that citizenship was unavailable because "the average man knows perfectly well" that Indians are not White. Thind's visible difference—which, as an observant Sikh, included his turban and beard—marked him as ineligible to be American.

Thus, at all stages, religion has served a role in the construction of Whiteness and non-Whiteness in America. Christianity's normative status allowed the extension of citizenship to certain groups, often those who had been in the United States for generations. On the other hand, the citizenship question for non-White immigrants became a deeper look into who could socially belong in an America where both religious and racial norms were deeply embedded in law, social expectation, and popular prejudice.

Racial ideologies and practices cannot be understood apart from their religious dimensions and roots, and Whiteness and Christianity are inextricably linked. Recall our earlier discussion about the difference between having the First Amendment's religion clauses on paper and making them as fully applicable to non-Christians as to Christians. The lesson of *Thind* and *Ozawa* is that Christianity, if not enough, is at least a necessary element of Americanness in the eyes of the law. The courts will construct an

American identity using whatever rationales they need to keep it both White and Christian—to keep both sides of the ribbon intact.

Religion cannot be understood apart from its growth within a racialized political and social world. Religion and race do not just come into contact with each other; each actually produces the meaning of the other through intersections in individuals, institutions, and ideologies. Thind's physical appearance, religion, and phenotype came together and were recognizable to the Court as *not White*. As a result, the Court would not accept "the best scientific evidence of the time"; rather, the justices would construct Whiteness however they wanted, notwithstanding *Ozawa* and lower-court precedents relying on the same pseudoscience. *Thind* codified the notion that to be religiously different from Christianity, even as a US Army veteran who had served during World War I, is to be non-White and therefore ineligible for citizenship.

The Past with the Present

The scholar Duncan Ryūken Williams, in his groundbreaking work *American Sutra*, has described the entwinement of religion, race, and questions of Americanness in the experience of Japanese and Japanese Americans in the mid-twentieth century. Japanese Americans' experience during WWII—known as "Japanese internment"—has most frequently been looked at through the prism of race. As Williams reveals, however, religion played a key role in why the majority of government officials, media outlets, and the general public perceived Japanese Americans as a threat to both national security and American national identity.

Both military and civilian governmental agencies considered Buddhist and Shinto priests to be groups that could undermine national security.[90] The vast majority of Japanese Americans at the time were Buddhist. For roughly 150 years, Buddhist immigrants from Japan had brought the teachings, practices, and institutions of a 2,500-year old religious tradition to the Americas, and by the mid-twentieth century, Japanese Americans were the largest group of Buddhists in the United States. Long before the attack on Pearl Harbor, the FBI was investigating different Buddhist communities as a potential threat to US national security. Decades of fear mongering by nativist politicians and the press about a "Yellow Peril"—the growing presence of inscrutable and uncivilized "heathens" and "pagans," as Asian American Buddhists were frequently labeled—was used to justify various immigration restrictions that targeted Asians. In addition to Japanese Americans' racial status, "the supposed incompatibility of their religious faith also played into their exclusion from America."[91] In the days after the Japanese military's attack on Pearl Harbor on December 7, 1941, nearly 200 Buddhist priests were rounded up by the FBI, part of a dragnet that had been planned after years of surveillance on temples, investigations of particular priests and organizations, and intelligence reports that measured the potential loyalty of Buddhists to America in the event of a war with Japan. Only a relative handful of Japanese American Christian ministers were arrested.[92]

Japan was not the only country with which the United States was at war in 1942, but it was the only majority non-Christian country and the only Asian country in that category. So, whereas Roosevelt's Executive Order 9066 included modest restrictions for Italian and German nationals in the US—excluding them from "military areas"—it led to the rounding-up and forced removal of only Japanese immigrants and their children, who were US citizens. When the constitutionality of Executive Order 9066 and Congress's enabling legislation reached the US Supreme Court in *Korematsu v. United States*, the internment of Japanese Americans was upheld by six justices, over the vehement dissents of the remaining three, each of whom noted the prejudice inherent in rules that made it criminal merely to be of Japanese ancestry and resist being rounded up.

US citizenship was thus no protection from questions about whether a person of Japanese descent was a real, or loyal, American. Nowhere in Roosevelt's order was it written that the Japanese Americans' Buddhism was what made them a national security threat. Yet they alone, among the *US-born* offspring of Axis nations, were rounded up. In the camps, non-Christian religious activity was permitted but those who practiced tried to do so quietly. In those camps, the Buddhist majority again experienced the suspicions and derision of those individuals who believed Americanism required abandoning anything linked to Japan and its religions or culture. In 1944 the Buddhist Mission of North America (BMNA) renamed itself the "Buddhist Churches of America," apparently in hopes that rebranding its temples as "churches" would make them sound less foreign, and thus less suspect.[93]

Today, seventy-seven years later, another group is targeted in the name of protecting national security: Muslims. As a presidential candidate, Donald Trump called for "a *total* and *complete* shutdown of *Muslims entering the United States*," and after his election he attempted to make good on this campaign promise. Because of the expressly religious nature of the targeted group, Trump was forced to revise his "Muslim Ban" twice to overcome Supreme Court objections that it violated the First Amendment. The original countries excluded were Syria, Libya, Chad, Iran, Yemen and Somalia. It took adding officially atheist North Korea and Catholic-majority Venezuela to the list of barred countries to persuade the Supreme Court that the Order was no longer a "Muslim Ban."

Yet when we read this executive order, and the Supreme Court's decision to uphold it, with the same critical eye as we read the Immigration Act of 1917, we must ask: what are its consequences? There is no real prospect of North Koreans reaching the US in material numbers. The addition of Venezuela appears to have been more of a snub of Venezuela's longtime anti-American leader than any actual US security need. By contrast, 160,000 people had entered the US from the newly barred countries in 2015 (the last year for which data was available), including more than 25,000 people seeking asylum or refugee status. The executive order gave preference to people suffering religious discrimination, but only if they were members of a religious minority in their countries of origin—a provision clearly designed to admit Christians, but not Muslims, from the affected countries. And while the executive order included an indefinite and complete shutdown of all Syrian refugee arrivals to the United States, the president nevertheless told a Christian Broadcast Network interviewer that he would make admitting Syrian Christians a "priority."[94] By ruling that this executive order passed muster, the Supreme Court again showed its willingness to bow to popular prejudices, and to selectively ignore the realities behind the legal language. Indeed, even in the majority opinion upholding the ban, Chief Justice Roberts acknowledged the historical wrongs in *Korematsu*, but did not actually overrule it.

Conclusion

National identity can draw from all kinds of sources: geography, ethnicity, language, or fealty to a particular ideal or leader. In all cases, the notion of nationhood raises the question of who belongs and who does not. For almost 250 years, the United States has answered that question by maintaining a system that on its face seems to discriminate based on race, while in fact defining the very notion of race, and of eligibility for admission and membership, in terms of religion.

One consequence of race generally being conceptualized in terms of Whiteness and Blackness is the lack of attention to Christian supremacy's role in constructing Whiteness, and the mutual support of Whiteness and Christianity for one another in defining national identity. We err when we think of "White" as meaning nothing but racial appearance. From the founding of the Republic, naturalization policy defined who could become a citizen of the new nation, and did so in a way intended to replicate the founders' identities: only a "free white person" of "good moral character" could throw his lot in with the new nation. The latter phrase ought not to be understood as modifying the first, but as defining it. Immigration policy was then used to replicate this version of America. When undesirable "hordes"—whether of Jews from Europe or of heathen "Chinamen"—appeared to threaten the established Protestant order, the nation responded by slamming its doors shut.

Signing the 1965 Immigration Reform Act, President Lyndon Johnson said it would "correct[] a cruel and enduring wrong." In that, he was correct. But Johnson also believed that the law was "not a revolutionary bill. It does not affect the lives of millions. It will not reshape the structure of our daily lives . . ." In that, he could not have been more mistaken.[95] In the past sixty years, immigration has reshaped America in fundamental ways: from Iowa to Texas, minarets now soar above our amber waves of grain. My parents helped to build the first Indian Hindu temple in Atlanta within my lifetime, and now Atlanta has at least twenty temples.

None of this means those old tests are gone, or that we cannot hear the echoes of history in the policies of today. Who exhibits "good moral character"? Seventy years ago the United States rounded up and interred Japanese Americans out of fears with religious and racial as well as political roots. Today, we speak of American Muslims in similar ways. In a 2016 presidential debate, Hillary Clinton was asked, "With Islamophobia on the rise, how will you help people like me deal with the consequences of being labeled as a threat to the country?" Clinton's response repeated Islamophobic tropes: "We need American Muslims to be part of our eyes and ears on our front lines . . . part of our homeland security." While Clinton's response theorized the existence of good Muslims, it still reproduced the deep idea that Islam represents a threat, implicitly at odds with America's "good moral character." That same deep idea led the New York Police Department to surveil mosques and Muslim-owned businesses in New York and New Jersey, and motivates law enforcement recruiting efforts directed at youth in these communities in ways that, functionally, amount to the government asking and encouraging American Muslims to monitor and record their own communities.

The common theme across groups and across the centuries is White Christian supremacy, the marginalization of and discrimination against various groups that fail to match the nation's dual identity as White and Christian. Even if White people become a numerical minority in the 2040s or 2050s, and the proportion of Americans who identify as Christian continues to decline, this demographic shift will not soon loosen the grip Whiteness and Christianity have on the country. The advantages built up over three centuries, and the structural preferences that shaped who could come and who could join the nation, will not disappear. Social power is more than population numbers; it is being able to create policy and replicate a national identity and worldview.

That enduring social power perpetuates the reality and perception of privilege for future generations. As we will see in the next chapter, the deep cultural norms of "us" and "them," and of who is or may be fully "American" are manifest in the *everyday Christian privilege* that shapes the very experience of living here, affecting both Christians and religious minorities in every facet of their lives.

4

Everyday Christian Privilege

There is a young man I have a lot in common with: we both grew up in the South, both of us Indian American Hindus and children of immigrants. We were both good students and varsity athletes. Suhas's religious identity was a source of tremendous conflict and disadvantage in high school. Despite his athletic prowess, Suhas was denied the chance to "start" on his public school's soccer team because he refused to join the coach and his teammates in Christian prayer:

> Every time, [before] we played a game, the coach would made us recite the Lord's Prayer. At a certain point, I stopped doing it, and I said, "I'm not going to do it," and I would walk away. And he would yell at me to get back in the group because, you know, "you're breaking up team spirit," yadda, yadda. I said, "No, I'm not going to do it, I'm not going to be there." So, I got benched and I was benched for the rest of the season, sat on the bench, and I would always come in within like two minutes, but he wouldn't start me because I wouldn't ever be in the huddle for the Lord's Prayer.[1]

When he challenged the coach's policy, he said, the coach responded: "'If you want to be an individual, you be an individual and you can think about it for the first part of the game, and when you're ready, when I think you're ready to be a team player, I'll put you in the game.'" For Suhas's coach, "team spirit" meant reciting a Christian prayer, and to reject that was punishable.

Then in his senior year, Suhas's Hindu identity cost him an academic honor he'd earned:

> I got kicked out of the National Honor Society because once a month on a Sunday they went to different churches so that you could have "a diversity of experience with different religions." That was the purpose behind it.[2]

When Suhas suggested the National Honor Soceity (NHS) attend a Hindu service at his temple, his classmates and the club's faculty advisor "said, 'No, no, we're not going to do that.'" After experiencing such a direct rejection of his religious identity, "I was like, 'Then I'm not going to these religious things.' . . . They didn't say anything, but when I fell out of the participation because I didn't go to the religious things, they kicked me out of the Honor Society."

This discriminatory act had academic ramifications for Suhas:

> I was very, very mad because I was graduating in the top five in my class. Everybody around me had the Honor stole on except for me, and I was upset because the only reason I didn't have the Honor stole was because I refused to go to church on one Sunday out of the month.

For Suhas, life as an Indian American Hindu high school student came with specific, consequential impacts. He was a high-performing athlete, but started every game on the bench after refusing to pray the Lord's Prayer. He was a top student, but after having his identity and family religion rejected by his faculty advisor and classmates he stopped going to National Honor Society events at churches, got kicked out of the society, and was finally denied the right to wear the NHS stole at graduation. Meanwhile, his Christian classmates enjoyed corresponding advantages because their identities were reinforced and endorsed by coaches and teachers in ways that excluded Suhas.[3]

Privilege is a product of institutional oppression and legacies of social power. Up to this point, we have been looking largely at those structures and legacies: the history, the legal precedents, and the ideas and social practices that embedded White Christian supremacy in US culture. Now we turn our attention to the present-day effects of these norms and power structures on religious minorities and Christians in their everyday lives. We will see how *Christian privilege*, the set of favors, benefits, and advantages bestowed on Christians, functions to embrace and endorse them. The corresponding effect is to marginalize and deny opportunity to religious minorities and their spiritual practices. We will explore where *Christian normativity* is found, and how society and its structures recognize and include Christians while burdening religious minorities.[4]

There are, of course, nuances within these structures, which distinguish the experiences of some Christians and religious minorities from others' because of the *intersectionality* of identities. Black, Latinx, Asian, immigrant, female, or LGBTQ Christians experience Christian privilege differently than do White male Christians. The simultaneous experience of Christian privilege and disadvantages based on factors like race, citizenship status, gender, or sexual identity changes the quality and extent of these individuals' Christian privilege. *Intersectional* analysis acknowledges that it is difficult to separate one social identity from others, and that our daily lives encompass multiple identities being experienced simultaneously. Christian privilege interacts with other privileges and cultural norms, such as heterosexual privilege, to create crosscutting patterns of benefit and detriment. While we cannot ignore or "suspend" intersectionality as part of individual experience, this chapter aims to focus on Christian privilege in particular.

Several years ago I interviewed a woman who identifies as a White Catholic lesbian. Janey is a proud Catholic. She attended

Catholic school and grew up immersed in the Catholic community: "I loved a lot of the rituals we had. We had chorus performances and sang at every holiday, and there were all these pageants in the church and it was so much fun." These experiences, and the privilege accompanying them, exist alongside her lesbian identity. When she was coming out in college, she recalled, "being a Catholic didn't work for me then and I couldn't reconcile it. . . . when I came out it was like, 'how can I be both at the same time?' I struggled with it a lot." Janey experienced marginalization, discrimination, and alienation from her Catholic community as a lesbian. In the interview, it was clear that facing homophobia over the years helped her recognize other forms of bias. She remarked that "a lot of the social norms that we follow," like "this whole fight over marriage for gays," arise because the country "is so Puritan and from our Christian heritage." Her experience as a gay Catholic enabled her to acknowledge how Christianity's influence over American culture disadvantages others.

The concept of privilege has both external (or structural) dimensions and internal (or attitudinal) dimensions.[5] The *external/structural* dimension of privilege refers to the construction of what is normal and not normal, what is acceptable and unacceptable, as decided by society. Privileged groups define the mainstream culture—behavior patterns, symbols, institutions, values, and other socially constructed components of society.[6] They are what is "normal"; groups that do not fit this mainstream norm are marginalized. Sometimes they are described as "subcultures"—literally, "under" the (mainstream) culture. This marginalization may be invisible for Christians. Suhas's coach, for example, was focused on team spirit and morale, and did not understand that because the Lord's Prayer is a Christian prayer it was inappropriate—and indeed illegal—to force a Hindu student to recite it in order to exhibit "team spirit." These embedded social advantages may also be invisible to members of the religious minority group; for example, while Suhas understood that he was being discriminated against, he may not have recognized that his Christian classmates were benefiting from Christian privilege by simply "fitting in."[7]

The *internal/attitudinal* dimensions of privilege are the beliefs and thought patterns that reify the idea that members of the dominant group have some specific right to their position and its advantages. When it comes to religion, Christians in the US have consciously and unconsciously internalized the message that Christianity is superior. In reality, what is normative or logical is often what is familiar. The ability to critique and judge others, like Suhas's coach and NHS advisor did, is abetted by the deep idea that Christianity is the ordinary and natural way of things, and by a lack of humility resulting from this power and from Christians' limited knowledge about religious minority groups.

It is intellectually and emotionally difficult to identify and acknowledge all these facets of Christian privilege, but it is necessary to map its full dimensions in order to grapple with it. For some Christians it can be a source of tremendous guilt, while it can engender a feeling of being blamed (or being blameworthy) for some religious minorities. Recognizing the problem as beyond any individual's ability to control or "repair" may be comforting. A well-meaning Christian cannot, for example, change the school calendar enough to make it fair; the calendar is the product of centuries-old laws and traditions, from the "weekend" to "Christmas break." However, the individual can control her internal/attitudinal privilege by understanding minority religious experiences and adjusting her thought patterns about topics like the days off her students or colleagues take or other accommodations for holiday observances.

A few years ago, I conducted a study in which I interviewed fifteen K–12 public school teachers who identify as White and Christian.[8] Their perspectives illustrate many dimensions of Christian privilege. One of the study participants teaches at a school with a large Arab Muslim population. The teacher expressed her pride at the accommodations her school offered Muslim students—such as a study room to sit in during the lunch period in Ramadan, and early dismissal on Fridays for *Jumuah* (Friday prayer). The teacher drew a line, however, when accommodating Muslims meant giving up a Christian tradition:

> But there was a time, at Christmas time it was Ramadan and we weren't allowed to have a Christmas party, because some of the teachers were also fasting. We had to wait to have a Christmas party in January, so in that case religion played a part in making that decision. *[Research Assistant: So, how did you feel about that?]* Well, I felt if you are going to have a Christmas party, it is in December. Celebrating in January [doesn't make sense, because then Christmas] is over. I felt they were given more priority over our beliefs. If they didn't want to come then don't come.

Here we see the external/structural dimension of Christian privilege in the construction of what is normal and not normal. "Normal," as Özlem Sensoy and Robin DiAngelo describe it, "is the line drawn around an arbitrary set of ideas a group determines as acceptable in any given place and time."[9] Christian privilege is embedded in this teacher's definitions of what is normal and abnormal, and in the assumptions conveyed through language: a "holiday" party is defined as a Christmas party and must therefore be held in December. The teacher felt entitled to have a Christmas party regardless of whether her Muslim colleagues were fasting for Ramadan. This teacher's attitudes may reflect how societal norms shape majority thinking on religious topics. Many American Christians, accustomed to a national calendar that matches their religious calendar, have never noticed that Muslim communities sometimes wait to have large Eid celebrations on the weekend, instead of on the date on which the Eid holiday actually occurs, or that Hindu communities have done the same with Diwali or Janmasthami.

These blinders are an example of the internal or attitudinal dimension of Christian privilege. They manifest as a sense of entitlement in relation to situating a diverse school faculty's winter holiday party in December. Such a party could take place at any time. But because the "holiday party" used to be called a "Christmas party," the Christian teachers feel entitled to have it scheduled in December. The teacher I interviewed occupies the comfortable space of the nominally open-minded American: willing to accommodate certain needs of her Muslim students and colleagues, but only up to the point where those accommodations collide with her own comfort and happiness. At that point, she shows her Christian privilege, expressing an entitlement to place her enjoyment over her Muslim colleagues' ability to eat at a faculty celebration. This entitlement expresses Christianity's normative influence over what the word "holiday" really means and when office parties ought to take place.

When Christian dominance is maintained so subtly, through the power of cultural norms and the influence of nominally secular or majoritarian phenomena, Christian privilege is not analyzed, scrutinized, or confronted. Centuries of Christian control over legal and cultural standards have successfully resulted in dominant social realities and social visions being accepted as common sense, as "normal" and universal. The teacher's statements reflect the belief that Christians have the right to their positions. She has internalized the messages of Christian superiority. Christian privilege here manifests in the lack of humility that results from a limited knowledge of religious minority groups and the invisibility of Christian privilege to Christians. The internal/attitudinal dimension of privilege is evident in the teacher's statement that her Muslim colleagues "were given more priority over our beliefs. If they didn't want to come then don't come."

This dimension is often invisible and a powerful force in everyday interactions. It carries particular weight in hierarchical relationships such as teacher/student and supervisor/employee. The same teacher reported the different ways Muslim and other religious minority students are accepted and accommodated in the school:

> Well if someone, like, is Jewish and they wear that Yarmulke on their head and they come to school, that is fine. We have had students who had to leave early on Fridays, the Muslim students to go to the mosque to pray. Plus, if they are fasting, like, for Ramadan, we give them a separate room where they don't have to go to lunch. *[RA: How do you feel about that?]* That is fine.

She went on to describe other accommodations, "like we even have a special menu in school"—that is, no pork is served in the cafeteria. Consider the attitude behind these words: All this is something "we" are doing for the Muslim students. See how *they* get "special" things. See how *we* make an extra effort to accommodate *them*. When religious minority groups want access to the same things that Christians have often had, these occurrences get framed as the religious minority group asking for special treatment— especially when the new accommodation involves the perception that Christians are "giving up" something. No pork in the school cafeteria also benefits the Jewish and Seventh Day Adventist students in the school, not to mention the cardiac health of everyone who eats there. But when prompted by an influx of Muslim families to the school district, it is a "special accommodation."

Understanding the attitudinal dimension of Christian privilege is critical to working for social justice. We can create polices and legislation that are fair, but we cannot legislate attitudes. As our country continues to change and respond to its post-1965 racial and religious diversity, we have yet to change or even consciously address the underlying power of the norm. So, we speak of "tolerance" and of "accommodations." The more important question is: how do we build a more equitable society, one that provides genuinely equal opportunity for people of all faiths? Often, the answer has been that Christians will accommodate others up to the point of Christian discomfort, but as soon as Christians feel that they are giving something up, resentment sets in, a line is drawn, and the power of the norm is invoked.

Christian privilege is one side of the coin; the other side is *religious oppression*. Religious oppression is more than an ideology of Christian superiority. It is a pervasive social creation. In the United States, Christianity exists as normative at three levels: the institutional, the cultural or societal, and the individual. These levels are dynamic, each affecting the others in ways that may be conspicuous or exceedingly subtle. *Religious oppression* is the end product of a process that begins with Christian normativity. In the United States, social norms and rituals, language, and institutional rules and rewards all presume the existence of an exclusively Christian sociopolitical history and a current Christian sociocultural context.[10] America's linguistic and symbolic vocabulary of faith, practice, prayer, belief, house of worship, and history largely ignore the existence of other religions, many of which are older than Christianity. To be nominally Christian in the United States requires no conscious thought or effort on the part of the Christian American; "business as usual" follows their schedule and reflects their theological understandings. The norms create comfort and propriety as well as familiarity.[11]

In the context of this norm, the belief systems of minority religions, along with their respective histories and cultures, are delegitimized, misrepresented, and discounted. In other words, Christian normalcy implies that what is not Christian is not merely different, but is different in a way that diminishes it. A *norm* defines and is defined by its opposite: the "other," the exclusion of which is simultaneous with, and mirrors, the inclusion of that which is normal. The norm encompasses everything from theological "truth" to manners and customs of practice; by comparison, the "other" religions come to be seen as deviant, wrongful, evil, or sick. That which is associated with the Christian norm is considered religious or spiritual, while that which is not is rendered exotic and illegitimate and relegated to cult status. By attributing to a population certain characteristics in order to categorize and differentiate it as an "other," those who do so also establish criteria by which they themselves are represented. In the act of defining religious minorities as deviant, Christians represent themselves as good, normal, and righteous.

The focus on the "otherness" of minority religions contributes to the delegitimization of these faiths. When the subject of religious practice or theology comes up, the Christian norm is applied and the beliefs, rituals, and practices of others are compared to it. Differences, real or imagined, from the Christian norm are found with respect to other religions' theology and manners of practice. For example, the Christian image of "prayer"—kneeling, with the fingers of both hands interlaced—is compared to Native American dance or the Jewish use of *tefillin* (phylacteries), and the latter are not recognized or are regarded as strange. Likewise, as in our discussion earlier, when compared to Christianity's normative images of God as a male human figure with a flowing beard, images of Hindu gods—with their colorful clothing and multiarmed bodies—are seen as "weird" and cultic. The combination of the Christian norm, which is associated by the Christian majority with the idea of "goodness" or righteousness, and the differentness of these other faiths fosters the belief that the latter are illegitimate by comparison.

Identifying Christian Privilege

In a seminal 1988 paper, educator Peggy McIntosh discussed White privilege and made it comprehensible by presenting it as a simple list, stated in the first person, of the advantages Whites enjoy over non-Whites. She described these privileges as "unearned assets that I can count on cashing in each day, but about which I was 'meant' to remain oblivious. White privilege is like an invisible weightless knapsack of special provisions, maps, passports, code-books, visas, clothes, tools, and blank checks." Similar lists have been constructed for Christian privilege.[12] These lists are helpful in generating discussion and raising awareness, but more explanation is needed to illustrate the existence of Christian privilege and its impact on various religious minorities.

This discussion is also necessary to illustrate the nuances and, in particular, the differences of experience among different religious minorities. Some of McIntosh's "white privileges" make sense only when understood as part of a Black-White binary. In the same way, some "Christian privilege" will only affect certain religious minorities, or only affect them in certain ways, depending on their specific religious identity. Some of the forms of Christian privilege may impact a Jewish person in one way and affect a Hindu in another way, or not at all. Some manifestations of the Christian norm may impact Native American spiritualities and yet not trouble a Muslim American. There is no universality of negative experience, but there is a common denominator: Christians always have these advantages. Whether the examples below[13] describe things experienced particularly by Buddhists, or Sikhs, or any other specific group, they have this in common: Christians do *not* experience them.

Readers who identify as Christian might find themselves saying "but this happens to Christians, too" or "this is not Christian privilege, it's secular society versus all of us." Denial is a common reaction to having one's privilege pointed out, but it is not a productive one. When dynamics are described, there is almost always an exception. That is why we have the saying "the exception proves the rule." Oprah's success does not mean that there is no racism or sexism or sizeism in television. Barack Obama's presidency does not mean that there are no barriers left for Black men in the United States. Rather than succumb to the urge to seek an exception, or to personalize the critique, engage with the ideas presented here and acknowledge that this book is describing broad societal phenomena and not any specific individual's life experience. Our analysis must not be driven by anecdotes that may be exceptional, but by data and trends that illuminate the typical.

Prayer: How and Where

AS A CHRISTIAN,

- the way I pray looks and sounds familiar to most Americans.
- the way I pray is reflected in media and popular culture.
- the way I pray is considered an acceptable or normal way of praying.
- my religiosity is not questioned because of the way I pray or where I pray.

What mental image does the word "prayer" conjure? Do you picture a person sitting or kneeling quietly, with crossed hands and closed eyes? Do you picture someone prostrating themselves on a carpet, facing toward Mecca? Do you picture someone burning incense or a ghee-fueled lamp in front of a deity's statue, while chanting in Sanskrit? All of these are forms of prayer. All of them happen every day in the US. Yet only the Christian way of praying—and specifically, the European Protestant way of praying—is generally depicted as the "normal" way to pray. If a television show needs to convey concisely the idea of a character at prayer, the actors will be sitting or kneeling with hands crossed, probably in a church or accompanied by a Christian religious image. Put that on a television screen and no further explanation is needed. It is just the way people pray. It is the norm.

This treatment reifies the idea that the Christian method of prayer is theologically correct. Likewise, "real" worship occurs in a dedicated building, a church, with multiple devotees participating and led by clergy. Here, the church represents both a place outside the home to go to for prayer, and the more fundamental phenomenon of congregationalism—the idea that prayer, properly performed, is done in groups and led by a person imbued by an institution with special theological authority. Practices inconsistent with this approach, such as solitary individual prayer in a home shrine, *pradakshina* (worshipful circumambulation of a *murti* or statue of a deity), or meditation in a natural setting are diminished and rendered invisible. The way that some Jews pray (davening), or the Muslim prayer tradition of facing east and repeatedly prostrating oneself on the floor, becomes something that is different— not unique, but "weird" and, by implication, less theologically valid. Unlike the Abrahamic faiths, religions such as Hinduism and Buddhism don't have a weekly Sabbath or a weekly gathering that adherents attend in order to pray. Prayer is something that is done at home. Many Hindus have an altar in the home where one will say prayers in the morning before going off to school or work. Is that too little prayer? What about too much prayer? A Muslim praying five times a day, as her religious tradition requires, may be viewed as excessive and, by extension, as fundamentalist—that is, as rigid, strict in ways that are not Christian, and therefore unable to fit in.

Beliefs versus Myths

AS A CHRISTIAN,

- I can count on most people to consider the stories in my religion to be credible.
- if I see an image of God in the commercial setting, it will usually be presented in an appropriate, respectful matter.

Most holy books and faith traditions include stories that can be described as supernatural. To believe they are truthful and accurate requires us to disregard some known fact or law of nature. Consider the way various religions' stories are talked about. Core Christian beliefs, such as the virginity of Jesus' mother Mary, the Resurrection and the Assumption, and many of the "miracles" attributed to Jesus, are treated as true and accurate. In the press, popular media, and in many everyday conversations, biblical stories are talked about as if they may have happened in the way the Bible describes. Even if someone doesn't believe in the stories literally, they are often given respect for being part of a familiar faith tradition.

The important beliefs of other faith traditions—Vishnu's periodic visitation of the Earth under different guises (Hinduism), the Prophet Mohammed's midnight flight to heaven on a winged horse (Islam), or various religions' beliefs in communing with the spirit world—are no more fantastical, scientifically speaking. The fact that some faith traditions have a multiplicity of stories, like Hinduism's multiple creation stories, does not mean that any of them should be taken less seriously than the biblical creation story, or that they are less holy or meaningful. Yet these religious minority beliefs are relegated to the status of "myths" and "folkways," terms that devalue them by removing their religious content. In the media, they may be prefaced with phrases like "Muslims believe" or "Sikh tradition states," subtle language that implies a lack of the truth and universality. Somehow only Christian beliefs carry the cachet of truth in the way we speak of and describe them.

When your beliefs simply *are*, while mine are represented as "myths" and "legends," you enjoy an implied legitimacy that I can never match. By implication, your "faith" is well-founded, because your beliefs are credible and legitimate. By comparison, my faith amounts to mindless clinging to old village stories. When any religion is devalued, it can be trivialized. Whereas the treatment of Christian stories in American culture and popular media tends to build up their legitimacy, members of minority religious communities receive messages that their beliefs and scripture are lesser, in a way that allows them to be disregarded and disrespected.

This disregard and disrespect can crop up itself not just in the "marketplace of ideas" but in the commercial marketplace. When deities lose their religious legitimacy, they can be commodified and trivialized.[14] When faith images become interior design fads or fashion elements, the spiritual dimension is removed. When Christians encounter their holy images in the marketplace, they will usually be on items that are intended to be purchased for religious use: votive candles, First Communion gifts, and the like. While Christian religious images may also be sold in ways that hold relatively little religious significance—jewelry, for example—their presentation will still generally be respectful,[15] and will generally be intended for consumption by Christians. By contrast, when Hindu or Buddhist images are found on T-shirts, scented candles, and home décor, these are items that are not created for religious use by believers but rather for popular consumption. The removal of the spiritual from these images becomes part of a cycle: robbed of spiritual legitimacy, holy images are commodified, further reifying the idea that they are something less than true religion.

Sales in gift shops of Native American "dream catchers," or figures of Hindu gods and goddesses on perfume, tapestries, and clothing sold for secular purposes, exemplify religious misappropriation. To be sure, there are some Native artists who reproduce cultural designs and whose proceeds support Native artists and communities. But in the mass market, Happy Buddha statues and Native traditions' spirit animals become cultish, fetishized, portrayed as cartoonish, despite their religious seriousness to believers as visible manifestations of the divine.

Scholarship, surveys, and other analyses are not immune to Christian hegemony. In 2014, the Pew Research Forum published the first-ever nationwide survey on Asian Americans and religion. As a member of Pew's academic advisory panel, I had access to the preliminary draft of the report. That draft grouped data on ancestral spirits, spiritual energy, yoga, reincarnation, and astrology under the heading "Eastern and New Age Beliefs," a phrase fraught with Orientalist connotations. The panel recommended replacing the heading with the phrase "Spiritual Matters" as a less offensive and more accurate description. In the published report, the data appear under the heading "Ancestral Spirits, Spiritual Energy, Yoga, Reincarnation and Astrology," and are referred to in the text as "other spiritual matters." Despite our panel's best efforts, however, the Orientalist "othering" of religious minority beliefs and traditions still surfaces elsewhere in the Pew report. For example, while beliefs in heaven and hell and angels and evil spirits are identified as such and discussed without an undertone of judgment, the fact remains that these beliefs, associated with Christianity, are never referred to as "Other Spiritual Matters." The normative status of Christianity runs deep, and recognizing its influence on social science research is important for truly understanding our religious landscape.

Civic Matters

AS A CHRISTIAN,

- When I swear an oath on my holy book, my credibility won't be questioned.

For centuries, the Bible has been seen as the world's constitution.[16] In the present day, that means that the Bible alone, among whatever other "holy" texts may be recognized, conveys the trust and seriousness that underlies concepts like the swearing of an oath. In numerous contexts, but particularly in the courtroom and in public service, the idea of an "oath" is essential. We have all seen it on television: a trial witness will place her hand on the Bible and swear to "tell the truth, the whole truth, and nothing but the truth." Elected officials place their hand on the Bible as well, and swear to perform their public duties, "so help me God." The act connotes seriousness and inspires trust.

What the data tell us, however, is that that seriousness and trust attaches only to the Bible and not to any other holy book. In the 2014 New Jersey lawsuit *Davis v. Husain*,[17] for example, one juror revealed after the trial that she found the defendant, an Indian American

Muslim, to be a less credible and trustworthy witness because he did not swear his oath on the Bible. As a result, she voted for the plaintiff to win the case. Adam Jacobs, a criminal trial judge, has urged the New Jersey Supreme Court's Criminal Practice Committee to eliminate the tradition of having witnesses swear an oath on a holy book, and instead have all witnesses "affirm" their intent to tell the truth. Despite what happened in *Husain*, the committee rejected Judge Jacobs' recommendation, preserving the Bible's role in courtroom oaths.

A similar issue arises when elected officials swear their oaths on holy texts other than the Bible, such as the Quran or the *Bhagavad Gita*. These occurrences of the swearer choosing a text other than Bible become noteworthy enough to earn news coverage. The fact that the Bible is the expected text and any other is "different" illustrates Christianity's normative power in our thinking about public oaths. Only the Bible, of all scriptures, is so ordinary a part of public oaths that it is considered a document with civic meaning, rather than only a reflection of the swearer's private religion.

AS A CHRISTIAN,
- my religion is reflected in the people who represent me in government, and it is familiar to them.

Political campaigns in the United States, whether at the local level of city council or the national level of running for president, entail visiting houses of worship. Candidates will attend worship services, and often stay to speak with the leadership and community afterwards. But many elected officials are uncomfortable in settings unfamiliar to them. Whereas an elected official may find a church of another denomination familiar and comfortable enough, the same may not be true of a minority religion's space. For some elected officials, this discomfort is a matter of avoiding the possible embarrassment of "doing something wrong"; for others, it's the fact that their own Christian faith makes them want to avoid "praying to a false god."

Whatever their reason, some elected officials are less open to visiting religious minorities' houses of worship. By not showing up, elected officials fail to get to know members of these communities in the same way as they get to know their Christian constituents. To use Civil Rights attorney and activist Bryan Stevenson's phrase, which we'll revisit later, they fail to "get proximate" to the concerns and needs of these constituents. The result: religious minorities' opportunity to participate in and contribute to local government, and to speak personally and directly to local elected officials, isn't equal to Christians'. As a result, members of these communities do not see themselves as being represented and a vicious cycle of less civic engagement is perpetuated. Elected officials' non-attendance also conveys the message that religious minority communities are less important.

AS A CHRISTIAN,

• I see faith leaders of my religion regularly at public events.

It is still more common than not in the US for local government meetings to begin with a prayer. This practice raises obvious Establishment Clause questions, but a bare majority of the Supreme Court has ruled, in *Greece vs. Galloway* (2014), that Christian prayer at public functions is acceptable because it is a long-standing tradition. The proposed compromise in that case, that "nonsectarian" prayer be offered, is really no solution at all. What prayer, that is a prayer at all, is truly "generic"? Even when prayers are stripped of conspicuous Christian references like "Jesus Christ" and "Savior," the prayers used in these context are generally based on Christian prayer and will sound clearly and conspicuously Christian to any listener. Consider, for example, the carefully nonsectarian prayer offered at the beginning of every meeting of Passaic County, New Jersey's governing body, which begins: "Oh God, who provides for thy people by thy power, and rules over them in love." "Oh God"?

"Thy people" and "thy power"? To any religious minority listening, this is a Christian prayer, and therefore one that excludes them.

Many local governments, attempting to be inclusive, will also include a Black minister to represent African American Christians, or a rabbi or imam to represent their respective faith communities. But even when minority faith communities are included in this way, White Christianity is never omitted. With rare exception, few would remark on the absence of a Hindu priest or rabbi, but if *only* those clergy participated and there were no White Christian cleric the event would likely be considered incomplete. If it takes a White Christian's prayer to make the religious element of a civic function complete, what does that tell us about the relative importance of other faiths? What message does it convey to religious minorities?

As noted earlier, when a Hindu priest was invited by then-majority leader Senator Harry Reid of Nevada to offer a prayer to a joint session of Congress in 2007, the Congressional gallery erupted with loud protests and attempts by Christians to shout down the priest as he prayed. One of the reasons for this sort of incident is that US national identity is bound so tightly to Christianity that religious minorities are seen as foreign and therefore objectionable in xenophobic discourse.

AS A CHRISTIAN,

- I can run for office and my religion not be brought into question.

For political candidates, being like one's constituents in any way, but particularly in religion, is politically preferable; being different results in questions that can derail a campaign. The first time second-generation Indian American politician Nikki Haley ran for the South Carolina Legislature, she seemed comfortable identifying both with her parents' Sikh religion and with the Methodist faith of her husband. As she grew in political stature, however, her campaign faced more and more questions that sounded something like this: "Okay, she's talking about God, but *which* God?" The language on her campaign website was revised, with a reference to "almighty God" changed to make specific reference to Jesus Christ. At one point, she added a section to her website titled "Is Nikki a Christian?" (The answer, of course, was yes!) South Carolina voters needed reassurance that their candidate would represent them, and for many, that meant praying to and believing in a Christian God.[18] Haley's story is also a perfect example of how religion can be racialized. As an Indian American, her appearance prompted some of these questions about her beliefs.

Christian candidates can profess their faith as a way to create a sense of identity between themselves and their voters. But except in very rare religious minority-majority districts, religious minorities cannot do the same. Whether asked aloud or not, certain questions are directed only at religious minority candidates—or at candidates who, because of their racial identity, are perceived to not be Christian. The voter's question in a democracy—"does this candidate represent me?"—is answered by White Christian candidates primarily through reference to political ideology, policy, and performance. For racial and religious minority candidates, the same basic question takes on a more skeptical tone, and invokes questions of identity. This person and I lack a fundamental thing in common. Can she really represent me, even though she is so different?

Patriotism and American Identity

AS A CHRISTIAN,
- I am assumed to be a patriotic American.
- I can protest and my patriotism is not questioned.

Christianity is a visible ingredient of US patriotism in times of war and conflict. During the height of the US–Soviet Cold War in the 1950s, atheism was viewed as un-American and Jews were regarded with suspicion. To emphasize this message and rebut the "godless communism" of the Soviet Union, Congress in 1954 amended the Flag Act to add the phrase "under God" to the Pledge of Allegiance. As compared to Protestants, people of other religions are often seen as having other allegiances, such as Catholics (including presidential candidate John F. Kennedy) to the Vatican, and Jews to Israel. The WWII-era internment mixed racial and religious factors in imagining Japanese Americans as the enemy other. In the present day, it is American Muslims who are suspected of being a potential "enemy within." Due to the immigration and naturalization policies described earlier, many Latinx and Asian Americans are part of immigrant communities—raising, again, the implied question of divided or un-American loyalties. By contrast, Whiteness and Protestant Christianity work together as American nationalism.

Religious minorities, and especially Muslims in the post-9/11 era, understand this all too well. A few years ago I interviewed a teacher who described her experience with Muslim students immediately after the September 11, 2001 attacks:

> My school was five miles away from the Pentagon . . . [T]he next day [of school, on September 13, 2001], I noticed that the groups of Muslims had all little flag pins and were really sensitive and they would say good morning and came up to us [and were unusually polite]. . . . [T]hey would come up to us wearing "God Bless America" pins. You would say, "good morning," and they would say, "good morning" and "God Bless America." And it was a very interesting experience how they would take that time to say that. . . . Almost as if to say, "this happened, but we aren't a part of it."[19]

The Muslim students and their families felt the need to prove their loyalty to America so strongly that they wore pins and made extra efforts to be polite to their teachers. In doing so, they expressed their fear of being targeted for scrutiny or worse because their religion marked them as suspect. Their Christian classmates did not feel the same need to engage in conspicuous patriotism; their privilege was to be presumed patriots by virtue of their religion.

Many of us noticed similar post-9/11 behavior in businesses and even houses of worship. Particularly as South Asian Americans began to realize that "backlash" attacks were often directed at non-Muslims, many South Asian-owned businesses began displaying American flags, "support our troops" banners, and other trappings of conspicuous American patriotism. One Hindu temple in New Jersey placed a neon "GOD BLESS AMERICA" sign in a window, facing the street.

The association of Christianity with patriotism, augmented by the immigrant status of many American Hindus, Muslims, and Sikhs—groups that are also racialized as foreign—and the assumed connection between American Jews and the State of Israel, results in religious minorities facing questions about their loyalty and commitment to the US that Christians do not. Whereas a Christian might be able to protest against American military intervention abroad or human rights issues at the US border, or for Syrian refugees, and not have her patriotism questioned in the bargain, the same is not true of religious-minority Americans. As a result, members of religious minorities may feel less able to participate and express themselves as fully as the First Amendment's speech and assembly clauses allow.

Language

AS A CHRISTIAN,

- American English idioms and metaphors incorporate my religion and religious stories.
- I don't encounter unfamiliar religious ideas in my day-to-day conversations.

The cultural impact of European Protestant Christianity on American norms has been so deep, it exhibits the paradox of being barely perceptible but also omnipresent. We find it in written and spoken metaphors all over our "city on a hill," where we often "turn the other cheek," where we sometimes "rob Peter to pay Paul," and where being a "good Samaritan," or even going through a "baptism of fire," is sometimes our "cross to bear." When we ask "WWJD?", it is expected that everyone knows what the letters stand for and why we should care what Jesus would do. These examples are so engrained in everyday life, they might seem inconsequential. But understanding them deeply, and knowing when and how to wield them, distinguishes Christians, and Protestants in particular, from all others. They hold the additional cultural capital of being "natives" of these cultural mores, while the rest of us operate from a place of relative cultural disadvantage as a result.

The relationship between Protestant Christianity and the English language reaches back to the publication of the King James Bible in 1611. Although not the first English translation, the King James version was commissioned by the King of England and distributed widely with the advent of the printing press. Along with the Book of Common Prayer, published in 1549 to provide a uniform, English-language liturgy for the newly constituted Church of England, the King James Bible became a major tool for teaching and learning how to write and read English. Centuries later, biblical stories remained part of basic literacy, including in the McGuffey Reader used to teach English in eighteenth-century "Common Schools" in New York, which became the model for public schooling across the US. Through all of this, and the influence of Western Christian narratives on the "canon" of great literature, from Shakespeare to *The Canterbury Tales*, society has absorbed Christian sayings and religious language.[20]

Due to Christian normativity, these sayings and stories are often used with the assumption that everyone understands what they mean. I remember a day in my ninth grade English class when the teacher was teaching us about metaphors and similes, and she brought up the story of the Good Samaritan. Now, using the Bible as literature and to teach language is not illegal; done right, it's a fine idea. But when my teacher assumed all her students knew this story—saying "We all know the story of the Good Samaritan. Can you identify a metaphor in that story?"—she left me at a loss for an answer. Unlike nearly all my classmates, I hadn't been to church or summer Bible camp, and I had no idea how to answer her question. Whether in class or elsewhere, a person who doesn't know or understand the metaphor can't participate in the conversation. It may feel inappropriate to ask, or they may not have the courage to ask, for fear of marking themselves as different or stupid.

Because Christianity is normative, its concepts also become the point of reference in discussions about faith and scripture. Religious minorities are asked, "What is your *Bible*?" and "When is your *Christmas*?" The normative force of these questions sets up the idea that other religions are also defined by one sacred text, one or a small number of major holidays and the connection of such holidays to the birth of a deity, or the idea of a messianic figure or the expectation of one. Hinduism, for example, has multiple sacred texts, multiple deities, and multiple creation and god-birth/origin stories. Judaism and Islam have numerous interpretive texts that function as religious authorities. Other religions celebrate different events, such the revelation of God's word, or the birth or death of a prophet or other leader, and not the arrival or resurrection of a messiah. The pressure on religious minorities to conform to certain norms forces them to distort their own faith to make it understood.

Christianity's normative power also creates a situation in which holidays that fall in or near December take on disproportionate religious importance due to their proximity to Christmas. The best example of this is Hanukkah, which has relatively less theological significance but often gets more attention than the more theologically significant High Holidays or Passover, simply because of Hanukkah's proximity to Christmas. We often observe the phenomenon of schools attempting to be inclusive by celebrating all religious holidays in December. The result, for Christians and religious minorities alike, may be a misunderstanding of holidays and their meanings, and a misestimation of their importance.

Members of religious minorities who understand what is wrong with such false associations are left with the implication that their religion and its holidays are considered less important. They may also find themselves unable to fully explain their own religion, and have it understood in its own right, because they are asked to create analogies to Christianity. Many universities, for example, refer to their staff clergy as *Chaplains,* regardless of whether they are Christian. Princeton's Vineet Chander, for example, is "the nation's first full-time Hindu Chaplain," according to the University's website. Terms like *chaplain* carry meaning; their origin is in church tradition, and they connote particular traditions—such as pastoral care—that are uniquely Christian. Those terms may not be accurate or appropriate, in relation to minority faith traditions.[21]

Rituals

AS A CHRISTIAN,

- I can have my religious event at a venue of my choosing without changing or giving up any rituals.
- I can display or talk openly about my religious practices without concern for how they will be received by others.
- I rarely have to explain why I am, or am not, doing things related to my religious faith.

When my husband and I were preparing to get married, we needed a hotel ballroom for our integrated Hindu–Christian wedding ceremony. As part of the Hindu ritual, a small, contained fire, called a *havan*, was a spiritual necessity; fire represents purification and the presence of the divine. However, when we tried to find a venue for our ceremony, our need for a havan became a point of contention. At hotel after hotel, the reaction to our plan was instant and absolute: "We can't do that." They said our ceremony would set off the entire hotel's sprinkler system, and that the fire marshal would never allow it. What they did not do was to try to understand the ritual. Not one hotel asked how big the fire would be, or how long we would need it lit, or offer any other question or suggestion to help us find a solution. I was one of the first in my community to get married, so I was not surprised or bothered that Atlanta-area hotel managers didn't know what a havan was. I was frustrated, though, that not one of them even tried to understand our needs or work with us to make our wedding possible. With the prospect of hosting a 500-guest wedding, why would any hotel not even try to find a way to earn that business? I wondered whether, despite our explanations, they were envisioning a bonfire in the middle of the ballroom rather than a few flames in a small bowl, fueled by grains and *ghee* (clarified butter). In the end, we could not book our wedding at any of the elite downtown Atlanta hotels my parents had always envisioned.

There's a happy ending to our story. We were married in a suburban hotel owned by an Indian American Muslim man. Having grown up in India, he was familiar with Hindu rituals, and he literally took us by the hand and said, "We'll work with the fire marshal, and everything will be fine." He shut off the ballroom sprinklers for an hour, and coordinated with the fire department, so we could have a beautiful blended ceremony with a havan. This hotel owner earned our business by understanding our needs, whereas none of Atlanta's elite hotels even tried. Their unwillingness to accommodate us, or to even seek a way to accommodate us, is a manifestation of the Christian norm that dominates US society. Its normative nature makes Christianity the religion that need not be explained, and for which society's rules were written. How many of those hotels had hosted weddings with candles? A candle, being part of Christian faith traditions, is normal; a fire, unfamiliar in Christian ritual, is not. In fact, I would argue that if Christian wedding traditions included a *havan,* there isn't a hotel in the United States that wouldn't accommodate it.

The line between known and unknown, or familiar and unfamiliar, also affects how minority religions are seen and understood. Most Americans understand that different people practice Christianity in different ways. By contrast, minority religions are not as well understood. They know, for example, that Islam prohibits the consumption of alcohol and pork, and mandates praying toward Mecca five times every day. They may know that Hindus won't eat beef. (Actually, complete vegetarianism, not just avoiding beef, is considered by many Hindus to be a religious obligation.) They may know that the Sikh religion requires adherents to keep their hair uncut and to wear a *dastaar* or "turban."

Due to this one-dimensional understanding of non-Christian faiths, many don't get that, just like Christians, some religious minorities observe the tenets of their faith more or differently from others. Second-generation Muslim Americans who drink alcohol report being challenged by Christian peers, or feeling that it was difficult to explain their decision not to follow that Islamic proscription; some have even told me they decided not to drink at a social function just to avoid questions about their religion. And while numerous turban-wearing Sikhs have reported discrimination or negative attention directed at their turbans, some Sikhs who cut their hair and don't wear the turban have reported being asked why. When I've eaten chicken at events, I've had people say, "I thought Hindus were vegetarian." When I'm feeling cheeky, I'll respond: "Do you go to church every Sunday?"

American Christians don't generally need to deal with similar questions and comments, and the implied moral judgments they represent. Few would take issue with a Catholic American ordering a steak at lunch on Friday, or being divorced, or using birth control—all prohibited under a strict reading of Catholic doctrine. Somehow, with Christianity, most Americans grasp that there is nuance and choice, and that not everyone will follow all the rules. Yet the same is not true when it comes to other faiths. Some might challenge that analysis as obsolete. Few American Catholics still observe all of the doctrine's obligations and prohibitions. But that very objection proves the point. We recognize, and accept without comment, a spectrum of observance and non-observance in Christian practice, while still expressing surprise or puzzlement when the conduct of a Hindu, Muslim, or Jewish colleague doesn't match our rudimentary understanding of their faiths' "rules."

The Christian way is the normal way and, as a result, even when there is a concept that overlaps with other faiths, other religions' practices can be seen as strange or deviant by comparison. For example, fasting as a Christian ritual is typically brief (one day) if complete, or selective when longer ("giving up" something for Lent). This concept of a "fast" is understood and accepted. Yet the Muslim fast of Ramadan—30 days of complete abstention from food and water in the daytime—is seen as extreme. The fasting I do as a Hindu is hard to explain. A Hindu holiday fast may mean abstaining from grains and vegetables, but not from dairy or fruits; some may observe the holiday by only drinking water. When I fasted as a child, I often worried about explaining this concept of a "fast" to my non-Hindu friends, or about facing the question "Is it really fasting if you're eating fruit and potatoes?" Nobody wants to be questioned for their beliefs, so I did not share with my friends the details of how I was fasting. It made it easier not to talk about it, but it was also frustrating because my holidays were fun and meaningful in ways I wish I'd felt comfortable sharing.

Religious Attire

AS A LAY CHRISTIAN,
• I don't wear attire that calls attention to my faith.

While some Christians make the personal choice to wear a cross or crucifix as jewelry, most contemporary Christian traditions do not require particular attire, head coverings, or other markings. Many other religions do, from the Jewish *kippa* (yarmulke) for men, the Muslim *hijab* or *niqab* for women, and the Sikh *dastaar* (turban) and *kara* (bracelet), among other things, for both men and women. Christian normativity, and the faith's lack of attire-as-practice, directs attention to religious minorities for engaging in visible faith practice by wearing particular items. This prompts the question: Why do religious minorities need to "call attention to themselves" or stand out from the crowd? People who observe these obligations of Islam, Judaism, and Sikhism may be seen as a refusing to "assimilate" and become "regular" Americans.

Sometimes, individuals are targeted as a result. Numerous Sikh men have been told to remove their turbans to receive service in restaurants or to go through security at buildings and airports, even though those requests violate Title II of the Civil Rights Act.[22] Prejudice against religious head covering, and its economic impact on one young woman, went all the way to the Supreme Court in a case involving clothing retailer Abrercrombie & Fitch. The company refused to hire a Muslim who wears hijab, because she did not conform to its "look policy"—a dress code that forbade religious head covering in its retail stores. In announcing the Court's ruling against Abercrombie, Justice Antonin Scalia—not always a friend of religious liberty—commented, "this is an easy one."[23] Maybe for the court, but not for the young woman and her lawyers who had to wage a costly years-long legal fight just to get a job at the mall.

At the level of culture and normativity, the line between Christian and other faiths' religious attire and visible daily practice will continue to define the barrier between normal and abnormal. The latter will remain exotic, "foreign," and potentially even the target of criticism or violence that enjoys social sanction due to Christian normativity. Christians experience their privilege when they think nothing of wearing crosses as jewelry, but the other side of the coin of privilege is the disadvantage, even danger, experienced by

Jewish people who may think twice about their safety before wearing a Star of David in certain areas and observant Muslim women concerned about wearing a head covering to a job interview. At the most basic level, relevant particularly for schoolchildren faced with peer pressure, the difference between what one wears and what one's classmates wear becomes an element of not "fitting in"—a social privilege that sometimes seems reserved for Christians.

Dietary Restrictions

AS A CHRISTIAN,

- I can attend a business luncheon, or eat at a school or workplace cafeteria, and not worry about whether there will be food that satisfies my religious dietary restrictions.

Protestant Christianity is virtually alone among major world faiths in having no dietary restrictions or guidelines. Individual Protestants may decide to "give up" a particular food during Lent, but there are no general dietary guidelines as are found in other faiths. For Catholics, a prohibition on consumption of meat (other than fish) applies during Lent and, for some, on Fridays year-round. Judaism's rules include *Kashrut,* the "Kosher laws" that restrict the type and preparation of food permitted. Islam has a similar set of restrictions known as *Halal.* Hinduism, as it is practiced in different parts of India and around the world, may include prohibitions on the consumption of beef or of all meat (religious vegetarianism).

As a result, the dietary restrictions of non-Protestants are seen as especially different; they render these faiths a noteworthy "other" because they have a body of rules foreign to the Protestant faiths. People who observe religious obligations cannot assume that their dietary needs will be met at a typical restaurant or buffet. For the observant, this creates the disadvantage of having to plan ahead, and to draw attention to oneself as a religious minority by requesting dietary accommodations. One could eat alone before-hand, so as not to be hungry, but will then endure questions and attention for having an empty plate. Sometimes, due to the dynam-ics of social power, a person may not be in a position to make the necessary request and may simply go hungry. And when it's time for grocery shopping, particularly for communities whose dietary laws include prescriptions for the slaughter and treatment of meats, like kashrut and halal, religiously compliant foods often cost more.

During Lent, dietary accommodations are often made for those Catholics and other Christians who might be observing the Lenten ritual of not eating meat on Fridays. Fish and poultry options are available in cafeterias, and it seems to be the one time of year when McDonald's advertises its Filet-O-Fish sandwich. Yet when accommodations are made for Muslims, some Christians react negatively to the "special treatment." One teacher I interviewed expressed frustration about a time when she brought Rice Krispy Treats into class for her students, but then could not serve them because a close inspection of the ingredients revealed that they contained gelatin, which violates the halal dietary restrictions. At her school now, she said, "you can't serve pork. And if you bring in treats for the kids, they read the labels, and 'does it have gelatin in it?'" Here, the religious practice of one group is viewed as an inconvenience by the Christian teacher. The line of Christian con-venience was crossed, and the resulting frustration—or, perhaps, embarrassment—affected the teacher but also her students, who could not eat the treats she brought and probably felt bad or differ-ent as a result.

These issues arise frequently on college campuses, where par-ticipation in the meal plan is often mandatory—and expensive—yet the cafeteria may offer no options, or little selection, for those ob-serving religious dietary restrictions. A cafeteria's open hours can also be a burden for the observant. About ten years ago, Ramadan (the month when many Muslims fast from sunrise to sunset) fell during the winter, affecting students in my classes with 4:30 or 5 p.m. start times. Muslim students came to me because the hour for breaking their fast came just as class was starting, and by the time class ended the cafeteria would be closed. They asked to bring food to class and break the fast rather than go hungry until late in the evening. Those same students also probably faced a dilemma every morning: the dining hall opens at 7:30 a.m., after sunrise.

Lifestyle

AS A CHRISTIAN,

- I can shop anywhere for items that represent my religious norms.
- my work schedule and religious calendar are in sync.
- my family can hear music on the radio and watch specials on television that celebrate the holidays of our religion.

In an area we can broadly define as "lifestyle," American Christians have a wide variety of choices when shopping for everything from jewelry to greeting cards. Even in a diverse state like New Jersey, I have shopped for Bar and Bat Mitzvah cards enough times to know that there aren't many choices. And good luck finding a Diwali card at Walgreen's! By contrast, Americans who are Christians have no problems finding Christmas cards or Easter baskets for every taste. These items are so normal that their presence is not even remarked on. Likewise, to consume these goods is normal and marks one as a member of the "in-group" and not the opposite.

Displaying these items is also ordinary: no one thinks twice of seeing a cross or crucifix pendant on the neck of a salesperson at the mall. Yet it took the US Supreme Court to tell Abercrombie & Fitch that its "look policy" was discriminatory. Notwithstanding the Supreme Court's ruling, at the institutional level of the workplace, employees whose religious identities are visible still may not be considered for "front desk" or "client service" positions in which grooming and dress policies reproduce mainstream cultural norms that clash with the kippa, turban, long hair and/or beard, required of observant Jewish, Sikh, or Muslim men, or the hijab worn by many observant Muslim women.

In workplaces and businesses, especially small businesses, the notion of taking time off is problematic. A small business owner cannot just close for Navratri; customers, employees, suppliers, and others count on them to be open on ordinary business hours and business days, which are fixed to the Christian calendar. A young professional with a looming deadline on an important project won't feel he can approach his boss and ask for a day off for Vaisakhi, yet that same young professional's Christian colleague would not be expected to work on Christmas—because on Christmas the office is closed.

Conclusion

Thumb back through the discussion of privileges in this chapter. Think about how many facets of life these privileges touch: professional advancement and economic success, academic achievement and social participation during the formative years of K–12 and higher education, commerce and the experience of consuming goods and services, personal interactions with neighbors and strangers, and of course worship and living your faith. Whatever your religious affiliation, consider how many times and places in a day you deal with any of these issues: from the workplace to your or your children's school, when you turn on the TV or log on to social media, when you are shopping at the mall or browsing the greeting card aisle at your local drugstore.

Some readers may be thinking, "But wait, Christianity is commodified in Hollywood films, too. A Christian cannot pray freely in public without judgment, or say grace before a meal at a business luncheon. Sometimes we are treated as stupid for believing, or assumptions are made about our politics because we profess our faith." That is all true, and there is probably no one in the world who gets through life without ever being made to feel uncomfortable or targeted or devalued for what they believe or do not believe. But for religious minorities in the US, these are everyday experiences that require them to exert energy on how to respond to, deal with, or accommodate their own needs—energies that Christians do not have to spend on such a daily basis. All this is reinforced at the level of institutions and public policy. White Christians alone can count on consistently seeing themselves reflected in the nation's structures, and enjoying calendars and expectations that coincide with their beliefs and practices. And sometimes the consequence is deadly serious fear or violence: the Muslim high school students in Virginia, wearing flag pins and greeting their teachers with the words "God bless America" after 9/11; the multiple Sikh men killed in 9/11 backlash attacks; or congregants at synagogues, gurdwaras, and Black churches who have been attacked with guns or bombs in recent years.

In talking about whether experiences like these "happen to Christians too," we must also keep in mind that individual experience is a reflection of social power. The difference between Christians' and religious minorities' experience in America is driven by the ability of the majority[24] to define what is normal and what is not. Life in the United States over the centuries has produced the social power that today makes it easier and safer for Christians, and particularly White Christians, to practice their faith. Christians may sometimes be made to feel bad, but they do not face systematic discrimination endorsed and augmented by nationally recognized rules and structures. By contrast, religious minorities face an entire system that, in its laws and language and standards, devalues and negates their faith.

The energy this consumes in the lives and minds of religious minorities can be enormous. Teens worry about fitting in. Busy working parents take the time, money, and effort to buy food and pack lunches because they and their children cannot eat what is served at work, school, or camp. At any age or setting, members of religious minorities must muster the psychic energy and deliver explanations for why they need some accommodation extended to them. They must worry about whether a supervisor who is Christian will understand the need, and they must also live with the feeling that they are counting on that person's generosity. All this, just to practice their faith.

Recognizing these privileges does not mean stigmatizing Christianity or saying that individual Christians are guilty of anything at all. Remember: privilege is an accumulation of systemic advantage and institutional discrimination. Christians' pride and positive self-image need not be replaced with shame or self-consciousness. Still, we need to make policy and social changes that better embrace the nation's contemporary religious diversity. These changes should become part of an overarching vision of social justice in which the current privileges Christians enjoy in the US become *rights* for everyone, regardless of what religion anyone practices or whether one practices religion at all.

5

Voices of Christian Privilege

When I was in high school, a community youth group would send its leaders into my school regularly to publicize student gatherings and social events held every Wednesday evening at a location called "Our Place." None of the leaders, and none of my friends who went out together, ever invited me to take part. I learned many years later that the organization, Young Life, was an evangelical Christian organization. But in high school, all I knew was that all my friends were hanging out together at "Our Place" on Wednesday nights and nobody seemed to want me there.

A few years ago, I was talking with my high school teachers about "Our Place." Some of them let me know that Young Life's recruiting visits had been the subject of discussion at a faculty meeting. Should a Christian youth group leaders be allowed into our independent (nonreligious) school to recruit for their youth group events? One teacher described arguing against Young Life because the school served students of diverse religious backgrounds, including me and my sister. However, most of the faculty believed Young Life's visits were harmless and they allowed Young Life to continue coming into our school. As people who were or had grown up as Christians themselves, they either did not recognize Young Life's language as Christian proselytization or they may have regarded it has harmless or not understood how it would affect religious minority students. In fact, Jewish students sometimes socialized with their peers at Our Place. When one of them was invited to a Young Life weekend retreat, one of her teachers—understanding that the weekend would involve intense preaching and proselytization—tried gently to discourage the student from going. The Jewish student went on the retreat anyway, and came home confused and upset by the experience. She was hurt and worried about what people thought of her and her religion. What did it mean for her friendships, if her friends' deeply held beliefs were that they were "saved" and she was not?

Socially and emotionally, the high school years are all about fitting in and feeling included. Feeling excluded, unwelcome, and different can cause turmoil and scars that can last a lifetime. For religious minorities like me and that Jewish student, Christian privilege exacerbates the social moments of exclusion. When authority figures do not address or understand why it is important to respond to proselytization or other elements of Christian privilege, they collude in the marginalization of religious minorities. In this instance, one teacher recognized a problem and tried to act, but was outnumbered and unable to protect her religious minority students.

Christian privilege affords Christians myriad advantages while leaving so many others on the outside looking in. It has a significant effect on the everyday lives and outlooks of Christians, religious minorities, and atheists. While there is no single or monolithic story to tell, there are trends and collective experiences that illustrate how Christian hegemony shapes the lives of all Americans. Being a member of a privileged majority group or of a marginalized minority group influences how people experience life and how they see the world, including awareness of and perspectives about social justice issues. Using individual voices, this chapter maps the spectrum of beliefs, approaches, and attitudes that both Christians and religious minorties in the US have regarding the supremacy of Christianity and of White Christianity. The word "spectrum" is very deliberately used here. What is laid out below is not generally a progression of thoughts or attitudes; people may be situated, unmoving, at any point on the spectrum.

The framing of this chapter around first-person voices should not lead the reader to view religion as merely a personal set of beliefs, choices, and experiences. Rather, as we have seen throughout this book, Christianity is deep in the legal and social infrastructure of America, and for many Christians it is deeply held as truth and moral structure, not just personal choice. The voices here illuminate those structures, and the modes of thought they form in all of us, while the voices at the end of this chapter—when I ask what a social justice approach to religious diversity sounds like—offer a starting point for the prescriptive thoughts in the final chapter that follows.

To engage with this material, we also need to acknowledge that many individuals who are pursuing social justice work—particularly people with Christian backgrounds—reject and avoid the topic of religion. Because of Christianity's historic role in the oppression of women, LGBTQ people, communities of color, and others, they regard faith as inherently at odds with liberatory consciousness. Such beliefs, and the attendant discomfort with talking about religion, lead many to overlook religion's relevance, either as an oppressive force requiring attention or as a liberating influence (as it was during the Civil Rights Movement) on issues like race, incarceration, immigration, LGBTQ rights, and women's reproductive freedom.

The voices of Christians and religious minorities are presented separately in the two sections that follow. Each section is framed around three themes: denial or avoidance, internalized superiority or inferiority, and the recognition of Christian privilege. Finally, the chapter concludes with voices that answer the question: What does a social justice approach to Christian privilege look like?

Christian Privilege and Christians

We are more likely to see religious discrimination than we are to see privilege and the structures that create it. Even those who can see discrimination against religious minorities at the one-on-one level do not necessarily understand how individual discrimination connects to larger structures of Christian hegemony, normativity, and privilege. Recognizing Christian privilege is not inherent in any stage of child, adolescent, or adult development; the dynamics of an individual's participation in situations where privilege appears do not correlate with age. Rather, seeing privilege requires both recognizing how individual experiences reflect deeper phenomena and having the language to express those connections to oneself and others. Here, the first category of voices is of those who cannot or will not acknowledge Christian privilege. Even among those who recognize it, there are people who regard Christian privilege as a warranted product of US history and Christian moral superiority. Moreover, even recognizing the privilege and rejecting it does not correlate with having the language or tools to dismantle the structures that create privilege in the first place.

Denial and Avoidance

"But I don't have privilege."
"But we have the First Amendment, so all religions are treated equally."
"But Christians are criticized for their faith."
"That's not my Christianity."
"I grew up Christian, but I don't identify as one today."

When Christians are unable or unwilling to recognize Christian privilege, there are generally two major reasons: the myth of meritocracy and the myth of religious freedom. Most American Christians regard the US as a meritocracy: a place where anyone can get ahead with skills and hard work. Many also continue to believe that the First Amendment actually protects everyone's rights to freedom of faith and practice; they may point to flourishing religious diversity as proof of actual equality. The idea of unearned privilege contradicts these myths: the deck is not supposed to be stacked against some and in favor of others. But it is. Just as many are challenging the myth of meritocracy with respect to race and class, we need to apply the same critical lens of religion to this analysis as well. Manifest Destiny, and the idea of personal industry being the path to success in the "New Israel," is ingrained in our culture. Christian identity and White identity have traveled the path of history hand in hand. Nevertheless, many Christians cannot see or do not understand the institutional roots that feed their privilege; they may refuse to acknowledge the individual practices and prejudices that perpetuate it. These Christians might say . . .

"But I don't have privilege."

When people first hear about having privilege, a common response is to reject the notion. One of the biggest obstacles to seeing one's own Christian privilege is the lack of understanding of systemic discrimination: bias that is structural, not interpersonal. Individual acts of meanness or kindness reflect individual bias, not systemic bias. The individual level is often where bias is easiest to spot, but it is not necessarily where it is most pervasive or most pernicious. Unless they have been taught real and accurate US history that discusses the pervasive role of Christianity in our laws and social history, including in the founding of our country, it is difficult for people to see Christian privilege. Instead, many Christians use their personal circumstances to explain it away. Many will invoke an identity in which they do not have privilege. For example, one might say: "I grew up poor." Or, "my great-grandfather faced discrimination when he immigrated." Or, "I'm the first one in my family to go to college."

Intersectionality often plays a role here. Christians of color, such as Asian American or African American Christians, may be quick to say that they do not have Christian privilege due to the racism they experience. University administrator Mamta Accapadi provides the example of how it is difficult for Christian students of color to see the hegemonic place of Christianity in cultural centers on college campuses at Christmas time. Describing conversations between Christian and non-Christian students about how to decorate these multicultural spaces for Christmas, Accapadi observed that students "toggled" their advantaged and disadvantaged identities around this conversation of Christian privilege.

When a student spoke in favor of Christmas, they used their "person of color" identity lens to articulate how Christmas decorations allowed them to be themselves as a person of color, rather than owning their dominant identity as a Christian person. This way, they did not have to hold themselves accountable for the oppression associated with Christian dominance. This phenomenon is not unique when it comes to people who have "one up/one down" identities, with one identity being dominant, and the other subordinated.[1] Christian individuals of color are not always able to see their Christian privilege. The Black church has been a wellspring of inspiration, community formation, and social justice. Nevertheless, bringing Christian celebrations into multicultural spaces asserts a Christian privilege and normativity that has an impact on students who are members of religious minorities.[2]

Others I have talked with about Christian privilege have rejected the idea, or tried to minimize it, by telling me, "I am a woman," or "I am a female clergy member." Yet a lack of male privilege does not eliminate Christian privilege. The struggle for equality is real, and it is also limited to its circumstance. Christians—even when they are women, people of color, immigrants, or identify as LGBTQ—do not generally have to make compromises, or invent work-arounds for practicing their faith, as religious minorities do. In other words, along with the disadvantaged identities Christians may hold, Christians still have Christian privilege.

"But we have the First Amendment, so all religions are treated equally."

Another vector for denying Christian privilege is to rely on the First Amendment's protections of "freedom of religion" and the "separation of church and state." This approach imagines the First Amendment to be evidence that Christian privilege does not exist. Christians may entertain this belief while also believing that Christianity is superior to other faiths, or that many religions are equally worthy. For the former group, belief in their own inherent superiority can coexist with believing that the law protects everyone and that therefore none suffer. For the latter, the First Amendment represents the founders' wise creation of a level playing field that must actually exist because it is right there on paper.

Of course, the First Amendment actually proves none of these points. A White Christian person who insists that anyone can practice their religion freely does not see the isolation and discrimination religious minorities face, such as not being able to build a house of worship where they want to, seeing their religion cheapened and commodified in the secular marketplace, or having their faith misunderstood on a frequent basis. She is also, either consciously or unconsciously, expressing the internalized superiority that Christianity's deep cultural power has taught her all along.

Not recognizing Christian privilege is itself a form of *implicit bias*. Implicit bias generally results in a preference for dominant group members and creates privilege for people in those groups. It informs our perceptions of a person or social group, and can influence our decision making and behavior. Formed by our socialization, our experiences, and our exposure to others' views, implicit bias leads to quick and often inaccurate judgment based on limited facts and our own life experiences. This perception gives certain individuals and groups both unearned advantage and unearned disadvantage in the workplace. People can consciously believe in equality while simultaneously acting on subconscious prejudices.

Christian privilege can also emerge as *microaggressions*: unintentional, negative slights toward people from marginalized groups.[3] The deep nature of Christian privilege sets the stage for religious microaggressions. These are commonplace, daily, verbal, behavioral or environmental indignities that intentionally or not communicate hostile, derogatory, or negative ideas and insults toward people who are not Christians. They crop up from Christian hegemony, and can appear as seemingly innocuous comments, or silences, that not only betray the Christian speaker's lack of knowledge about the significance of others' holidays and rituals, but also convey a trivialization of the beliefs and identity of the religious minority to whom she is speaking. I have experienced these kinds of microaggressions in the workplace. When sharing with colleagues that Diwali is coming up, I have been met with silence. They neglected to ask when is the holiday or wish me a Happy Diwali, or even ask, "What does that celebrate?" Just silence, and its message of disinterest. Microaggressions stick with you, like the tune of a song you hate. An atheist friend told me about the aggravation she anticipates, and experiences, when sneezing in public: "Someone is going to say 'God bless you,' and that's going to annoy me, and all those thoughts just go through my head every time I'm out in public and feel a sneeze coming on. In my own head, I can't even sneeze in peace."

"But Christians are criticized for their faith."

There are Christians who will perceive this book as another example of how our culture today is against Christianity. "It is *our* religion that is constantly being discriminated against," say these Christians. "We are treated as unintelligent because of our faith." This cohort sees working for social justice as a personal critique and an attack on their way of life. Some immediately bring up parts of the world where Christians are discriminated against and even face danger and death for their beliefs. While absolutely true in many other countries,[4] that is not the situation in the United States. Nor is it true in most places where Christians are the majority and where Christians have the overwhelming social power, as they have had throughout US history. Even when popular culture offers negative portrayals of Christians, particularly evangelical Christians, these images, ideas, and critiques do not contradict the existence of Christian privilege in the United States.

Christians can be discriminated against or derided in certain social spaces, including in the academy and in politically progressive dialogues.[5] There is a bias in these circles against religion and religiosity.[6] People may express surprise when intellectual people mention Scripture in conversation, or discuss attending church, or participate in a mission trip. Over the past twenty-five years, I have noticed that in social justice and human rights initiatives, many White Christians believe that in order to work for justice they must renounce their faith, because they see how Christianity has been weaponized for oppressive purposes. They struggle with how to both identify as a Christian and work for social justice.

The real story of Christians' perceived oppression is the story of small steps US laws and thinking have taken in the direction of social justice. Because of a 1962 Supreme Court ruling, *Engel v. Vitale*, public school teachers can no longer force Jewish children to pray to Jesus. The Supreme Court has also ruled that county clerks who believe homosexuality is evil can no longer deny service to gays and lesbians (even if bakers still can).[7] Christians construe these cases as an attack on their beliefs and their way of life and thus now may see themselves as fighting for their "religious freedom." However, limits on Christians' ability to use government to enforce their religion's rules against others do not oppress Christians. If your faith includes the tenet "I don't have to accept you if you do something I don't believe in," you will eventually collide with legal limits on putting that faith into practice. The line between my First Amendment rights and a Christian's will always be a contested one. But that ongoing contest does not discriminate against Christians, nor is it anti-Christian to say that one's right to practice faith ends at restricting another person's freedoms.

"That's not my Christianity."

Some Christians, particularly those who are politically progressive, may deny their privilege through deflection. They will think of the extreme forms of Christian supremacy, such as the neo-Nazi march and violence in Charlottesville in the summer of 2017, and say *that's* Christian supremacy but that's not what *I* believe. They might point to the Southern Baptist Convention's anti-Hindu literature,[8] and the prejudice expressed by conservative political figures Jerry Falwell or Franklin Graham, and say, "but I'm not like them." They may identify the literature on how to proselytize, like the Intervarsity Fellowship booklet "Internationals On Campus," which identifies Indians as requiring "special care" and offers advice "training students to reach Hindus" and "bringing the gospel to our Muslim friends," as offensive. Pointing to the extreme in order to prove that they are not extreme, these Christians ignore legal structures and everyday Christian privilege. They use their political identity or their theological disagreement with politically right-wing Christian ideas to deny their dominant social status. Alternatively, they may point to religious minorities who have achieved positions of influence—a Sikh attorney general, a Muslim mayor, a Hindu CEO—to prove the negative. Yet violent extremists are not the only manifestation of Christian privilege, and one religious minority's success is not proof that his entire social group has overcome disadvantage.

"I grew up Christian, but I don't identify as one today."

Some people will try to minimize Christian privilege, or separate themselves from it, by distancing themselves from the faith of their upbringing. But just because an adult does not identify with the Christianity his parents or grandparents practiced, or dislikes "Christianity" as he sees it today, does not mean that he does not benefit from Christian privilege. Christian privilege is social capital. Whether or not she attends church today, someone familiar with Bible stories can easily understand the analogy her boss or colleague is making in a board room; as a result, she enjoys an advantage over her colleagues who belong to religious minorities, who may not be familiar with them. Society makes it easy for her to walk through life, because—to quote Peggy McIntosh again—she still has all the tools in her invisible backpack of Christian privilege.

Superiority and Entitlement

"Well, of course. We were here first, and there are more of us."
"Our dominance is the result of our superiority."
"Look at all the religious diversity we have."
"Yes, that's why this is a White Christian country."

A number of responses to Christian privilege reinforce Christian hegemony and White Christian supremacy. Christians exhibiting superiority and entitlement endorse Christianity as being at the center of American life and intricately linked with national identity, and believe that Christians are superior people who make the US great. This set of ideas combines Christian supremacy with American exceptionalism and sees an imagined pre-1965 America comprised of predominantly White Christians as preferable to increasing religious diversity or movement toward social justice.

"Well, of course. We were here first, and there's more of us."

There are those individuals whose eyes are open to Christian privilege and see it as nothing but the natural order of things in a majoritarian democracy. Christians have been here the longest, and where there are more Christians than anyone else, Christian normativity should be both expected and accepted. Those who exhibit this mindset ignore the fact that European Christians weren't here first. Native Americans were. With conquest as its agenda and Christianity as its rationale, Manifest Destiny led to the genocide of Native Americans and the colonization and settlement of the entire continent by people of mostly European background. Christianity's role in the conquest narrative is minimized, subsumed entirely in a racial narrative, or sanitized through stories of kind missionaries carrying out God's promise. An occasional response of my White Christian students to the subject matter of religious diversity and social justice is reflected in the following statement: "Religious minorities can't expect the dominant culture to change. If someone is going to live in America, then they need to understand that we are a Christian country, and the majority rules." Americans who belong to religious minorities, these students and many others have argued, must accept Christianity's dominant status.

"Our dominance is the result of our superiority."

Many White Christians accept their group's socially advantaged status as normal and deserved, rather than recognize how it has been constructed through policy and laws in our society. *Internalized Christian dominance* refers to the belief of Christians that they are more capable, intelligent, and entitled than atheists, agnostics, religious minorities, and the unaffiliated. Christian rituals, traditions, and stories are regarded as superior to other beliefs.[9] The ideas underlying this belief system hark back to European notions of what is "civilized"—progress, technology, and Western thought. By comparison, the cultures of the populations that were historically colonized, occupied, or enslaved, including Native traditions, are perceived as backwards.

Internalized dominance may be unconscious or conscious. It also may not feel malicious in the mind of the believer. Some Christians who feel spiritually and socially superior nevertheless appreciate the diversity around them—albeit as mere novelty and entertainment. Most are, to some degree, White Christian supremacists.[10] Their narrative of American history is the victor's narrative, the owners' narrative that takes credit for the work of non-Christians, whether slaves or coolies, who built much of what we now recognize as our country on land confiscated from other non-Christians. These individuals do not connect their Christian privilege to the historical injustices, such as the exclusion of religious minorities and forced conversion, that caused it. They therefore see themselves as superior and deserving of their privilege.

These individuals do not deny the United States' growing religious diversity, but they are likely unhappy, resentful, or upset about it. They may long for a mythical time when all Americans were White, Christian, and heterosexual. They believe immigration is causing America to lose its identity, and that accommodating diversity is a surrender of American greatness. They don't want other religions and cultures to be recognized in the workplace or schools. In a discussion of harassment experienced by women in hijab or men wearing turbans, their solution will be: "Take it off." They will deliberately and consciously commit acts of prejudice and perpetuate negative stereotypes of religious minorities: the greedy Jew, or the Muslim terrorist.

"Look at all the religious diversity we have."

Observing the nation's growing religious diversity with a positive or appreciative tone, many Christians believe that the presence of religious diversity proves the absence of religious discrimination. They may express a superficial pleasure with the presence of religious diversity when it suits them, but will make no genuine attempt to be inclusive or to develop knowledge of or engagement with minority faith communities. They probably know the right words for polite conversation, but they ultimately regard minority religions as artifacts to consume—Holi traditions commodified into a "color run" or Buddha statutes to help "find your Zen" at the office. These individuals are fine with the Christian privilege they have. Some clergy and seminary faculty are well-intentioned Christians who, when they encounter the subject matter of this book, will happily point out: "We have a world religions class in seminary." In other words, "look, even our clergy are being taught to respect other religions." But *how* is your seminary's world religions class being taught? From whose perspective? What is the message in the end? If the frame of reference is still Christianity, and the treatment of the subject assumes Christian superiority, it is still operating from a place where any notion of religious equality will be tempered by the quiet thought "but we're still the best."[11] That idea countenances all the norms and advantages of Christian hegemony.

"Yes, that's why this is a White Christian country."

Some people acknowledge Christian hegemony and respond, "Well, this society was built for us. We made this country what it is, and others can leave if they don't like it." Upon surveying the span of American history, with what we have learned about the theology of Manifest Destiny and the use of Christianity to isolate, oppress, or destroy various groups, the idea that God wishes White Christian America well is not a fringe idea. These ideas help buttress White Christian supremacy. Indeed, White supremacist organizations will use the same historical moments I discuss in this book to show the presence of White Christian privilege, but draw a different conclusion: that the US is *supposed* to be a White Christian nation.[12]

This sentiment is also shared by people who would not identify themselves as White supremacists. Many White Christian Americans who rarely encounter people of different faiths, know little more than what they learned in the traditional US history curricula that promotes American exceptionalist ideas: that generous European colonialists "civilized" the savage Native Americans, and that masters took care of their slaves and were good to them. (This is the education that many of us received, not realizing at the time that it promotes White Christian supremacy.) Their only source of information about other religions is through television news or entertainment, in which other faiths are still presented as foreign, exotic, and unpatriotic. If they are aware that Christianity is not the United States' official religion, they think it should be.

Even declaring Christianity to be the United States' official national religion would not be enough for the White supremacists, because they would prefer to get rid of Christians who are Black, Hispanic, Native American, or Asian. They also want many Christians—the ones who aren't White—kept out of the US, so much so that one of their movement's most popular figures, the forty-fifth President, shut down the US government in 2018–19 to advocate "building a wall" to close the United States' southern border.

The Recognition of Christian Privilege

"I see it, but I do not know what to do about it."
"It's great to have religious diversity, but it isn't practical to accommodate every religion."

Attitudes and behaviors emerge when a Christian starts recognizing the Christian privilege, normativity, and hegemony present in our society. These attitudes are shaped by a combination of anger, guilt, confusion, and resistance to the changes that challenging Christian privilege might require. As a person begins to acknowledge and understand Christian privilege, they may remain skeptical about its actual impact. They may even embrace religious diversity, while continuing to apply traditional frameworks of response, like accommodation, that avoid or accept rather than confront the underlying imbalance of power and access.

"I see it, but I don't know what to do about it."

For many Christians, discovering privilege and acknowledging it still doesn't answer the question: now what? In this mindset, a person may be able to name Christian privilege and identify it. Others grasp that something is wrong—they are troubled by Hollywood's fixation on the Muslim terrorist, or by the deadly violence directed at American synagogues and gurdwaras in recent years—but they cannot see or articulate the nexus between those phenomena and their own privileged status. Many are not able to challenge Christian privilege because they do not believe that they know enough about the problem or cannot envision any solution. Others don't feel empowered to speak up, because the dynamics of privilege do not affect them personally enough. Some may say, "I do not like that I have this privilege. But what can I do about it?" All these dilemmas may be accompanied by feelings of guilt, shame, or helplessness in the face of a phenomenon so much larger than themselves or their community. Without an answer to what can be done, even those who recognize Christian privilege can become mentally stuck within a state of being aware of their privilege yet feeling powerless to move forward.

"It's great to have religious diversity, but it isn't practical to accommodate every religion."

People may have positive feelings about religious diversity, while simultaneously not taking it seriously when it comes to the policy changes needed to create equity in diverse communities. For example, My teacher's colleagues knew my sister and I were Hindu, but being part of the Christian majority allowed them to ignore our rights rather than have a difficult conversation with the people from Young Life. For these individuals the abstract positive of religious diversity becomes a concrete negative when they try to incorporate and recognize it in policy. Questions typical of this group would be: "When does it stop?" "How many religions are we going to recognize?" "How do I run my business if all these different people need all these accommodations?"

One common response to the issue of how much accommodation is "reasonable" is to eliminate all religion rather than make physical or social space for religious minorities. Such thinking is often driven by the flawed theory that religious inclusion is a zero-sum game: to make space for B, we must make less space for A. The archetypal example of this approach is the high school "Winter Concert," held in December but devoid of any Christmas music. Settling on an extreme solution, rather than do the difficult work of exploring what is possible, yields its own problems. Members of religious minorities get blamed for Christianity's removal from public spaces (in this case, the winter concert), resulting in Christians feeling that their "rights" are eroding. Religious minorities are portrayed as wanting "special rights," the same dismissive language used to silence the fight for equal rights for LGBTQ people, such as marriage equality. These "special rights" are nothing more than the opportunities and treatment that Christians have always received. The perception that equal rights for religious minorities somehow constitute defeat or marginalization for Christians can lead to hostility toward the increasing religious diversity in communities.

Eliminating religious expression is not a solution. It only causes resentment on both sides. Location- and situation-specific solutions can be found to fit the needs and circumstances. Millburn, New Jersey, for example, contains a large Indian American Hindu population with kids in the school system, but virtually no Hindu faculty. The district has made Diwali a school holiday but also a professional development day for teachers. This nuanced policy serves everyone's interest, at least for now.[13]

Religious Minorities and Christian Privilege

Growing up in suburban Atlanta in the 1980s, I was surrounded by megachurches; I passed roadside marquee boards on the way to and from school every day, all of them reminding me that I needed to accept Jesus. Still, I didn't recognize the Christian normativity and privilege that I was surrounded by, on the road, in my school, or in social spaces outside my ethnoreligious community. I got used to feeling different, inadequate, and alone. Being different at school resulted in being bullied, and I knew that my religion was part of what made me different. Still, it took my collegiate study of religion, and then a year living abroad as part of a religiously diverse graduate cohort in Jerusalem, to fully understand my childhood experience. I knew something wasn't right, but until graduate school I didn't have the language to name or explain my experiences as belonging to a religious and racial minority.

Developing a critical consciousness[14] is a difficult process, both intellectually and emotionally. Grappling with the realities of religious minority status in a Christian normative nation can be difficult, and it may prompt a range of emotions, from shame and embarrassment to anger and outrage. Being able to name privilege, and finding the language that helps express one's experience and recognize that others have shared it, feels liberating and even exhilarating. Many religious minorities have never developed awareness or understanding of how Christian privilege affects them. We need to remember that many members of religious minorities are aware that they are different, but lack the language and perspective to name it or to see the edifice of Christian privilege that disadvantages and marginalizes them.

The impact of Christian privilege on religious minorities or atheists is not "one size fits all." It is experienced differently, and has different impacts on people's lives and identities, depending on the specific Christian privilege at hand and the way the person of a minority religion is affected. As we consider the individual experiences of members of religious minorities, it is critical to consider the intersection of different social identities, including not just race, gender, or immigration status but also factors like generational, socioeconomic, and geographical differences within immigrant and second-generation communities. The presence of Christian music and decorations in December, for example, may affect Jewish people differently than it does people of other faiths, because of specific factors—notably the theological disagreement between Christians and Jews on Jesus' status as the divine messiah. That is not to say that other religious minorities do not have a reaction or an opinion, but the tension that exists between Judaism and Christianity on the question of Jesus' messianic status does not exist for most other minority religions.

Denial, Avoidance, and Internalized Inferiority

"This is just life in America."

"Christianity is normal and my faith is not."

"I want to be part of that."

"This is just life in America."

The response of religious minorities to Christian privilege depends on several factors, including the specific religion, context, and length of time in the US in years or in generations. Immigrants understand discrimination, alienation, and injustice. They can recognize that not getting a building permit for a temple, when permits are easily issued for churches in the same neighborhood, is wrong. They know harassment or violence on the street is wrong. At the same time, many may not recognize how history and law created those individual injustices, and that discrimination results not from immigrants being new or different but from an underlying Christian privilege that predated their arrival by centuries.[15] Here, immigration history is often part of the equation. The thought, "well, we're just not familiar yet" is more prevalent among immigrant communities than among religious-minority communities with longer histories in the US, such as Jewish Americans. Whereas nineteenth-century Jewish immigrants might have said, "this is just life in America," a century of advocacy and organizing against antisemitism positions Jewish Americans differently from Hindus, Jains, Sikhs, and others with more recent immigration stories.

Immigrants may be proud of their faiths—indeed, it is often the major means of replicating and transmitting the home culture to their children[16]—and yet they may nevertheless decide to put up with harassment and disadvantage rather than challenge it. The immigrant generation, both children and adults, may have reduced expectations of being understood and of having their beliefs accommodated. As it did for me, feeling different becomes normalized: we lower our expectations, and anticipate misunderstanding and rejection. A Muslim might not think it practical to be excused from work or school to observe a religious holiday. Some may deny their religious background in the guise of assimilating to the dominant culture.

As victims of marginalization and religious oppression, religious minorities are susceptible to the effects of *internalized oppression*.[17] They can begin to view themselves through the lens of the Christian group, which can lead to consciously or unconsciously internalizing attitudes of inferiority or "otherness." Internalized religious oppression results in negative feelings like low self-esteem, shame, and depression, but also in behaviors such as exhibiting prejudiced attitudes toward members of their own religious community, trying to "hide" their home religion and home life from Christian peers, avoiding religious participation entirely, or even converting to Christianity. Internalized religious oppression can be hard to identify because some of its behaviors look like a rational decision not to observe one's faith. For example, a Sikh man who keeps his hair short and does not wear the turban may just be deciding not to abide by that particular tradition, or he may be acting out the internalized oppression of wanting to hide his differentness. More examples of internalized religious oppression appear below.

"Christianity is normal and my faith is not."

Religious minorities, particularly youth, may see the White Christian way as normal and their family faith as odd and different. Religious minorities may begin to accept and conform to White Christian religious and cultural standards. The acceptance, or internalization, of the Christian norm manifests in different ways. For example, Bindu, a young Indian American Hindu woman I interviewed years ago, recalled finding Christianity appealing because it "has . . . one single god. . . . I really have a hard time believing in multiple gods." The idea of multiple deities conflicted with what she saw and heard in school and society: God depicted in the singular. In addition, Bindu described negative experiences with her Hindu faith, and contrasted them with the enjoyable experience of quiet and order of church services: "I would go to church with my friends sometimes just because I'd be spending the night on Saturday. It was such a nice, quiet ceremony. I go to Indian weddings and they're so loud and people walk around and talk and stuff during it, and I didn't like that." Attending an independent school, with few co-ethnics or co-religionists, this woman was surrounded by White Christian normativity. She absorbed Christian ideas (e.g., monotheism) about what religion and religious practice should look and sound like (e.g., silent prayer). As her comments indicate, such experiences can diminish religious minorities' interest in and enthusiasm for their home religion.

Religious minorities may express apologetic attitudes about their religious rituals or blame their own religious group for making itself a target. One Muslim American said this about the violence perpetrated after a Danish newspaper published cartoons about the Prophet Mohammed in 2005:

> I think it's been negative because the Muslims haven't been handling it well, like with this whole Denmark, the thing about . . . the cartoons or whatever, and whatever else just happened to happen, Muslims are always, they start riots and stuff like that. And that's the stupidest thing I have ever seen because instead of doing it peacefully and showing how true Islam would be, they go and they start riots and stuff, that's just making Muslims worst, worst off. So who would want to convert to Islam?[18]

Even by presenting his opinion this way, this young man was reflecting the influence of the present day and media coverage. Street protests are a means of political self-expression around the world, in numerous religious communities, yet he associates them with Islam because of the particular riots most often covered by the US media. Internalized oppression can cause religious minorities to blame their own faith community for the effects of Christian normativity. Another Muslim American described his feelings about the post-9/11 "backlash" attacks:

> I mean, I did feel sorry for Muslims maybe a year after 9/11 but it's honestly our fault. . . . why aren't there channels out there being sponsored by Muslims to get the word out to the average American who sees on fourteen different channels a negative view of Muslims? Yes, it is a shame that it has to be that way. But you know, Muslims too have to change over time. And it's our own fault.[19]

This young man believes the Muslim community is responsible for the negative backlash against Islam due to of the lack of organization within the community when it came to countering post-9/11 misconceptions and falsehoods about Islam. His thinking absolves Christians, whose viewpoints dominate US news coverage, of responsibility for "a negative view of Muslims" because Muslims have not effectively disseminated a pro-Muslim counter-narrative.

"I want to be part of that."

Surrounded by Christian norms, finding little validation outside the home for the theological principles of their minority faiths, adolescents and young adults particularly could doubt the legitimacy of their family's faith. Consider the example of a young Hindu woman I interviewed when she was in her twenties about her upbringing in the South. Sweta recalled conversations with her high school classmates that caused her to question Hinduism:

I feel like those years I was having conversations about Christianity and whether or not I was going to go to hell if I did not believe in Jesus Christ as my Lord and Savior. I would totally get paranoid about things like that.

Not understanding Hinduism's ideas about death and eternity, Sweta found herself confused and wondering whether her Christian friends were right. That confusion is the power of the Christian norm: her classmates' faith, combined with ignorance about her faith, led her to genuinely worry that she faced damnation for being Hindu. Beyond the question of her own mortality, encounters like this young woman's can cause people of minority faiths to adopt negative views of themselves, their communities, and their beliefs. Sweta was typical of many people for whom being part of a religious minority in a society where Christianity defines theological truth causes feelings of inferiority, self-hatred, resignation, isolation, and powerlessness. Many who react this way are less likely to embrace their home faith.

Surrounded by Christian normativity, young people will sometimes try to make sense of their religion through the theological lens of Christianity. Attempting to understand their home faith using Christian language and concepts can occur because young people are unfamiliar with the ritual language of their home faith—which could be Arabic, Gurumukhi, or Sanskrit. Not understanding the words used in prayers and teaching, they have difficulty grasping the rituals, their theological meaning, and the underlying religious principles. By contrast, Christian principles and expressions are ubiquitous in schools and society, and American Christianity's "native language" is English. As a result, the only vocabulary these individuals have to make sense of their family faith is the language of Christianity. Often religious-minority youth wish to be presented with something from their home faith that is "along the lines of the

Ten Commandments." Those were the words of Anita, an Indian American Hindu woman I interviewed years ago. Lacking that sort of articulation of her family's faith, Anita said, "I'm just as religious, but less Hindu."[20]

One reaction to feeling invisible is to crave validation. Religious minorities rarely see themselves represented in popular culture in a positive light, so much so that the memory of being represented sticks with you. When I was in my twenties, the High Museum of Art in Atlanta publicized an event: a puppet show of the *Ramayana*, one of the two major epics that are sacred texts for Hindus. Now, I am not an art person. I do not "get" art and, up to that point in my life, had never willingly gone to an art museum. But when the High Museum advertised their event, it caught my eye and made me want to attend. It was the first time I had ever seen an aspect of my religion being promoted for a US audience. I "felt seen" for the first time I can remember.[21]

In certain circumstances, religious minorities will subsume visible aspects of their religion in order to appear assimilated, or seek ways to demonstrate their similarity to Christian friends or colleagues through behavior consistent with mainstream cultural norms. For example, I know a Muslim who, early in his career, drank alcohol with his co-workers after work and at business networking functions. This was not a personal rejection of his faith, and he did not feel negatively about being Muslim when he was at home or with his ethnoreligious community. Rather, he chose to hide his faith and "fit in" in circumstances that felt important for developing a professional community and advancing his career. Religious minorities may avoid asking for things, such as holidays off from work, that call attention to their religion. Finally, *conscious collaboration* can also occur when religious minorities knowingly (if not always voluntarily) accept mistreatment or inequality in order to maintain social status, livelihood, or some other perceived benefit of "not rocking the boat."

The Recognition of Christian Privilege by Members of Religious Minorities

"I want to be at the meeting and be part of the conversation."
"I need to go my grandmother's funeral."
"I am an American too."
"There's a cost to saying something, and not saying something."
"I'll stand up for my faith."

For religious minorities, there are innumerable paths to recognizing Christian privilege. It can come from conversations with a colleague about taking a religious holiday off that trigger the realization that Christians never have to make that choice. It need not be a full understanding of US history and the historical origins and legal foundations of Christian privilege. Indeed, it rarely is. But like so many things we learn, the initial realization grows and expands. The invisibility of privilege—that quiet sense for a person of a minority faith that there's something not right, not fair, or not balanced, about how things work—may trigger the next step: as an individual's experiences of Christian privilege accumulate over time, the larger structure of advantage and disadvantage can become visible in a great "a-ha" moment. That moment of awareness happens in different ways for different people in different contexts. Very often, it feels liberating to know what you've been feeling all of your life is real, shared, and based in history and other factors beyond your control. The "a-ha" moment is just a starting poinqt. From there, members of religious minorities recognize more of the ways White Christian supremacy disadvantages them and others who are not Christian. Here are some religious-minority voices who have recognized and have begun responding to Christian privilege.

"I want to be at the meeting. I want a say."

A few years ago, not long after I earned tenure, my department chair scheduled a faculty meeting on Diwali. She hadn't set out to disrupt my holiday; she had scheduled a meeting on a weekday during the semester. It was an important meeting where the direction of the department would be discussed, and decisions would be made affecting me and my students. I faced a dilemma: do I observe my holiday and get shut out of these decisions, or do I take part in the faculty meeting at the expense of not participating in rituals at the Hindu temple? In my chair's selection of the meeting date, we also see another advantage American Christians enjoy over others: everyone knows when their holidays are. Although she is Jewish, my chair would never have chosen December 25 for a meeting; she is American and would know better. She also would not have chosen a major Jewish holiday—such as Rosh Hashana or Yom Kippur—for the meeting. Those holidays appear on her calendar, literally and figuratively. But Diwali was unknown—invisible on the calendar. When I told my chair about the conflict, she said it would be okay for me to miss the meeting. I knew it wouldn't be a problem for others if I missed a faculty meeting. However, by missing the faculty meeting, I would be denied the opportunity to have my voice heard in important departmental matters. If someone cannot attend a team or departmental meeting due to a religious obligation, the *meeting* should be moved. Yet that idea did not even occur to my chair or my colleagues.

The privilege springs from the deep implicit norm of the Christian calendar. As an American, my Jewish department chair knows the Christian calendar. Accommodating it is inherently appropriate and expected, in ways she may not even be able to articulate. Allowing me to skip a meeting on Diwali solves less than half of the problem: It fixes my scheduling dilemma, but it denies my voice in the governance of my department, and it denies

Hinduism's holidays the ability to be seen and understood as equally worthy of attention in the schedule as Christian holidays are. This ordinariness of the Christian calendar, and the fact that we will defer to it but not to other faiths' calendars, illustrates the normative power of Christianity in the United States.

"I need to go my grandmother's funeral."

In her essay "My Grandmother and the Snake," Nicole Adams, a member of the Wenatchi Band of the Confederated Tribes of the Colville Reservation, shared her experience of facing Christian privilege as an undergraduate, after her grandmother passed away. She was familiar and proud of the traditions in her family and community. "I had been taught by my mother and grandmother alike to follow our traditional customs," she wrote. "I could not allow myself to cry until my grandmother's body has been placed into the ground. I have been taught that to cry would not only be a sign of disrespect for my grandmother, but it would also impair her journey into the spirit world."[22] Adams flew home to help her family with preparations for her grandmother's funeral and to perform rituals in the longhouse, a gathering places for tribal functions, such as feasts, dances, and funerals services. "I had difficulty staying awake during the final night of drumming and singing before my grandmother was to be buried. The drumming lasted throughout the night." Exhausted, she returned to campus. She met with each of her professors and explained her absences from class. Most were sympathetic and understanding. Adams, however, said that her professor "had difficulty comprehending why it had taken me a week to travel home and take part in my grandmother's funeral. Because of her own cultural bias, she could not understand why I had not simply flown home, attended a service, then flown back to school. Taking an entire week was unnecessary and unheard of to her."[23]

When students' loved ones die, professors will often provide extra help, accommodate missed classes, or assign make-up work. Here, however, Adams's professor was unaware of the religious or spiritual customs of her Native American student.[24] As a result, the professor viewed *a week off* as excessive. This is the Christian norm—in this case, the Christian traditions of one-day funeral rites—influencing the professor; she therefore denied Adams the courtesies Christian students receive when relatives pass away. Perhaps without even realizing that she was applying the lens of Christian funeral traditions, the professor treated Adams differently from her Christian peers. This Christian normative behavior, dismissive of Adams's religious identity as a Native American, contributed to a hostile academic environment.

"I am an American, too."

The power of Christian religious norms can prevent minorities from practicing their religions fully and freely, particularly when aspects of the minority religions are incongruent with the Christian norms expressed in US culture and practice. For example, the absence of any Christian tradition analogous to the Sikh prohibition on cutting one's hair (including facial hair) and the obligation to wear a turban has again and again forced US Sikhs to counter discrimination with legal advocacy. Because of their visible difference, and the US cultural association of short hair and shaving with cleanliness and hygiene, Sikhs have been denied employment and have been turned away from restaurants and other public accommodations, in violation of the law.

In police departments, the US military, restaurants, food production and other manufacturing fields, and elsewhere, Sikhs have been forced to choose between employment and religious observation. Restaurants have denied jobs to Sikhs and defended their positions by stating that long hair or facial hair presents health and safety concerns. Sometimes restaurants can point to state or local regulations regarding hair or headgear in food preparation jobs. But just as often, service industry employers like restaurants just want a "uniform look" to convey a particular "image"—and a Sikh's appearance doesn't fit.[25]

Sikhs pursuing public service careers have fought their way into such positions so that they may serve and observe their religion the way they want to.[26] Through advocacy and organizing, Sikhs have pushed various major city police departments, including in New York and Washington, DC, to enact policies allowing Sikhs to serve while keeping their beards and turbans. The accommodations should not have been difficult—in New York, for example, Sikh officers simply wear uniform-blue turbans, with the New York Police Department's standard hat shield affixed—yet in each case, years of advocacy, and sometimes litigation, were required. "Litigation in the Sikh community is unlike litigation in any other community you can think of," they explained, "because what we're doing . . . is beyond arguing the law; we're giving a little mini-history and religion lesson" on Sikhism.[27] After years of advocacy by individual Sikh officers seeking the opportunity to both serve and observe, the US Army adopted a new policy permitting Sikhs to serve with their beards and turbans intact. What must be pointed out here is that the Army repeatedly granted these permissions one officer at a time, which required each new Sikh officer to re-fight the same battle.[28] Only in 2017 did the Army actually adopt a policy of accommodation available to any soldier seeking to wear a religiously mandated beard and turban while in uniform.[29]

"There's a cost to saying something, and not saying something."

Consider the experience of Elizabeth Carey,[30] a Native Hawaiian student who identified and was classified as a Native American at Dartmouth College. Dartmouth has a history of Native activism because of its history: the nation's ninth university was founded as a Congregational boarding school for Native Americans. As an undergraduate, Carey worked for the on-campus catering company in a year when Dartmouth faced a vigorous controversy over murals depicting Native Americans. The murals depicted Native Americans as uncivilized and savage "heathens," with a White colonizer coming to take care of them and give them alcohol. Due to the mural dispute, the graduating senior class decided not to hold the "clay pipe ceremony" that had historically been part of graduation exercises.[31] Native Americans had long advocated abolishing that tradition, in which seniors gather to "smoke" clay pipes provided by the college then smash the pipes on a tree stump. The pipe is a sacred symbol in many native religions. Carey explained: "The pipe is like a sacred altar that can be used to pray to the creator anywhere and at any time. Breaking the pipe to us is like smashing a cross to a Christian."[32]

Dartmouth's pipe-smashing tradition is an example of the appropriation and abuse of a minority religious practice. Here, college students many years ago saw something that looked cool and decided to make it a graduation custom. They took a Native American ritual, stripped it of its spiritual meaning and corrupted it by breaking a sacred object, thus establishing a "Dartmouth tradition." When religions are robbed of their sacred authority, their artifacts can be devalued and destroyed because they are merely objects for consumption and not—as Carey described—"sacred" like a cross or altar. This commodification is particularly true for religious elements and rituals tied to nature, which are found in numerous religions.

As a member of the catering staff at an alumni gathering that spring, Carey overheard discussions about the mural controversy and the pipe ceremony. One alumna approached her and asked, "Why is it that the Indians here are so offended by everything? My husband said there was an Indian in his class who is proud of the murals. Why do you think the Indians are offended today?" Carey described her dilemma: "even if I wanted too, I wouldn't have known where to start to educate her on the Native American struggle. She exuded arrogance. Everything was simple in her mind. Everything was done her way, or something was wrong." The alumna eventually asked Carey if she was Indian. Unable to hold back, she responded: "I am proud of my heritage, yet I am unhappy, as are my native brothers and sisters, because people like you do not take our struggle seriously. And you think anyone could answer for us, taking as truth whatever is said that fits your way of thinking."[33]

When "Dartmouth tradition" was challenged as offensive and wrongful, many alumni rejected the idea that that the pipe ceremony violated sacred elements of Native American tradition. Likewise, the alumna Carey encountered exhibited the Christian privilege of being able to disregard others' lives and experiences. That alumna asked a question about Native American perspectives, but not because she wanted the answer. It was an argumentative question. The alumna felt no obligation to hear or respect minority perspectives. Carey thus found herself in the conundrum so many members of religious and racial minorities experience from time to time. Should she speak out and risk getting fired, or should she stay silent and endure the humiliation and outrage of her faith being mischaracterized and disrespected?

"I'll stand up for my faith."

Many people of minority faiths have described interactions with Christians proselytizing them: college clergy, hometown neighbors, or zealous high school classmates.[34] Some responded with self-doubt, like the young woman quoted earlier in the chapter, who came away from such encounters feeling "totally . . . paranoid" about going to hell. For others, however, the constant questioning and proselytization opened their eyes to Christian privilege and prompted a "self-defense" posture when it came to religion. One young woman I interviewed described how her neighbors' proselytizing "really pushed me to learn about Hinduism." She asked her parents more questions about the religion, and read books about Hinduism, in order to have "ammunition": She wanted to be able to respond credibly to proselytizers' appeals to accept Christ or go to hell. Another, Saleena, described a similar response to a campus missionary who distributed Bibles at her college: "That experience has changed the way I see religions now. I feel that it has made me more opinionated."[35] What Saleena described as becoming "more opinionated" is her development of a sense of strength in her identity as a Hindu and a readiness to respond to Christian proselytization when she encounters it. Where she might earlier have accepted the pinpricks of religious discrimination and Christian hegemony, the experience of being targeted with proselytization helped her foster a desire and willingness to speak up for herself and her family.

What Does a Social Justice Approach to Christian Privilege Sound Like?

> "We shouldn't have a meeting on _____ holiday."
> "What are the food choices for those who might have religious dietary restrictions?"
> "Is the prayer actually needed?"
> "Is that an American tradition, or it is Christian?"
> "We shouldn't make judgments about someone's morality or patriotism."
> "It's not just White supremacy, it's White Christian supremacy."

Thus far, this chapter has shown that the optical illusion of "religious freedom" remains in place for many in the US—religious minorities and Christians alike. To challenge White Christian supremacy, we must begin by displacing the optical illusion with a clear-eyed look at our own advantages and disadvantages and a willingness to point them out to those who do not yet see. Only by recognizing systemic inequality in history and in the present day will we build a more just and equitable society for people of all faiths and achieve authentic engagement between people of diverse religious and racial backgrounds.

One popular approach to diversity, including religious diversity, is *pluralism*. Pluralism sets its goals as appreciation, awareness, and learning about minorities and their cultures, including some of the challenges they face, such as discrimination. This objective puts the focus on learning about the "other," without analyzing how the *status quo* maintains Christian normativity and hegemony. A pluralistic approach may acknowledge discrimination, but does not recognize White Christian supremacy or the institutional nature of inequality. It also does not address race and intersectionality.

To address structural inequality, and to move past analysis to action, we need a *social justice approach* to religion in America. A social justice approach is intersectional; it acknowledges religious difference and emphasizes examination of social structures and historical legacies. It recognizes and challenges Christian privilege and the larger framework of White Christian supremacy. At the individual level, it involves Christians examining how they live their faith—not to abandon it, but to make sure it is not a belief system that oppresses others. At the institutional and societal levels, a social justice approach challenges White Christian supremacy and uses individual and social action to interrupt and eliminate oppression. In a social justice approach to religion, Christians can find within their privilege a direction for a new course of action. Just as some White Americans have realized that they must wield their White privilege in the cause of racial justice and equality through *ally and accomplice work*, Christians must do the same: deploy their access and social power to authentically engage with religious diversity and forge new possibilities, by making Christian privilege work for religious equality and social justice.

As mentioned earlier, my family is active in our Episcopal church community. It is an Episcopal congregation with some racial diversity, where everyone is welcome to take Communion, including this Hindu congregant, and where the Sunday school teachers loved it when our son talked about the Hindu deities Hanuman and Krishna. One day a few years ago, our minister asked if I would be willing to present my research on Christian privilege for our community. Although I had been a member of the church for almost a decade, I felt apprehensive as I began my presentation. I knew that this was sensitive material, and I did not want to offend a community that I consider myself a part of. It's one thing, as a researcher and an academic, to talk about Christian privilege in the college classroom, at an academic conference, or on social media. It is an entirely different matter to walk into church, where Christians go to express their faith and connect with God, and tell them how Christianity's social power results in injustice for others. I felt more nervous talking about Christian privilege in a church than I'd ever been in any academic or public forum. My concerns were allayed when my community engaged in a respectful, candid, and thoughtful discussion of religion, race, and social power. The follow-up conversations continue to be illuminating.

A few years later, I was invited to speak at a church in Lynchburg, Virginia. I discussed Christian privilege through stories from my own immigrant experience and the perspectives of my interfaith family. The event was open to the public, and had been publicized through the Lynchburg clergy network and the local newspaper. I walked into the church that evening and the pastor told me I'd be speaking from the pulpit. "Are you sure about that?" I asked. I was in their home—the part of the church literally called the "Sanctuary"—and I was being invited to speak from the honored location typically occupied by clergy. He said, "Absolutely. You speak from there." He knew my views, because he'd heard me speak at a chamber of commerce luncheon the day before, and we'd had a conversation about my talk a few months earlier. Putting me in the pulpit was his endorsement of my message. It was a rainy, thunderous day, yet at 6:30 p.m. the pews were mostly full, and about sixty mostly White congregants, and a few African Americans as well, heard the minister say, "Our community needs to wrestle with this." His endorsement sent a powerful message, and the audience was attentive and engaged—as demonstrated by the "Q & A" lasting a full hour after my prepared remarks. Conversations like this are a first step, and equip Christians to see their privilege, engage with existing power structures, and challenge the assumptions and policies that reinforce White Christian supremacy.[36]

To make headway on these deep, vexing, and complicated issues, I had to go into uncomfortable places. For anyone who works on social justice issues, the old realtors' saying—"location, location, location"—is not just about houses. It is about finding the places where we can make change happen. Location matters. The histories and realities in this book have to get to the people who need to hear them, where they are. That will take a willingness—like that shown by the Rev. Dennis Roberts of Lynchburg, Virginia—to engage, to deal with uncomfortable truths, and to welcome and endorse a challenging message even in sacred space.

Just as we need to bring the messages where they are needed, both religious minorities and Christians need to address White Christian supremacy in the subtleties of our culture and the crevasses of our laws and traditions. Christian privilege might not often hit you over the head like the marshal of the Supreme Court crying, "Oyez! Oyez! God save this honorable Court!" Here are some of the places to look, and questions to ask, when you are trying to locate Christian privilege:

- Is Christianity being conflated with American national identity?
- Are people of religiously diverse backgrounds being asked to participate in a Christian practice? There are numerous American civic traditions that emerged from Christian practice, such as removing one's hat or covering one's heart in certain circumstances. Many of the same rituals are observed when a prayer is offered. When people are asked to bow their heads, remove their hats, or engage in some other ritual, make sure what is being recognized is a secular and not a religious obligation.
- What religious perspectives are being ignored in your community? Certain religious beliefs, such as recognizing nature or ancestral homes as sacred, are unfamiliar to Christians and might not even be considered when infrastructure projects like pipelines and roads are being designed.
- Are your elected officials visiting faith communities? Which communities are they visiting? Which elected officials do not attend religious minority community events? What is their behavior like? What do they say in remarks and speeches?
- Do your elected officials describe their decisions by reference to the Bible or Christian moral principles? Are those principles actually unique to Christianity?
- Would a public function be complete if the only prayers offered by were by a rabbi or imam, or is the participation of Christian clergy required? Having clergy take part in public functions is common, And while Christian clergy do not represent the religious minorities in the audience they are often the only clergy invited to attend—or the only ones whose participation is regarded as essential.
- Universities are doing a better job of providing the social and physical spaces for religious minorities, but are those spaces still called "chapels"? Is the building architecturally Christian, characterized by stained glass windows, crosses, pews, and the like?

Here are some examples of statements and questions that inter-rupt Christian hegemony. In some cases, allies and *accomplices* making these statements will be important. In other cases, they are statements or questions we all might speak, in a country that was genuinely applying a social justice approach to religious diversity.

"We shouldn't have a meeting on any religious holiday observed by a member of our team."

As a Hindu, I have asked for a meeting or other important event coincides with a holiday I observe to be changed. Doing so is nei-ther easy nor comfortable, and I have the job security of tenure. The request is more difficult for people who worry that their jobs could be at stake if observance intrudes on an important proj-ect or deadline. It is time to take the onus off people of minority faiths to be the ones always asking for accommodation. Instead, Christians need to learn and know when their colleagues, stu-dents, or clients need to be accommodated. In some months—like October, when Navratri, Diwali, Rosh Hashanah, Yom Kippur, and other holidays often coincide—it won't be easy. But it needs to be done.

"What are the food choices for those who might have religious dietary restrictions?"

Special accommodations can feel almost as isolating as not being able to eat at all. Consider the needs of those attending your lun-cheon or dinner meeting, and how a dish that satisfies those needs might be appealing to all. A vegetarian main course, for example, avoids issues around kosher/halal meat requirements for Muslims and Jews and accommodates Jains, Hindus, and others.

"Is the prayer actually needed?"

In addition to taking into account people of other faiths, remember that some people are atheists for whom any religious element, particularly in a government or other public forum, is an unwelcome imposition of religious belief. Omit prayer from meetings that are not for or about a specific religious community.

"Is that an American tradition, or it is Christian?"

An alien dropped into an American shopping mall around the holidays could be forgiven for thinking that Christmas celebrates the birth of Santa Claus. Christians may perceive Santa as a secular figure, and Christmas trees and mistletoe as not being "about" the story of Jesus' birth. But for those of us who are not Christian, all these images and traditions revolve around a holiday that is not our own. So when you are deciding whether something is "religious" or not, and thus whether it is appropriate for a religiously diverse group, remember that anything associated with a Christian holiday will be seen as Christian and not "secular" by religious minorities. If you are recognizing a Christian holiday, so be it, but do not entertain the fiction that Santa Claus, Rudolph the Red-Nosed Reindeer, or the Easter Bunny are not part of the Christian holiday just because they aren't figures in the Bible.

"We shouldn't make judgments about someone's morality or patriotism."

From an atheist perspective, there is not just Christian privilege but also religious privilege. Religions are recognized as moral codes, and by extension someone who is an atheist is often assumed to lack a moral code or compass. Because one can have a moral code without believing in a deity, do not engage in these assumptions and avoid language that connects morality to religiosity. Likewise, do not conflate Christian belief with American patriotism; our nation has patriots of all faiths, and of none.

"We cannot just talk about White supremacy, without talking about the role of Christianity in creating and maintaining White supremacy."

For all the reasons you have read about in this book, we cannot talk about White supremacy without acknowledging Christianity's role in creating and maintaining it. Because religion is so deeply meaningful for people at a personal level, talking about "Christian supremacy" can be harder than talking about White supremacy. Still, we must recognize religion as part of the structure of privilege. We must see through the optical illusion and acknowledge the intimate way in which Whiteness and Christianity coexist in our legal structures in order to begin dismantling White Christian supremacy. The Klan does not burn poles, it burns crosses. The federal government did not just send teachers to eradicate Native American identity, it sent Christian missionaries. The last peoples to gain the right to naturalized citizenship were those least likely to be Christian. Violent men upset about racial and religious diversity do not just target shopping centers, they shoot worshippers at synagogues, gurdwaras, and Black churches. Until such problematic interconnections are acknowledged they cannot be addressed. Acknowledge the interconnectedness of race and religion in America's worst moments and inclinations, and insist that others do as well.

Conclusion

This chapter has offered a window on the voices, attitudes, and approaches that both Christians and religious minorities may exhibit regarding Christian privilege in America. Understanding the

spectrum of experiences and viewpoints is a starting point for analyzing the different ways Christian privilege affects people. Striving
toward social justice, and discerning what conversations to engage in,
requires understanding the perspectives of those you are interacting
with so that you can engage effectively and take meaningful action.

Christians may be dismissive or defensive when someone points
out the presence of Christian privilege or normativity. But stop,
pause, and acknowledge that your ability even to see a problem
may be limited because you have not experienced disadvantage
due to your religious identity. Resist labeling social justice work or
inclusive language as "politically correct," a phrase that devalues
any question by making it merely about words and feelings. Two
points on the "politically correct" slur: First, language creates and
conveys our perceptions of reality, so word choice is not just about
the words; it conveys our assumptions and intent, and gives real-
world impact to what we say. Second, feelings matter.

Sometimes, it is hard to believe privilege exists or to acknowledge when you benefit from it. Whether it is Christian privilege
or White privilege or straight privilege, having privilege does not
mean you are wealthy, or carefree, or a bad person, or that you have
not had obstacles to overcome. Privilege *does* mean there are some
struggles you'll never have to deal with. The personal impact and
sometimes practical consequences of Christian privilege are very
real in the lives of religious minorities, even when they are invisible
to those who benefit from the privilege.

Working for social justice also means being ready to confront
White Christian supremacy even when you don't want to. For religious minorities, this is not a choice. We deal with it whenever it
hits us, even if that is the last thing we want to do at that moment,
even if we are tired or stressed out or right in the middle of dealing
with something else entirely. By contrast, the beneficiaries of privilege get to choose when they feel like dealing with the injustices of
Christian privilege. If a White Christian is comfortable and I am

uncomfortable, that White Christian is in a position to just "let it ride" without consequence, because of her privilege. But to strive for social justice, Christians need to be ready to deal with their privilege at all times, to be allies and accomplices whenever allies and accomplices are needed, and to affirmatively make space for religious minorities. With these thoughts in mind, we can embark on the discussions needed to illuminate the social forces at play and spark the personal and policy changes that will begin to undo Christian supremacy's legacies.

6

Making Meaning and Making Change

In 2016, the Republican candidate for president, Donald J. Trump, called for "a total and complete shutdown of Muslims coming into the United States." Less than a year later, the newly elected president delivered on this promise, issuing an executive order better known as the "Muslim Ban," effectively closing the United States' doors to visitors and refugees from seven Muslim-majority countries. The order prompted a nationwide mobilization of religious and civic leaders, lawyers, and rank-and-file activists opposed to the ban. Across religious and racial lines, communities and leaders organized and spoke out against the ban. Crowds gathered at airports and on the streets, carrying signs and chanting slogans decrying the Muslim Ban as un-American and un-Constitutional. Many Christians, including religious leaders, added another criticism: it was "un-Christian." Although clergy of the right-wing conservative movement stood with the president, religious leaders of numerous Christian denominations wrote that it was "A very sad day in America. We stand with all of our Muslim sisters and brothers and against all who would enshrine and canonize bigotry into law. God give us wisdom and courage for this hour."[1] Jewish faith community leaders also spoke out: "Scapegoating people of one religion, restricting their travel, separating families across international borders—the Jewish community has seen this before, and we must raise our voices now."[2] Muslim organizations, along with secular civil rights organizations like the ACLU and others, also denounced the ban.

Policy makers responded: two dozen state attorneys general sued the US government, initiating litigation that led the

Supreme Court partially reversing the ban. The states' litigation was supported by a host of civil rights organizations, including the Korematsu Center,[3] which filed an *amicus* brief referring to the Japanese American experience during World War II as an example of the misguided collective punishment of an imagined enemy. The version of the ban that survived was prompted by these court challenges: the president removed Iraq and added Venezuela and North Korea. This ruse was sufficient to persuade the Supreme Court that the order was no longer anti-Muslim.

Opposition to the Muslim Ban galvanized one of the largest nationwide, multi-ethnic and multi-religious movement for civil rights since the movement for racial justice in the 1950s and 1960s. As a movement reflecting the country's post-1965 era religious and racial diversity, it offered a first glimpse at how today's US population could respond to a civil rights challenge on a par with the immigration bans of the early twentieth century. Change follows challenge; movements of this size rarely arise except in response to a specific challenge, which was supplied by a newly elected president's decision to enact and endorse religious discrimination at a national scale. Responding to that adversity, this activism gave us a preview of what an emerging and enduring network of clergy, policy makers, and others with social power could accomplish. Some of them understand their Christian privilege; they can acknowledge the presence of White Christian supremacy, and recognize the Trump era as a reemergence of the nation's worst historical turns: using the law to exclude and marginalize religious minorities.

While living in a world where White Christian supremacists can still sieze and wield power in support of racist and discriminatory agendas, it important to ask the question: What does a liberated world look like? Is it the return of the Black Hills to Native Americans? Is it houses of worship never being targeted again for violence or vandalism? Is it new court decisions that protect LGBTQ people from discrimination in private transactions? Is it all

Americans being able to observe their holidays without fear of professional repercussions? Envisioning a world where the religious diversity in our country is not just valued but where all have genuinely equal opportunity is difficult, precisely because it is so hard to step entirely out of the nation's history and legacies of injustice.

On the night before he was assassinated, Rev. Dr. Martin Luther King, Jr., preached the story of Moses and the Israelites. He exalted that he had "been to the mountaintop," and had seen the promised land. What did he see? King's promised land involved not just racial justice, but economic justice and peace rather than war. We need to form this type of vision for twenty-first-century communities, much more diverse than in King's time. We should live outside of today's patterns, and learn "new patterns of thought and behavior."[4] While living in a White Christian supremacist society, we ought to articulate an ambitious idea of where we are going—of a society beyond White Christian supremacy. In working for social justice, let us make our goals audacious.

A Social Justice Approach

A social justice approach requires what noted Brazilian educator and social justice activist Paolo Friere, and more recently feminist writer bell hooks, have called *critical consciousness*. To be critically conscious is to recognize systems of inequality and to take action against these systems—"to intervene in reality in order to change it." In other words, critical consciousness is the ability to see where you are while also envisioning and pursuing ways forward. To find that escape from ordinary patterns of thought, even as we exist within them, and to identify and help others to identify the actions that will free us from them, a liberatory consciousness is required.[5]

My approach to social justice involves the head, the heart, and the hands. The *head* represents knowledge. When it comes to Christian privilege, the essential first step is understanding the ways in which the *status quo* of institutional advantage has been built through centuries of laws and social norms, and acknowledging that we have been educated to accept these standards. Challenging privilege is about challenging assumptions, confronting structures, and dismantling them. When I speak of "dismantling" I mean taking down the edifice of White Christian supremacy, brick by brick: repealing a law, changing a policy or standard, discarding outdated and Christian normative turns of phrase, questioning the assumptions that allow those with privilege to lazily get by while those with disadvantages fight these fights without allies. We cannot fully and effectively accomplish that dismantling without knowing where the assumptions came from, why the laws were written, and how the structures were built. Doing so requires developing historical knowledge and understanding the patterns that show the structural foundations of bias. Too many conversations about prejudice, privilege, or equity revolve around opinions and personal observations. Subjective individual experiences matter, but if we only share or listen to individual stories and personal perspectives we are as likely to reproduce misinformation as information. Anecdotes are not the same as data and scholarship, and opinions are not necessarily analysis. Grappling with a phenomenon as complex and deep as White Christian supremacy requires study.

Acknowledging history does not mean blaming ourselves or others today for the past. We can identify oppressive characteristics of our society without impugning anyone today as an oppressor. Blame is unhelpful, and voicing it is usually counterproductive. Those with privilege are not to be blamed for the past. Still, they must take responsibility for having benefited from the oppressive practices which produced their privilege. Part of taking responsibility is seeking opportunities to be an ally and accomplice to the dismantling of privilege in the present day.

The *heart* takes into account the emotional component of learning about and working on social justice issues. The first connection between the head and the heart is this: there is an affective response to knowledge. Laws, history, and current events are not emotionally neutral topics. They evoke emotional responses. These reactions to newly gained awareness and information are important and should not be dismissed or trivialized, whether in activist circles, the workplace, or the classroom. Every time I teach the *Bhagat Singh Thind* case and think about its impact on South Asian Americans, I feel angry all over again. Likewise, I have been challenged academically and personally by White Christian students whose emotional reaction to learning about the dynamics of racial and religious privilege affected their experience in my class.

Recognizing the emotional component of learning real US history is important both for those doing the learning and for the teachers helping them through it. A few years ago in my advanced undergraduate class "Race, Religion, and the Law," my 15-student cohort included students of color of different racial, religious, and ethnic backgrounds and three White students, all male, including two immigrants from Eastern Europe. Course topics included critical race theory; the history of racism and religious oppression; the role of Christianity in development of Whiteness in the United States; and an exploration of the many places where we can find the influence of race and religion in the development and interpretation of statutes and case law. As part of the course, I encourage students to reflect on their own social identities (race, class, sexual orientation, gender). I do this for two reasons: first, so they become aware that how they react to information affects how they think through that information, and second, because it helps them consider how the identities of those in power have shaped public policy and court decisions. The self-reflection can be uncomfortable. This discomfort can manifest in a rejection of the material, doubting its validity or accuracy, and questioning the motivations and *bona fides* of the professor presenting it.[6]

In this particular cohort, the White students' response to the material was to act out more and more as the semester went on. In addition to the subject matter, they were also reacting to my identity. My students can see that I am a woman of color. I share that I am Indian American, an immigrant, and Hindu. As we applied the skills of critical race theory to identify and explore the Christian normativity and privilege embedded in US law, some of the students, particularly the three White Christian men, were connecting the coursework with my own identity. Their discomfort with the revelation of their privilege turned into a rejection of the subject matter and specifically of me as the one teaching it. The result was not just back-talk and attitude in class, which I am accustomed to. These students also went to other faculty and other White students on campus to express the opinion: "Professor Joshi hates white people."

While their behavior was inappropriate, I do not fault these students for reacting emotionally to the information. On the contrary, as social justice educators and activists, we need to anticipate reactions like theirs and help people experiencing those reactions navigate the emotional elements of learning about privilege and history. For example, after discussing some pivotal First Amendment cases, I usually ask my students, "How are you feeling?" Early in the semester, they do not know how to respond. Why is a professor asking how they are "feeling"? But as they come to understand the emotional potency of the subject matter, they also recognize that learning it will cause them to feel certain things: anger, despair, frustration, guilt, rage, remorse, joy, relief . . . All of those feelings can be part of the learning experience. By mid-semester, my students are used to the question, and talking about their feelings can lead to wonderful reflections on the present-day relevance of past events.

Unfamiliarity with this material is one of the reasons for the resistance and the visceral, often negative reactions of individuals like my students. As a social justice educator, I have made the decision to engage: to walk people through their discomfort, and to not take negative reactions personally because I understand them to be part of the learning process. In our communities and in government, some of the rage and raised voices around issues of religious oppression, xenophobia, and racism is similar to my students' behavior: people acting out their emotional reactions. Some of it is those same people expressing their bias or their investment in the system as it is. Striving for social justice means being willing to interact with all kinds of people. You have a decision to make: are you ready to engage?

Discovering tumultuous truths about history and the present day can bring up guilt and sadness for Christians, and for religious minorities it can mean a motivation to blame and a sense of betrayal for being wronged and misled. It is a challenge to own history without feeling guilty about it or betrayed by it. Guilt can be immobilizing for the dominant group. It is a powerful emotion that often surfaces when consciousness-raising is taking place. For members of the minority, betrayal can become blame, and often drives the impetus to withdraw or seek "payback" rather than engage constructively and seek solutions. Coming to terms not only with US history but with our emotional reactions is essential. In particular, for White Christians doing social justice work, there is an obligation also to work as an ally, and better yet as an accomplice, by holding other White Christians accountable for their actions and reactions to these issues.

The work of the head and the heart are brought to bear on the world through our *hands.* We cannot simply believe and hope our way into a just and equitable world. Just like it is not enough to be *non*-racist, we must be *anti*-racist. Merely being better people in our heads and our hearts may feel good but it will do nothing to challenge White Christian supremacy. Only the work of our hands will achieve the goal of social justice and religious equality.

That objective may mean welcoming a challenging voice, like Lynchburg's clergy did. It may mean lobbying a local board of education to adopt curricula with a social justice focus, or a state legislature to begin undoing laws that elevate Christian concerns over those of others. It may mean Christian business-owners wielding their authority and privilege to respond proactively to the needs of their employees who are religious minorities. In the past, and today, it has often involved litigation, such as by Sikhs seeking the opportunity to serve in uniform and atheists challenging long-standing practices of forced Christian prayer in public schools.

Bryan Stevenson, the prominent attorney and civil rights activist, talks about the need to "get proximate" to the things we seek to change—to engage, personally and directly, not just abstractly, with the social challenges we face.[7] Policy makers and government officials, for example, must not just read about the changing demographics in their districts, but must get out there and understand what it means to be Buddhist or Hindu or Muslim in America. This work needs to happen not just reactively—after an incident of violence or bias, for example—but proactively, to build relationships and a reservoir of understanding and trust that can be drawn upon in trying times. Getting proximate means becoming comfortable with feeling uncomfortable. Until we get proximate, it is impossible to fully understand someone else's reality.

For members of the majority, there is a necessary step before getting proximate: doing your homework. Getting proximate to a minority community without first reading and developing an understanding of the issues that affect them is the ultimate act of White Christian entitlement. Getting proximate starts with religious literacy but does not end there. It includes understanding how intersectionality and issues beyond religion affect the community(ies) you are getting proximate to. Understand that people live religion in all kinds of ways, and even in ways that seems like contradictions; all of us lead lives that combine following the rules and not following them. Building authentic relationships with people can also help you learn what you need to know. Acknowledge that what you are setting out to do can be nerve-wracking, and nobody wants to show up in an unfamiliar faith setting and do something wrong. For me, that sense of worry comes with attending Christian funerals. They are emotionally intense settings that involve rituals I am not accustomed to, and even unfamiliar visual cues like black as the color of mourning. (In Hinduism, mourners wear white.) At the very least, enter these dialogues with educated questions that show you have done some homework. That information will be seen as a sign of respect. Check your privilege, do your own learning about faith and faith systems, and do the thought work and study to consider what those other communities are experiencing. Then, get proximate.

It is not only Christians who can be in the role of outsider. Religious minorities also need to get proximate and learn about neighboring faith communities. While religious minorities share some experiences in the United States in common, there are differences—including immigration histories, national origin, differing theologies, and race—that make our experiences very different from one another. So not just for Christians but for everyone, preparing to get proximate is a necessary first step.

Inclusivity is a big part of working for social justice, but only if it is done right. Authentic representation matters, and so does meaningful listening. Getting proximate does not just mean inviting a Hindu or Jewish representative into the room; if you are not going to take what they say seriously, then do not patronize them by making them window dressing. "A seat at the table" only helps produce real change when the person in that seat holds a real voice—even, and especially, when that voice may make you uncomfortable. Getting proximate is not a one-time experience: you cannot get proximate in one Saturday afternoon. You cannot claim to implement an inclusive governing philosophy just by having a rabbi or shaman deliver a prayer at a function.

The principles laid out above are what most social justice work will bear in common: the need to better understand different religious communities, the need to recognize lived religion, and the need to authentically engage the head, heart, and hands. Beyond that foundation, getting proximate and doing social justice work will look different in different places and circumstances. Providing more specific examples here would be limiting, because there is no single way to work with different religious minority communities; in each circumstance, participants must respond to the particular circumstances and concerns of individuals, religious groups, and the wider community. It is important to remember that the work of our hands, the work of "getting proximate," is a tool and not an outcome. We engage not for the sake of engagement, but to create the kind of transformation needed at all levels of society to create a world with more justice.

The Change We Need

How then do we make meaning of our times, and enact the changes we need? We begin with a framework for thinking about what it will take to create our more perfect union; we seek examples of change people have made or are attempting to make at the institutional level; and we consider the personal work we can all do to recognize and combat Christian normativity in our viewpoints, language, and assumptions. The individual level matters not only from the standpoint of self-improvement, but also because individual actions and inactions collude together to perpetuate institutional structures. There are some concrete changes that people have envisioned and effected already. More school districts are recognizing religious minorities' holidays in ways that avoid the disadvantages of a "day off"—such as with rules regarding testing and homework on minority religious holidays in schools with a critical mass of students of a particular religion. More colleges are making sure that Muslim students can eat at cafeterias open early and late during Ramadan, and are constructing spaces for prayer and bathrooms with space for foot washing in dining hall floor plans. More hospitals, even in places with small observant Jewish populations, are providing Sabbath elevators, which automatically stop on every floor on the Sabbath so that observant Jews may ride without violating the prohibition on work.

What further changes will be effective as we seek to dismantle structures of White Christian supremacy and challenge Christian hegemony and privilege? There are as many answers to that question as there are dilemmas and challenges facing US religious minorities. Right now, Christians gain social privileges while religious minorities and atheists face discrimination on the basis of religion. Moving toward social justice is not a matter of "flipping the script," so that Christians encounter discrimination while others enjoy new privileges. The goal is to build a more equitable society where all are able to worship, pray, and live freely, whether that means going to mass, seeking the divine through a connection with sacred lands, invoking the blessings of one's ancestors, or in some other way—or in no way at all.

In the following sections, I offer a way to activate our liberatory consciousness and rethink our current reality, whether in research, government, or everyday life. This five-element framework is a useful way to think about how our conduct and thinking as a society will adapt to replace White Christian supremacy with social justice.[8] The five elements are:

1. Change the language
2. Change the questions
3. Change the focus
4. Change foundational assumptions
5. Change the paradigm

Change the Language

There are two substantial ways that changing the language of faith in America can help achieve social justice. First, we need to re-think what we mean when we speak of "morality" in the public square. In policy debates, ideas that are contested in *Christian* communities become *America*'s moral issues. This pattern has formed as a result of the increasing voice of evangelical Christians in politics since the mid-twentieth century; that voice has spawned the framework for public debate on "morality."[9] As a result, US politics and society have largely defined "moral questions" in terms of the issues evangelicals prioritize and characterize as "moral" or scriptural, such as abortion and homosexuality. This bias infects the entire public debate over moral questions and presents a notion of morality insistent on restricting the rights of individuals: women, LGBTQ people, and so forth. A morality of increasing rights would touch on different issues, from the death penalty to poverty to the treatment of immigrants and refugees. Striving for social justice demands reframing the debate on defining our nation's "moral issues." A new language of "morality" will elevate other policies and priorities as moral questions: preserving natural resources and preventing mass extinctions caused by climate change; recognizing women's autonomy; and treating sustenance and dignity as a human right.

Second, as we educate ourselves about religious diversity and pursue inclusiveness, we need to change how we talk to each other and the vocabulary we use about matters of faith. This takes "homework"—gaining knowledge about the faiths around you. It also takes practice to develop the skill of having the conversations and using the new vocabulary you've learned. When people do not know about other religions, they may be hesitant to ask. Afraid of saying the wrong thing or not knowing what to say, people say nothing. Silence comes across as disinterest, leaving religious minorities feeling devalued and disregarded. But too often, Christians who ask questions about others' faiths are really asking religious minorities to describe themselves using Christian references. I have been asked, for example, "What is your Bible?" or "Where is your church?" The word choice adopts and assumes the Christian norm. A social justice paradigm of religious language invites each to express and describe faith in its own right, not by reference to the majority's framework. So, more appropriate questions would be "What do you believe?" "How do you worship?" "When are your holidays, and what do they celebrate?" "What's important about your faith for you?"

Change the Questions

From time to time throughout my life I have been asked: "Is Hinduism monotheistic or polytheistic?" The reason this question is even asked is because there is an implied right answer, shaped by Christian normativity. The underlying question is: "Are you like Christians, or not?" The question itself implies a judgment. If one answers "Hinduism is polytheistic," then Hinduism becomes categorized as a heathen, primitive, and therefore less legitimate religion. To be viewed as legitimate, the answer needs to be "monotheistic," because that makes it more like Christianity. In my teens and twenties, when the topic came up, I would launch into an explanation that many Hindus have offered and many believe: Hinduism's "many gods" are different expressions of the same unitary divine, and while our religion may appear "polytheistic," it is at its core monotheistic. In adulthood, I found a simpler and more satisfying response: "Why does it matter?"

When we are talking about religion, changing the question also means appreciating religion's role in people's lives—not as abstract theology, or text and rituals, but as *lived religion:* how faith, spirituality, and religious identity are practiced in our everyday lives.

For example, the question "How Sikh is she?" applies metrics that may not fit, ignores intersectionality, or implies a measuring stick or checklist by which a person can be tested. If we really want to embrace America's diversity of faiths and practices, the far more important question is: "How is she Sikh?" That is where rich, personal, fulfilling and meaningful answers will be found. Through lived religion, we can understand how religion shapes identity, even for those folks who do not consider themselves to be religious.

Our society also needs to stop framing policy discussions around whether and when rights or opportunities may be "given" to a particular religious minority group. When policy makers are discussing, for example, "Should we stop serving pork in prisons to accommodate Muslim inmates?" or "Should Sikhs be allowed to serve in the military with *kesh* (unshorn hair) and *dastaar* (turban)?" they are really debating whether Christians should grant civil liberties to non-Christians.[10] That debate relies on entirely the wrong framework. The very question of whether the Christian majority should "let" religious minorities practice their faith assumes White Christian supremacy as normative. It imagines civil liberties as something that the dominant group can choose to extend to or withhold from a minority group. Framing questions this way represents a preemptive surrender on the most basic questions of religious freedom in the United States. Instead, we need to abandon this and other questions that arise from and assume Christian supremacy.

Change the Focus

Changing the focus means deliberately accounting for and examining religion and its roles in places where we now hide or disregard it. We live in a world of structures—not just literal edifices like buildings, but structures of thinking and analysis that place us at a certain vantage point from whatever we are "looking at." To view any structure from a different angle, to consider what is around the structure or hidden by it, or to form a more integrative understanding of what comprises it requires a change in perspective. One must ask, "What haven't we considered?" or "What don't I know?" In a social justice framework, changing the focus means specifically seeking and taking into account the impact of bias and privilege affecting religious minorities. In the view of a particular project, has religion's role been ignored, or has it been conflated or subsumed?

For example, when *National Geographic* apologized for decades of "racist" coverage, it still ignored the role of religion and Christian supremacy in the magazine's treatment of others. The magazine acknowledged a colonialist outlook that had set up a dichotomy between the moral, civilized west and the depraved, uncivilized other. From its twenty-first-century review of this history, *National Geographic* derived the lesson: "how we present race matters." But *National Geographic*'s orientalist and White supremacist writing and photography were not just biased and offensive racially but also in their treatment of the religions of Asia, Africa, and indigenous peoples worldwide as backward, superstitious, idolatrous, and deluded. When *National Geographic*'s editors ignored Christian supremacy's role in its biased coverage, they failed to apologize to religious minorities as such. They racialized Christianity as White, subsuming religious difference within racial difference and conflating European Christianity with Whiteness. This singular, racial focus also ignored how Christianity was complicit in the European colonial enterprise. *National Geographic*'s apology would have been more complete and accurate if the magazine had acknowledged the role of religion in the magazine's treatment of its non-Western subjects.

Often, changing the focus means pulling back to find a more expansive and inclusive version of events, stories, or policies. In 1994, for example, federal agencies were instructed to implement land management systems that were "respectful to tribal sovereignty." One way to implement this instruction would be to include Native American concerns in environmental risk assessments, which precede any major public works project or policy change in land management. Such "Environmental Impact Statements" are often scientific and highly technical. They may consider the possible effect on groundwater of a pipeline leak, project the air quality impacts of an increase in truck traffic, or describe the current environment and its importance, such as the presence of particular wild habitats or breeding grounds. In addition to those issues, respect for tribal sovereignty also means including a discussion of the spiritual relevance of natural spaces sacred to Native peoples, and the effects that development or resource exploitation would have on sacredness. Instead, the US government continues to push for, among other things, the Keystone XL Pipeline, a project Native groups oppose because it would cross their ancestral lands and the sacred sites of the tribes of Fort Belknap. A social justice approach to environmental issues requires an examination of whether a proposed action will perpetrate violence on lands and nature held sacred by Native Americans.

For faith communities, changing the focus can mean conceiving and enacting a new, more expansive and inclusive vision of what it means to "do interfaith work." Most of the current work of this sort is what I call "Interfaith 1.0." It involves intergroup dialogues, reciprocal visits to houses of worship, eating meals together to learn about each other's cultures. It can also involve readiness to provide mutual support in times of crisis, like we have seen after shootings at synagogues, mosques, and gurdwaras in recent years. Participants in Interfaith 1.0 may be ready to lock arms around a mosque to protect it from vandalism, but are ill-prepared to challenge the paradigms that making attacking an American mosque possible and even popular. It is high time to pursue "Interfaith 2.0," which acknowledges the American context of White Christian supremacy. Interfaith 2.0 takes an intersectional approach and moves beyond coming together only in adversity, toward taking action even *before* that happens.

It understands that there are differences between the religions, and is ready to have conversations from that standpoint while also grappling with race, class, gender, and privilege where they appear in theology and society. Interfaith 2.0 shifts interfaith work from "we are here to support each other" to "we are working together to create a social justice paradigm." For White Christian participants, Interfaith 2.0 requires exploring, owning, and beginning to fix White Christian supremacy with endeavors like that of the Lynchburg Clergy Association, which has developed a list of guidelines for participation in interfaith work designed to help Christians think through and check their privilege before entering interfaith spaces.[11] Authentic interfaith engagement pursues not just dialogue but action and service—or *seva*, as it is known in the Hindu, Jain, and Sikh traditions. For example, in the San Francisco Bay area in the 1990s, evangelical Protestants collaborated in coalition with Latinx Catholics and Cambodian Buddhists for equitable housing.[12] *Seva* work must also move beyond leaders, like clergy and vestry boards, to involve members of the community, such as by involving young people in interfaith community service.[13]

Finally, any interfaith work—indeed, any faith work—must give the right answer to the question: "Is this about justice, or just us?" A faith community whose focus does not extend beyond protecting and expanding its own rights and opportunities is not doing social justice work at all. By contrast, when the president of the Interfaith Alliance, a rabbi, called on Secretary of State Mike Pompeo to answer the question "Are you biased against Muslims?",[14] he was doing interfaith work as an ally. Numerous Jewish groups have spoken up for the protection of Muslim communities, just as Muslim organizers raised funds for the Tree of Life synagogue after it was attacked.[15] Speaking up for each other is Interfaith 2.0.

Change the Foundational Assumptions

We are not all the same. Our religions are not the same. There are differences between our belief systems. There is a tendency, particularly in tense times, to fall back on comforting fluff about our common humanity. In the aftermath of 9/11, for example, many Muslims emphasized that theirs is an Abrahamic faith, like Christianity, and talked about Islam's recognition of Jesus as a prophet. These connections needed to be stressed, many American Muslims believed, to reduce their chances of being seen as potential terrorists. At the church I attend with my family, we speak of "many paths, one journey." Ideas like that are nice to bring people together, but do not deal with reality and with the more complicated truth: we are not the same.

Appreciating human similarities cannot obscure the need to understand and talk about our differences. Being able to talk frankly about the differences among our faiths, in a manner that is free of judgment, is important. Just as important is acknowledging misconceptions and stereotypes about others. This discussion is difficult work—hence our tendency to fall back onto common ground, because we fear talking about the differences. For all its difficulty, it is also important for social justice. Acknowledging and talking about our differences helps us better understand each other, which results in more authentic relationships; such relationships are vital when getting proximate. Relationships among people of different faiths reduce misinformation and misunderstanding and build the trust that helps move us from encounter to collaboration.[16]

An essential first step toward changing our foundational assumptions, and talking about difference, is knowing something about what those differences are: *religious literacy*. Setting out to learn about religions can be daunting. There is so much to know, and so many religions in the world. A place to start is to understand the basics of your neighbors' and friends' faiths, by learning the "ABCDE's":

- Architecture: know what a faith's house of worship is called—like mosque, synagogue, or temple
- Books: know what a faith's holy text(s) are called—like the Bible, Torah, or Guru Granth Sahib
- Cities: know a faith's most important places, like Jerusalem, Mecca, or Varanasi, and why they are important
- Days: know the names of faiths' holy days, and what they recognize or commemorate
- Everyday religion: *lived religion* is what religion looks like in the lives of your students and their families. This may or may not resemble what you know, or the way Wikipedia describes the belief system. This approach takes into account the impact of culture and family traditions. For example, holidays may be celebrated in different ways by members of the same religion whose cultural traditions differ.

In presenting this framework, I acknowledge that not every religion has all of these components, or values them in the same way. Nevertheless, these facets serve as entry points to begin exploring different religions, their histories and the source of their beliefs.

On the subject of holidays, it is also important to know which holidays are celebrations and which are solemn. A classroom teacher shared with me that she was always trying to do the right thing for her students, but because she did not know better, she wished her Jewish students a "happy Yom Kippur." Because Yom Kippur is a solemn day of fasting and atonement, this wish was not an appropriate greeting. Do not hesitate to ask: "Can you tell me a little bit about your holiday? How do you recognize or commemorate your holiday? Is there a greeting that goes with your holiday?" Finally, recognize that everyday religion, what faith looks like in people's lives, is often what matters most. It may or may not resemble what you know about the belief system. This approach takes into account the impact of culture and family traditions. Holidays, for example, may be celebrated in different ways by members of the same religion whose cultural traditions differ.

Change the Paradigm

When you change the *paradigm*, you change how you and those around you think about something in a way that can lead to new patterns of thought and action. Paradigm is like the infrastructure of an argument: it encompasses an outlook that shapes the thinking, viewpoint, and language used to respond to a particular problem or issue. Here is an example of one of the most destructive paradigms of the last few decades: the idea that more religious diversity should mean less talk about religion—that religion should be ignored or set aside, rather than embraced and discussed. This paradigm does a grave disservice to Christians and members of religious minorities alike.

One common manifestation of the current, flawed paradigm is the idea that communities should respond to religious diversity by having "Winter," not "Christmas," concerts and activities, and that we should all say "Happy Holidays" at Christmastime. These changes brush a thin veneer over the privileges that Christians alone enjoy in the United States. Taking this approach disrespects and dilutes the meaning of Christmas, without making religious minorities feel authentically included. It creates resentment among Christians, who long for the Christmas concerts of old, worry that Christmas's sacred aspects are disappearing, and may associate these losses with the new mosque or gurdwara down the street. The inclusive impetus behind "Happy Holidays" is a good sentiment, and for people who often interact with people they do not know at all, like receptionists or retail staff, it is fine. But in our social spheres—work, school, neighborhood—we should know our colleagues, clients, friends, neighbors well enough to know their religion, and therefore what to say to them. Bringing other faiths authentically into your interactions with others means doing so in their own time and on their own terms—using your head first, and your heart.

At the social level, the attempt to ignore religion, or render it generic, trivializes the significance of the religious diversity in our country. One of the reasons behind the use of "Happy Holidays" in December was to be inclusive of the Jewish holiday Hanukkah. This sentiment was a good intention, but it created a false equivalence. Hanukkah is not as significant for Jews as Christmas for Christians; numerous other holidays, including Rosh Hashanah, Yom Kippur, and Pesach (Passover) are more theologically significant than Hanukkah. We need to move away from idea that the most important holidays take place in December. We also need to acknowledge and embrace Christmas as a Christian holiday, sing Christmas music at Christmas concerts, and embrace other religions on their own terms and calendars.

Changing the paradigm means not just not saying "Merry Christmas" to everyone in December. It also means knowing when and why to say Eid Mubarak, Happy Diwali, and Happy Vaisakhi, and when to wish your Jewish colleagues a "happy new year" or an "easy fast." It means so much more to me to hear "Happy Diwali" in October than to hear "Happy Holidays" when I am doing my Christmas shopping. In government, lawmakers should not focus on taking Christianity out, but on bringing everyone else in. Christianity already permeates all facets of our society and our laws. An even-handed silence that ignores that fact only perpetuates it. A social justice approach to religion is positive and additive—including the religious holidays, rituals, and practices of all Americans. This paradigm shift will improve how we talk about religion in the public square.

Here is another important change in paradigm: We need to stop resorting to binary frameworks for understanding complex problems. One extremely powerful element of US culture is our tendency to frame questions in either/or terms, like a light switch with only "on" and "off." A person either agrees with another or does not; another country is either our friend or our foe. People who think in more complex ways are considered unable to make up their minds: answers that begin "yes, and" or "yes, but also . . ." are taken as frustratingly ambivalent rather than as exemplifying a necessary and praiseworthy consideration of nuance. The dilemmas of White Christian supremacy will not be solved by thinking in the dualities of "White" and "Black" (or "White" and "people of color") or "Christian" and "not Christian."

Monotheistic religions that claim there is only one God, and one text from which God's immutable instructions can be derived, tend to support a binary thought process. One either adopts or rejects the particular set of beliefs about God, even though there is a wide range of willingness among the different faith traditions to permit variations in interpretation of the demands God places on believers. In practice, complete submission to religious authority is relatively rare in lay communities, but in theory, the authorities of the monotheistic religions demand adherence. This cultural and religious tendency makes understanding and appreciating differences of perspective very difficult. If we expect that there is a right answer to a problem or a right way to do something, what do we do when a third or fourth possible approach appears? To accept, or even explore, the possibility of additional answers when we are conditioned to expect only one answer is both cognitively and emotionally unsettling. Yet it is also vital to embrace complexity and difference.

The Path to Our More Perfect Union

A common response, when we begin talking about undoing White Christian supremacy, is: "Why would Christians, or men, or White folks, want to give up their privilege and social power?"

But that is the wrong question. Remember, we're supposed to change the question. That question starts from the *status quo*. It starts from the assumption that this country belonged to Christians, or to Whites, in the first place. On the contrary, Native peoples were here first. White Christians took the country and made it theirs. The Doctrine of Discovery told arriving Europeans that this continent, full of people, nature, and cultures, was in fact empty: it was a wilderness awaiting someone to possess it, and then to keep others out (like Asians) or in servitude (like Blacks). The other fundamental flaw in the question is that it assumes privilege to be a zero-sum game. It treats privilege like pie: if I get a bigger piece, then you necessarily must end up with a smaller piece.[17] The question defines the answer, and as long as we frame conversations about "giving up privilege," we start from the assumption that privilege should exist or should be enjoyed by anyone.

Envisioning a more perfect union requires us to change the entire framework. It is not about some people giving up privilege, or others seizing it. Rather, it is about working together in meaningful ways, each from our own position, to fulfill our nation's founding promises. The aim is not to share privilege, so that more people have it. Nor is it to reverse the polarity of privilege, so that now somebody else has it. As a nation, we should be pursuing and enjoying the absence of privilege, replacing it with opportunity, dignity, and safety that are equally available to all. The more perfect union is an America where the First Amendment really means what it says. We must dismantle the structures in place, not to redistribute privilege but to replace the very notion of privilege with a fulfillment of the ideals of equality.

It is about fixing the American social structure of Christian privilege and replacing it with a nation where all may feel included and live freely with all of our histories, ancestries, and beliefs respected. That will be our more perfect union.

Acknowledgments

I have been fortunate to encounter fellow travelers whose own life experiences also shape their outlook on religion, identity, and the scholarly enterprise. Almost since its founding, I have been part of the Asian Pacific American Religions Research Initiative (APARRI). My fellow APARRIstas have nurtured and encouraged me in exploring this subject matter, and I am grateful for the friendship and support of Rachel Bundang, Rudy Busto, Carolyn Chen, Joe Cheah, Sylvia Chan-Malik, Brett Esaki, Russell Jeung, Tammy Ho, Grace Kao, Jeffrey Kuan, Sharon Suh, Jane Naomi Iwamura, Janette Ok, Tat-Siong Benny Liew, Kwok Pui Lan, Jerry Park, Bandana Purkayashtha, Jadeep Singh, Paul Spickard, Justin Tse, Frank Yamada, David Yoo, Duncan Ryūken Williams, and Janelle Wong. I have also been sustained and encouraged by the support of other colleagues and friends: Shanelle Henry, Glenn Cassidy, Jonathan Zur, Nadia Ansary, Hany Mawla, and the ever-inspiring Jigna Desai. I have surely forgotten someone, and to those supporters and colleagues who are not listed, you have my apologies as well as my gratitude.

Throughout my career and today, I continue to reap the benefits of two professional development opportunities. Very early on, I was part of Indiana University–Purdue University in Indianapolis's Center for the Study of Religion and American Culture Young Scholars' Program. Phil Goff, the Center's director, has been consistently supportive of my work. After earning tenure, I was fortunate to part of the Mid-Career Asian/Asian American Faculty program hosted by the Wabash Center for Teaching and Learning in Theology and Religion, and I benefitted from the mentorship of Kwok Pui Lan and Rudy Busto. At both IUPUI and Wabash, I connected with colleagues from across the nation and built communities of mutual support and encouragement.

Three people deserve a special thanks. Maurianne Adams: our conversations over the past two decades and more, which resulted in various other publications, also helped much of the material in this book to gel. Two scholars I've known since my undergraduate years at Emory University and my master's studies at the Candler School of Theology, who continue to be great mentors and supporters, are David Blumenthal and Deborah Lipstadt.

I've been thinking about the material in this book for more than twenty years. Christian privilege emerged as a recurring theme in the forty-one interviews I conducted for my doctoral dissertation in the late 1990s, and in some of my earliest work with public school teachers. Over the past two decades, particularly as I began to speak more extensively beyond the classroom, I found the same experiences and concerns emerging in my dialogues with policy makers, judges, lawyers, and fellow scholars in a variety of fields. Together, all of these encounters, along with the support of colleagues, friends, and family, have made this text possible.

I began writing about Christian privilege in my first book, *New Roots In America's Sacred Ground* (Rutgers, 2006), which conveyed the voices of second-generation Indian Americans of diverse religious backgrounds. I explored the ideas in this book further in numerous other writings, including essays published in James A. Banks's *Encyclopedia of Diversity in Education* (SAGE, 2012); chapters in second and third editions of *Teaching for Diversity and Social Justice* (2007, 2016) and *Asian Americans in Dixie* (co-edited with Jigna Desai): and material presented in the *New York Times*, *Washington Post*, and elsewhere. Portions of this book have been presented to a variety of audiences, including at the biannual conference at IUPUI's Center for the Study of Religion and American Culture, the Association of Asian American Studies, the American

Academy of Religion, and before other audiences in the United States, India, and Lebanon.

I thank the Dean of Fairleigh Dickinson University's University College and the Director of the Peter Sammartino School of Education for their support for the writing of this book. I am also grateful to FDU's librarians for their guidance, good cheer, and patience with overdue books. My FDU colleagues Allen Debren, Kate Spence, Sorah Suh, Randall Westbrook, and Jamie Zibulsky have provided support in a variety of ways as the manuscript took shape.

David Blumenthal, the Revs. Diana Doyle Clark and Peter Jackson, Adam Jacobs, Russell Jeung, and Vijay Shah read the entire manuscript, providing not only rich reflections on the subject matter but also numerous questions and challenges that helped me improve my analysis. Mohan Ambikaipaker, Murali Balaji, Anne Joh, Sharon Suh, and Randall Westbrook each read portions of the draft and provided critical feedback. These readers' insights and questions pointed me toward resources that proved invaluable and helped me to engage deeply with the subject matter. Thanks also to the two anonymous reviewers, one of whom in particular provided crucial feedback that pointed out some blind spots and, in doing so, made this book stronger. My editor at NYU press, Jennifer Hammer, championed this project from the beginning and helped me focus on the material that mattered most. Thanks also to Veronica Knutson at NYU Press. I sincerely appreciate the care and precision Martin Coleman brought to copyediting my manuscript.

This book is the fulfilment and confluence not only of my scholarly work but also of all the years before that. These pages grew from deeply personal origins. I grew up as a little brown Hindu girl in Atlanta, Georgia, with almost no one else like me in my classroom or even the schools I went to. I lived with one foot in that world and the other in the world of ethnoreligious community: Atlanta's network of Indian American Hindu families, which was small but whose members worked hard to support one another and make meaning of culture and faith for their children, including me. The daily experiences and sensations of being neither White nor Christian, in a country where Whiteness and Christianity are normative, shaped my life in very personal ways. The fact that those experiences and sensations have continued into adulthood—from being unable to persuade a mainstream hotel to host my Hindu/Christian wedding ceremony, to being presumed Muslim while traveling, to having a Post-It Note stuck on my father's office door in November 2016 that read "Niggers and Towel-heads serviced here" reminds me constantly that this work is still needed in our imperfect union.

Special thanks to two people who are friends and family and everything in between: Elise Salem in Beirut and Kavi Desai in Bombay for the friendship and love that fueled the writing I did in your homes.

My family nurtures me every day. My parents Yogesh and Madhu Joshi and my father-in-law Glen Bartlett have been role models, showing me the many ways each of us can work for the greater good. My sister Hetal and brother-in-law Fergus along with my dearest Jaya, Henry, and Manu have all provided much needed respite and entertainment. Over the course of the writing process, my son Kedhar grew from a little boy who needed me into a teen who was there for me to provide "fun breaks" as I was finishing the manuscript. It is clear to me that, as a young person, Kedhar sees the inequities in the US today but often, like many students, does not have the language to articulate what is going on. He inspires me every day to build an America worthy of him and his generation.

Finally, there are not enough words in all the world's languages to express my gratitude to John, my husband, life partner, greatest support, and first-round editor. Fate brought us together in Jerusalem—possibly the least likely place for a Christian and a Hindu to find each other and fall in love—and in that I find hope and inspiration. Through me, Kedhar knows the immigrant story of his mother and grandparents. Through John, he traces his lineage to the Mayflower. John's ability to own all the history in this book, and to let it feed his legal and public service work to increase liberty and opportunity gives me faith that we can indeed throw off history's yoke and achieve the American promise for all.

Notes

Introduction

1 Joshi, *New Roots in America's Sacred Ground*; Joshi, "Patterns and Paths"; Joshi, "Christian Privilege in Schools and Society."

2 Blumenfeld, "Christian Privilege."

3 Foucault, *Discipline and Punish*; Foucault and Gordon, *Power/Knowledge*.

4 Smith, "Heteropatriarchy and the Three Pillars of White Supremacy." Smith argues this model also destabilizes some of the conventional categories in ethnic studies or racial-justice organizing—categories such as African American/Latino/Asian American/Native American/Arab American. For instance, in the case of Latinos, these logics may affect peoples differently depending on whether they are Black, Indigenous, Mestizo, and so on.

5 Gilder Lehrman Institute of American History, "The Doctrine of Discovery, 1493: A Spotlight on a Primary Source by Pope Alexander VI."

6 Fletcher Hill, *The Sin of White Supremacy*.

7 Dunbar-Ortiz, *An Indigenous Peoples' History of the United States*.

8 Joshi, "Brick by Brick"; Singh, "The Racialization of Minoritized Religious Identity"; Joshi, "South Asian Religions in Contemporary America."

9 Jones, *The End of White Christian America*.

10 After 9/11, professors in Asian American studies rushed to perform research and write about Islam, terrorists, and discrimination. But most of these publications rarely dealt with, or would even go near, the faith aspects of religion. Most of the articles in the field of Asian American studies did not touch on how such treatment resulted in people viewing their own faiths differently.

11 Yoo, "Racial Spirits"; Yoo, "For Those Who Have Eyes to See"; Yoo, *New Spiritual Homes*.

12 Edwards, "Perceptions of Power and Faith among Black Women Faculty"; Yancey, "Yes Academic Bias Is a Problem and We Need to Address It."

13 Joshi, *New Roots in America's Sacred Ground*.

14 See the works of Jack Shaheen, including *Reel Bad Arabs* and *The TV Arab*.

15 Joshi, *New Roots in America's Sacred Ground*, 187.

16 Bayoumi, *This Muslim American Life*; Selod, "Citizenship Denied."

17 Johnson, "Donald Trump Calls for Total and Complete Shutdown of Muslims Entering the United States."

18 Corbin, "Terrorists Are Always Muslim but Never White."

19 Stone, "Pittsburgh Synagogue Shooter Identified as Christian Nationalist Robert Bowers"; Brown, "Dylann Roof."

20 The Pluralism Project at Harvard University has been documenting the growth of religious diversity in the United States since 1991. Since 2004 most information has been available digitally at www.pluralism.org.

21 The US Census Bureau does not collect data on religious affiliation in its demographic surveys or decennial census. In 1976, Congress passed Public Law 94–521 which prohibits the Census Bureau from asking a question on religious affiliation on a mandatory basis. In the past, from 1906 through 1936, the Census Bureau conducted censuses of religious bodies at 10-year intervals. Bialik, "Elusive Numbers."

22 This is a 2019 update to Pew's "America's Changing Religions Landscape" (2015) report. It presents the US religious affiliation in percentages, which have been applied to the total US population in 2018 (US Census Bureau)—327,167,434—to generate the figures in Table 1.1. Although Pew polled adults (population over 18 years of age), I have applied the percentages to the total US population based on the reasonable assumption that children will share their parents' religious affiliation in most cases.

23 Cox and Jones. PRRI's report presents the US religious affiliation in percentages, which have been applied to the total US population in 2016 (US Census Bureau)—322,762,018—to generate the figures in Table 1.1. Although PRRI polled adults (population over 18 years of age), I have applied the percentages to the total US population based on the reasonable assumption that children will share their parents' religious affiliation in most cases.

24 There are several methodological obstacles in the obtaining demographic information on Buddhists (and other Asian American religious groups) in the US. Since most Asian Americans today are immigrants, and since a large proportion of them are not proficient in English (especially in answering a phone survey), Jerry Park argues most surveys since 1965 have no accurate recording of the Buddhist population. See Park and Davidson.

25 This percentage includes the following groups: White evangelical Protestant, White mainline Protestant, White Catholic, Mormon, Orthodox Christian, Black Protestant, Hispanic Protestant, Jehovah's Witness, Other nonwhite Protestant, Hispanic Catholic, Other nonwhite Catholic.

26 Pew Research Form, Basheer Mohamed 2018.

27 Rosenthiel, "How Many Sikhs in the U.S.?" The article is from 2012 and the author notes that the number should be viewed as a floor and not a ceiling. This number includes adults and children.

28 This number has been used by the Sikh Coalition, and therefore has been cited in many places. However, the Sikh Coalition makes no mention of methodology for obtaining this statistic. See www.sikhcoalition.org

29 Cox and Jones, "America's Changing Religious Identity."

30 Pew Research Center, "Political Polarization in the American Public."

1. Christianity and American National Identity

1 Parekh, "A Faith Driven Governor in a Secular Society."

2 Parekh, "A Faith Driven Governor in a Secular Society."

3 Bellah, "Civil Religion in America."

4 Blumenfeld, "Christian Privilege"; Feldman, *Please Don't Wish Me a Merry Christmas.*

5 Blumenfeld, Joshi, and Fairchild, "Introduction."

6 https://religionnews.com.

7 Seanan Fong et al., "The Roots of Chinese American Religious Nones."

8 Focusing on the decrease in the proportion of Americans who identify with a Christian faith also ignores the continuing increase in the number of adherents of other faiths, largely as a result of immigration.

9 GhaneaBassiri, *A History of Islam in America*; Dinnerstein, *Antisemitism in America*; Reeve, *Religion of a Different Color*; Snow, "The Civilization of White Men"; Johnson, *African American Religions*; Sands, "Territory, Wilderness, Property, and Reservation."

10 330 US 1 (1947). Feldman mentions that Jefferson's Danbury letter is referenced for the first time in *Reynolds v. U.S.* (1878). Feldman, *Please Don't Wish Me a Merry Christmas.*

11 The Constitution itself makes only one reference to religion: "no religious test shall ever be required as a qualification to any office or public trust under the United States." (Art. VI, § 3).

12 Some might argue that the Second Amendment is stated as absolutely as the religion clauses in the First. The Second Amendment does ends with the absolute-sounding verb phrase "shall not be infringed." But it also speaks of a "well-regulated militia," which implies a set of limitations akin to military discipline. As we'll read later in this book, the military's internal rules have been found to supersede numerous constitutional rights, including even the free exercise of religion by those who serve.

13 Fraser, *Between Church and State.*

14 The Anglican Church was the official state church of New York, Maryland, Virginia, North Carolina and South Carolina. The Congregational Church (Puritan) was the official state church of New Hampshire (1817), Massachusetts (1833) and Connecticut (1818). Rhode Island, New Jersey, Deleware, Pennyslvania, and Georgia did not have offical state churches. Wills, *Christianity in the United States.*

15 Feldman, "Religious Minorities and the First Amendment"; Narayanan, "Sacred Land, Sacred Service"; Lal, "Sikh Kirpans in California Schools."

16 Gotanda, "A Critique of 'Our Constitution Is Color-Blind.'"

17 The myth tells us that everyone in the US is free to practice whatever religion they want, whenever and wherever they want. Its underlying story, which we all learned in elementary school, goes something like this: The Pilgrims and Puritans, fleeing

sectarian religious persecution in England, arrived on American shores to establish a haven of religious freedom. Rejecting the treatment they had received in England, they sought to create a place of religious freedom "for all." If only this were true. In fact, the Puritans established in the Massachusetts colony a place to practice *their* religion without fear or persecution, but where non-Puritan practice was forbidden and religious heresy rooted out. Puritanism was in effect the first of many ethnocentric and parochial "immigrant faiths" planted on US soil in opposition to the Native American religious traditions already practiced here, and also in conflict with the Spanish and French Roman Catholic outposts and missions earlier established throughout the Americas.

18   Barton, "Church in the US Capitol."

19   Miller, "Enforcement of the Sunday Closing Laws on the Lower East Side."

20   Ravitch, *School Prayer and Discrimination.*

21   Dinnerstein, *Antisemitism in America*; Dinnerstein, Nichols, and Reimers, *Natives and Strangers.*

22   For a detailed discussion on Christian normativity and the phrase "Church and State," see Adams and Joshi, "Religious Oppression." For a general discussion on the history of the phrase, see Fraser, *Between Church and State.*

23   Feldman, "A Christian America."

24   Feldman, "A Christian America."

25   Feldman, "A Christian America."

26   Little India Desk, "Indian American Becomes First Turbaned Sikh to Be Inducted in Trump's Security Team."

27   Employment Div., Dept. of Human Resources of Ore. v. Smith (1990).

28   While their Anabaptist roots made the status of the Amish as Christians contested in years past, they regard themselves, and are now generally regarded, as Christians.

29   Wisconsin v. Yoder, 406 US 205 (1972).

30   Wisconsin v. Yoder, 406 US 205 (1972).

31   Scholars have shown how the court tends to conceive of religion in distinctly Christian, especially Protestant, terms. Feldman, "Religious Minorities and the First Amendment"; Greenawalt, *Does God Belong in Public Schools?*

32   United States v. Bhagat Singh Thind, 261 US 204 (1923)

33   Galloway v. Town of Greece, 1682 F.3d 20 (2d Cir. 2012).

34   Town of Greece v. Galloway, 572 US 565 (2014).

35   Haynes and Thomas, *Finding Common Ground*; Greenawalt, *Does God Belong in Public Schools?*

36   Abington School District v. Schempp, 374 US 203 (1963).

37   Joshi, "Because I Had a Turban."

38   Sensoy and DiAngelo, *Is Everyone Really Equal?*

39   Jones, *The End of White Christian America*, 49.

40   Cox and Jones. "America's Changing Religious Identity."

41 We must acknowledge that the White Christian majority is itself very diverse, both theologically and ethnically.

42 Murji and Solomos, *Racialization: Studies in Theory and Practice*; Kane, "Frantz Fanon's Theory of Racialization."

43 Alsultany, "The Prime Time Plight of the Arab Muslim American after 9/11"; Jamal and Naber, *Race and Arab Americans before and after 9/11*; Shaheen, *Reel Bad Arabs: How Hollywood Vilifies a People*; *The TV Arab*.

44 Said, *Orientalism*.

45 Gotanda, "The Racialization of Islam in American Law." Gotanda further argues that when Islam is racialized, as in the case of the "Muslim terrorist," the traditional analysis of both religion clauses of the First Amendment does not apply. See also Volpp, "The Citizen and the Terrorist."

46 Hispanics in the US have also had such experiences.

47 Singh, "A New American Apartheid"; Sian, "Gurdwaras, Guns and Grudge in 'Post-Racial' America"; Dhillon, "Covering Turbans and Beards." Researchers Model and Lin have found instances of "mistaken identity" in the religious targeting of minorities in Great Britain and Canada, concluding, among other things, that "outsiders can't tell them apart." Model and Lin, "The Cost of Not Being Christian."

48 Singh, "A New American Apartheid"; Hafiz and Raghunathan, "Under Suspicion, under Attack."

49 Page, "Sikhs Head for the Barber and Turn Their Backs on Tradition."

50 Jamal and Naber, *Race and Arab Americans before and after 9/11*; Alsultany, "The Prime Time Plight of the Arab Muslim American after 9/11."

51 Mehta, *Karma Cola*; Suh, *Silver Screen Buddha*; Sandhu, "Instant Karma."

52 Hafiz and Raghunathan, "Under Suspicion, under Attack," x.

53 Iwamura, *Virtual Orientalism*, Kindle loc. 195. Ellipsis added.

54 For a discussion of the Christian normativity in the Pew Survey on Asian Americans for the 2010 report, "Asian Americans: A Mosaic of Faiths," see Iwamura et al., "Reflections on the Pew Forum on Religion and Public Life's Asian Americans."

55 Bayoumi, *This Muslim American Life*.

56 Grewal, *Islam Is a Foreign Country*.

57 Bayoumi. Bayoumi points out that the 9/11 Memorial provides pamphlets and audio tours in nine languages, but that Arabic is not one of the languages.

58 Freedman, "Muslims and Islam Were Part of Twin Towers' Life."

59 Talking Points Memo, "Poll: 68% of Americans Oppose 'Ground Zero Mosque'"; Fox News, "Fox News Poll."

60 Jackson and Hutchinson, "Plan for Mosque near World Trade Center Site Moves Ahead."

61 Brown, "Gingrich Denounces Ground Zero Mosque."

62 Resnick, "All Muslims Are Often Blamed for Single Acts of Terror"; Serwer, "The Terrorism That Doesn't Spark a Panic"; Zauzmer, "The Alleged Synagogue Shooter was a Churchgoer Who Talked Christian Theology."

63 Scaminaci, "PRRI Survey."
64 Conason, "Coalition of Fear"; Vogel, "Mosque Debate Strains Tea Party."
65 Allam and Ansari, "State and Local Republican Officials Have Been Bashing Muslims."
66 Wong, *Immigrants, Evangelicals, and Politics in an Era of Demographic Change*, 52.
67 Rajghatta, "Christian Activists Disrupt Hindu Prayer in US Senate."
68 Rajghatta, "Christian Activists Disrupt Hindu Prayer in US Senate."
69 Singh, "American Apartheid for the New Millennium."
70 Tuan, *Forever Foreigners or Honorary Whites?*
71 Liptak, "Court Orders Removal of Monument to Ten Commandments."
72 Costello, "The Trump Effect."
73 Costello, "The Trump Effect."
74 Those findings were echoed by Brian Levin, director of the California-based Center for the Study of Hate and Extremism. See Allam and Ansari, "State and Local Republican Officials Have Been Bashing Muslims."
75 Spencer and Stolberg, "White Nationalists March on University of Virginia."
76 Spencer and Stolberg, "White Nationalists March on University of Virginia."
77 Frontline, "Documenting Hate: Charlottesville."
78 Frontline, "Documenting Hate: Charlottesville."
79 Lipstadt, *Antisemitism: Here and Now*, 220–221.

2. Christianity and the Construction of White Supremacy

1 Goldberg, "For Decades, Our Coverage Was Racist."
2 Banton, *The Idea of Race*; Fredrickson, *Racism*.
3 Muslims began arriving in the New World long before the rise of the Atlantic slave trade. The first arrivals date to the turn of the fifteenth century, when European explorers and colonists crossed the Atlantic in search of new horizons and trading routes. GhaneaBassiri, *A History of Islam in America*.
4 Native Studies scholars use the term *settler colonialism* to refer to imperialistic US policies and actions related to Indigenous peoples. Smith, "Indigeneity, Settler Colonialism, White Supremacy"; Dunbar-Ortiz, *An Indigenous Peoples' History of the United States*; Deloria, *God Is Red*.
5 Cannon, "Cutting Edge."
6 Omi and Winant discuss class and gender as they relate to or are part of the process of racial formation, but religion is visibly absent from their analysis and discussion. In a 2014 follow-up anthology on racial formation, religion was again overlooked. I believe this omission is due to the anti-religious bias in ethnic studies. Omi and Winant, *Racial Formation in the United States*.
7 Fredrickson, *Racism*, 12.
8 Carr, "Spain's Moriscos."
9 Rana, *Terrifying Muslims*.
10 Rana, *Terrifying Muslims*, Kindle locations 475–476.
11 Rana, *Terrifying Muslims*.

12 Harvey, *Muslims in Spain.*

13 Delgado and Moss stress the importance of moving beyond purity of blood to think constructively about the different ways the intimate historical linkages of race and religion were the foundation for elaborate hierarchies of essential difference that impacted the racialization of different groups in the Americas. Delgado and Moss, "Religion and Race in the Early Modern Iberian Atlantic."

14 Raboteau, *Slave Religion.*

15 Kaiwar and Mazumdar, *Antinomies of Modernity.*

16 Cannon, "Cutting Edge."

17 Rana, *Terrifying Muslims*; Johnson, *African American Religions.*

18 Cannon, "Cutting Edge."

19 Omi and Winant, *Racial Formation in the United States.*

20 Rana, *Terrifying Muslims,* 472–474, 499–500.

21 Dunbar-Ortiz, *An Indigenous Peoples' History of the United States.*

22 Said, *Orientalism.*

23 Allen, "The Globalization of White Supremacy," 480. See also Cheah, *Race and Religion in American Buddhism.*

24 Bryant, *The Quest for the Origins of Vedic Culture,* 15.

25 Trautmann, *Aryans and British India*; Trautmann, "Does India Have History? Does History Have India?"

26 See Trautmann, *Aryans and British India*; Trautmann, "Does India Have History? Does History Have India?" In his 1998 book, Jonathan Kenoyer states that "many scholars have tried to correct this absurd theory." Kenoyer, *Ancient Cities of the Indus Valley Civilization,* 174. In a 2006 article, he mentions that by scholarly consensus, the Aryan invasion and migration theories are no longer considered to be true. Kenoyer, "Cultures and Societies of the Indus Tradition."

27 Cheah, *Race and Religion in American Buddhism.*

28 Key scientific and philological texts from the age of European imperialism in the nineteenth to twentieth century include Gobineau's *Essai sur l'inégalité des races humaines* and Robert Knox's *The Races of Man.*

29 The word "barbarian" derives from the Arabic *berber,* which originally referred to the regions of North Africa populated primarily by Arab Muslims.

30 Fletcher Hill, *The Sin of White Supremacy.*

31 See Omi and Winant, *Racial Formation in the United States*; Smith, "Indigeneity, Settler Colonialism, White Supremacy"; Menand, "Morton, Agassiz, and the Origins of Scientific Racism in the United States."

32 Gross, *What Blood Won't Tell.*

33 The phrase "Indians not taxed" created a distinction between Native Americans who remained affiliated with their tribes and outside of terrirorial reach of the colonies, on one hand, and Native Americans who had integrated into colonial society and were subject to being taxed by the federal government, on the other.

34 Steve Martinot, *The Machinery of Whiteness*; Roediger, *The Wages of Whiteness*; Jacobson, *Whiteness of a Different Color*.

35 While clearly not at the forefront of the forces that shaped modern America, they signify confluences between Europe, Africa, and the Americas at the onset of the history of American Islam. GhaneaBassiri, *A History of Islam in America*.

36 The colonial mindset is reflected in this statement: "When men and women are brought into perfect harmony with God, it was thought, they become authentic White Americans." Lee, "A Great Racial Commission."

37 Takaki, *A Different Mirror*, 176–77.

38 Cannon, "Cutting Edge," 130.

39 I draw here on Smith, "Heteropatriarchy and the Three Pillars of White Supremacy."

40 Frichner, "The Preliminary Study on the Doctrine of Discovery," 341–342. For a list and description of each papal bull, see the website The Doctrine of Discovery, accessed May 5, 2019, https://doctrineofdiscovery.org/papal-bulls.

41 Harvey, "'A Servant of Servants Shall He Be.'"

42 Gross, *What Blood Won't Tell*.

43 Spring, *Deculturalization and the Struggle for Equality*.

44 Deloria, *God Is Red*.

45 Miller and Furse, *Native America, Discovered and Conquered*.

46 Many missionaries, of different denominations, were opposed to the violence against native communities. They stressed that "civilization" was possible without slaughter. They urged government officials to have patience and to act humanly toward Indian nations engaged in the process of cultural change. But more and more American sought land for homesteads and argued for removing all Indians living, leading to a continuing and repeating process of dispossessing and moving Native populations to "Indian country" far from their holy places. See Graber, "Religion and Racial Violence in the Nineteenth Century."

47 Clark, *Race and Religion in America*. The attempt to eradicate Native American cultures backfired, and the federal and social repression of Native cultures stimulated a growing Native American prophetic tradition: the "Ghost Dance." This prophetic tradition envisioned the restoration of Native lands to a pre-European arrival state. Living and deceased Indians would be reunited in a Native paradise, while Whites vanished, died in the world's regeneration, or moved back across the ocean.

48 Wenger, *Religious Freedom*.

49 Takaki, *A Different Mirror*.

50 Lincoln, *Race, Religion, and the Continuing American Dilemma*.

51 In the nineteenth and early twentieth century, as we'll see below, modern "scientific" thought helped develop a thorough and sometimes intricate set of theories to denote broad divisions of humankind, marked by physiological difference.

52 Lincoln, *Race, Religion, and the Continuing American Dilemma*.

53 Raboteau, *Slave Religion*; Lincoln, *Race, Religion, and the Continuing American Dilemma*.

54 Johnson, *African American Religions*, 149–150.

55 Gerbner, *Christian Slavery*.

56 Baum, *The Rise and Fall of the Caucasian Race*, Kindle location 771; see also Johnson, African American Religions. The curse of Ham's son Canaan seems to have been first used to link slavery to "blackness" in the Islamic world during the Middle Ages.

57 Baum, *The Rise and Fall of the Caucasian Race*, Kindle location 783.

58 Harvey, "A Servant of Servants Shall He Be"; Gerbner, *Christian Slavery*.

59 Graber, "Religion and Racial Violence in the Nineteenth Century."

60 Raboteau, *Slave Religion*; *Oxford Research Encyclopedia of American History*, s.v. "Religion in African American History" by Judith Weisenfeld, accessed October 9, 2019, https://oxfordre.com/americanhistory/view/10.1093/acrefore /9780199329175.001.0001/acrefore-9780199329175-e-24.

61 Lincoln, *Race, Religion, and the Continuing American Dilemma*.

62 Lincoln and Mamiya, *The Black Church in the African American Experience*, 1. There are predominately Black local churches in White denominations such as the United Methodist Church, the Episcopal Church, and the Roman Catholic Church, among others.

63 While many churches, both Black and White, were a venue for progressive social activism during the Civil Rights Era, other churches fomented opposition to the Civil Rights Movement. Raced-based exclusions remained common in some American Christian institutional policies into recent decades. For example, the Church of Jesus Christ of Latter Day Saints (the Mormons) did not permit African Americans to become clergy until 1978, and have attributed Blacks' misfortune to a holy curse. Similarly, it was not until late in the 1990s that a major White Christian denomination issued a statement repudiating slavery. Emerson and Smith, *Divided by Faith*.

64 Martin Luther King, Jr. Research and Education Institute, "Communism."

65 In addition to its descriptions of Black Muslim organizations, the manual imagined an entire history of African Americans' "great migration" to northern cities in the early twentieth century that reified legacies of racial and economic disadvantage into nothing more than the natural way of things. As Johnson writes, "the training monograph rationalized the repression of African American Muslims. The manual established three major points: (1) poor, mostly illiterate African Americans raced to the urban North during the early 1900s to pursue the American dream of material prosperity; (2) these Blacks failed to realize they simply lacked the proper education and cultural sophistication required for gainful employment and aspirational success; and (3) they began to resent the superior, successful White race." Racial resentment, coupled with religious difference, became the rationale for the FBI's targeting of Civil Rights-era Black religious organizations, but

particularly Black Muslim organizations, to be surveilled and discredited in America's imagined national interest. Johnson, *African American Religions*, 379.

66 Johnson, *African American Religions*, 379.
67 Mazur, *The Americanization of Religious Minorities*.
68 Mueller, "An Evolving Mormon Church Finally Addresses a Racist Past."
69 Fletcher Hill, *The Sin of White Supremacy*.
70 Dunbar-Ortiz, *An Indigenous Peoples' History of the United States*.

3. Immigration, Citizenship, and White Christian Supremacy

1   Hope Yen, "Rise of Latino Population Blurs US Racial Lines."
2   Resnick, "White Fear of Demographic Change Is a Powerful Psychological Force."
3   Wong, *Immigrants, Evangelicals, and Politics in an Era of Demographic Change*, 52.
4   Pew Research Center, "America's Changing Religious Landscape."
5   Cox and Jones. "America's Changing Religious Identity."
6   Public Religion Research Institute, "PRRI Releases Largest Survey of American Religious and Denominational Identity Ever Conducted."
7   Wishon, "A Shifting America with a New Minority."
8   Resnick, "White Fear of Demographic Change Is a Powerful Psychological Force."
9   Wong, *Immigrants, Evangelicals, and Politics in an Era of Demographic Change*.
10 Johnson, "Donald Trump Calls for Total and Complete Shutdown of Muslims Entering the United States."
11 Munshi, "Beyond the Muslim Ban."
12 US Census Bureau, "Quickfacts: United States, Population Estimate July 1, 2018."
13 Cox and Jones. "America's Changing Religious Identity."
14 Ngai, *Impossible Subjects*, 72.
15 Jacobson, *Whiteness of a Different Color*; Ignatiev, *How the Irish Became White*.
16 The US Census did not record whether a person was an immigrant or native-born until 1850. Painter, *The History of White People*. The Census of 1790 did not include information about national origin or ancestry. The Census did not differentiate the foreign-born until 1850 and did not identify places of birth of parents of the native-born until 1890. Immigration was unrecorded before 1820 and not classified according to origin until 1899. Ngai, *Impossible Subjects*, 71.
17 Pew Research Center, "Modern Immigration Wave Brings 59 Million to US."
18 Jacobson, *Whiteness of a Different Color*, 70.
19 Dinnerstein, *Antisemitism in America*, 65.
20 Painter, *The History of White People*; Dinnerstein, *Antisemitism in America*, 32.
21 Dinnerstein, *Antisemitism in America*, 39.
22 Dinnerstein, *Antisemitism in America*, 95.
23 Dinnerstein, *Antisemitism in America*, 69.
24 Not all White Supremacist organizations have a Christian component; many in fact identify Nordic ideas and beliefs as core components of their White Supremacist

ideology. Damon Berry argues that what the organizations do share is the thread of racial protectionism. Berry, *Blood and Faith*.

25 McCoy, "'Saviors of the White Race.'"
26 Bald, "Selling the East in the American South"; Lee, *The Making of Asian America*.
27 Lee, *The Making of Asian America*.
28 Moon-Ho Jung, "Outlawing 'Coolies.'"
29 Jung, *Coolies and Cane*, 35.
30 Jung, *Coolies and Cane*, 66.
31 Takaki, *Strangers from a Different Shore*; Lee.
32 Lee, *The Making of Asian America*.
33 Chang, *The Chinese in America*, 66.
34 There are numerous historical stepping stones that help map the path to the Chinese Exclusion Act. The Page Act was passed by Congress in 1875; then-President Ulysses Grant said it should prevent "the importation of Chinese women, but few of whom are brought to our shores to pursue honorable or useful occupations." Grant's words reflected Congressman Page's arguments in favor of his bill, which invoked the image of "immoral Chinese women." Of course, the ban also had the effect of discouraging Chinese men—who could not become US citizens—from remaining in the United States by making it impossible for them to marry and establish families. Meanwhile, alien land laws, passed by various mostly western states in the second half of the nineteenth century, prohibited Asians from acquiring title to land. This policy kept them in the position of laborers, kept them segregated in neighborhoods where they could live as renters, and made certain professions more available to them than others. The irony, of course, is that these laws and their effects reinforced each other. The laws enabled Chinese only to live in certain places or engage in certain businesses, and then the charge that Asians "aren't integrating into our society" and cultural clichés like the image of the "Chinese laundry" were applied to reinforce the notion of Asians as separate and deviant.
35 Asiatic Exclusion League, "Proceedings of the Asiatic Exclusion League." The Asiatic Exclusion League was founded in San Francisco in 1905 as the Japanese and Korean Exclusion League but changed its name in 1907 in anticipation of the "flood of immigration from India."
36 Snow, "The Civilization of White Men," 274.
37 Collier's Weekly, "What the World Is Doing."
38 Jensen, *Passage from India*.
39 Lee, *The Making of Asian America*, 171.
40 The Middle East was not included in the "barred zone," and Arab immigrants, some of whom were Muslim, were still allowed to enter the country until 1924.
41 Daniels, *Coming to America*; Lee.
42 Dinnerstein, *Antisemitism in America*.
43 Grant, *The Passing of the Great Race*, location 172.
44 Painter, *The History of White People*, 324.

45 Later, the two-percent rule was replaced by an overall limit of 150,000 immigrants annually with countries' proportions determined by "national origins" as revealed in the 1920 census. Takaki, *Strangers from a Different Shore.*

46 Prewitt, "The Census Counts, the Census Classifies."

47 Ngai, *Impossible Subjects.*

48 These were the Luce-Cellar Act in 1946, which allowed for up to one hundred Indians and Filipinos to immigrate each year, and the 1952 McCarran Walter Act, which permitted up to one hundred people from each country in the world to immigrate *per annum* while also allowing a small number of specific, larger admissions such as 2,000 Palestinian refugees permitted to immigrate in 1953. See Ngai, *Impossible Subjects.*

49 Pew Research Center, "Origins of the U.S. Immigrant Population, 1960–2017."

50 Herberg, *Protestant, Catholic, Jew.*

51 Prashad, *The Karma of Brown Folk.*

52 Pew Research Center, "Origins of the US Immigrant Population."

53 As a matter of law, the Canal Zone was probably US territory, but no one even credibly raised the question, or seriously debated whether McCain—who, like Obama, served in the US Senate—belonged. Why? McCain was White and Episcopalian, with US citizen parents who were also White and Episcopalian.

54 See Tuan, *Forever Foreigners or Honorary Whites?*; Ng, Lee, and Pak, "Contesting the Model Minority and Perpetual Foreigner Stereotypes."

55 James Madison on Rule of Naturalization, 1st Congress, February 3, 1790.

56 Jacobson, *Whiteness of a Different Color,* 68.

57 Haney-López, *White by Law,* 11–12.

58 See several chapters/essays in Goldschmidt and McAlister, *Race, Nation, and Religion in the Americas*; Lum and Harvey, "Introduction"; Gualtieri, "Becoming 'White.'"

59 Snow, *Protestant Missionaries, Asian Immigrants*; Haney-López, *White by Law.*

60 Paddison, *American Heathens*; Harpalani, "*Desi*crit."

61 Gross, *What Blood Won't Tell,* Kindle locations, 2953–56.

62 The elimination of a racial or national-origin criterion for citizenship was the only progressive element of the McCarran-Walter Act, which perpetuated existing laws' preference toward immigrants from northern and western Europe. The act made slight revisions to the quotas from the 1924 Immigration Act and eliminated the racial restriction for citizenship, thereby ending Japanese and Korean exclusion. (Chinese, Indian, and Filipino exclusion had been eliminated with the 1946 Luce-Cellar Act.) Furthermore, even before Congress passed the Citizenship Act, many Native Americans had achieved citizenship through treaties, military service, and receipt of land allotments.

63 Ngai, *Impossible Subjects,* 237.

64 Congress passed the act over the veto of President Truman, who opposed the law principally for its racist features but nevertheless called for the continuation of the national origins quota of the 1924 Act.

65 Lee, "A Great Racial Commission," 93. See also Foner, *In a New Land*; Roediger, *Colored White.*

66 Gross, *What Blood Won't Tell.*

67 Fox and Bloemraad, "Beyond 'White by Law.'"

68 Fox and Bloemraad, "Beyond 'White by Law.'"

69 Mexicans' Whiteness remained contested well into the twentieth century. In 1930, the Census Bureau included among residents' possible "color or race" status a new category: "Mexican." This was a one-time appearance for "Mexican" as a racial category. "To not cause stress on diplomatic relations with Mexico, in 1940 Congress amended its naturalization laws to include 'all races indigenous to the Western Hemisphere'" in the federal legal definition of "White." Molina, *How Race Is Made in America.*

70 Menchaca, *Recovering History, Constructing Race.*

71 For Mexicans to be eligible for citizenship they had to have resided in Texas prior to 1845; any person migrating after that date was ineligible for naturalization. State and private actors attempted to ensure that Mexican immigrants would become ineligible for US citizenship by having them officially categorized as non-White. "Under pressure from a California nativist organization, a New York judge upheld an immigration officer's denial of the naturalization petitions of three Mexicans in 1935 because they were not white, but rather individuals 'of Indian and Spanish blood.'" Lukens, *A Quiet Victory for Latino Rights*, 121. Other groups in the former Mexican territories that were now part of the US, such as the *Afromestizos* (persons of mixed African and native heritage) were not considered eligible for citizenship. In sum, acceptance of Christianity and practicing Catholic rituals, along with non-Black and minimally native racial identity and a history of residency in the annexed territories and not of immigration, was key to citizenship for Native Americans. Molina, *How Race Is Made in America*, 44.

72 Paddison, *American Heathens*, 17.

73 Ironically, some Christian missionaries praised Chinese Buddhism and Confucianism for their morality and intellectual rigor, while still emphasizing that ultimately there were limitations to any non-Christian faith, in that none could provide the spiritual salvation found only in Jesus. While some missionaries advocated for citizenship for Chinese men if they converted, it was not a prevailing viewpoint.

74 Paddison, *American Heathens*, 12.

75 Paddison, *American Heathens*, 23–24; Kim, "Engaging Afro/black-Orientalism."

76 Paddison, *American Heathens*, 23–24.

77 In the decades after the Civil War, the then-emerging pseudoscience of eugenics was applied to raise the question of just how broadly the term "white person" should be interpreted. Italians were perceived in racial as well as religious terms, and in 1899 the US Bureau of Immigration began distinguishing between "Keltic"

northern Italians and "Iberic" southern Italians. In 1911 the House Committee on Immigration and Naturalization debated whether to regard "the south Italian as a full-blooded Caucasian." There was racial prejudice against southern Italians, and occasional threats to their status as "white." Still, no federal court or government official ever seriously suggested that any immigrant from Europe, no matter how swarthy, should be excluded from citizenship. "If US congressmen openly debated whether southern Italians were 'full-blooded Caucasians,'" writes Guglielmo, they never went so far as to deny southern Italians naturalization rights based on their doubts. Italians may have been Catholic, and thus a culture apart, but they shared the color status of Whites. There was, for example, a 1903 attempt in Louisiana to exclude Italians from voting in "white" primaries. Gross, *What Blood Won't Tell*, Kindle locations 3207–3209; Guglielmo, *White on Arrival*.

78 Haney-Lopez, *White by Law*.
79 Baum, *The Rise and Fall of the Caucasian Race*.
80 Gualtieri, "Becoming 'White,'" 32. See also Rogoff, "Is the Jew White?"
81 Kayyali, *The Arab Americans*.
82 Gualtieri, "Becoming 'White,'" 33.
83 Gualtieri, "Becoming 'White,'" 37.
84 Gualtieri, *Between Arab and White*, 158.
85 Gualtieri, *Between Arab and White*, 57.
86 At the end of the nineteenth century, only 2,050 residents of the US had been born in India. Jensen, *Passage from India*.
87 Takaki, *Strangers from a Different Shore*.
88 Haney-López, *White by Law*.
89 Snow, "The Civilization of White Men," 268.
90 Williams, *American Sutra*, 52.
91 Williams, *American Sutra*, 21.
92 Williams, *American Sutra*.
93 Williams, *American Sutra*, 146-148.
94 BBC, "Trump's Executive Order."
95 Indeed, one wonders whether, if Johnson had had a crystal ball and could see the racial and religious diversity that has resulted from the 1965 Act, he would have signed the law at all.

4. Everyday Christian Privilege

1 Joshi, *New Roots in America's Sacred Ground*, 133.
2 Joshi, *New Roots in America's Sacred Ground*, 134.
3 Joshi, *New Roots in America's Sacred Ground*, 133–34.
4 Joshi, *New Roots in America's Sacred Ground*; Blumenfeld, "Christian Privilege"; Schlosser, "Christian Privilege."
5 Sensoy and DiAngelo, *Is Everyone Really Equal?*, 65–68.
6 Adams et al., *Teaching for Diversity and Social Justice*.

7 Tochluk, "'But I Just Don't See It!'"; Johnson, "'My Eyes Have Been Opened.'"

8 My research sample consisted of fifteen White Christian women who taught in public schools in Bergen, Hudson, or Middlesex County, New Jersey. I chose White Christian women because they are the majority of the teaching force. Additional criteria included: having three to ten years of teaching experience, having or earning a master's degree in education, and being "church-going" (defined as attending a worship service not less than once per month).

9 Sensoy and DiAngelo, *Is Everyone Really Equal?*, 85.

10 Beaman, "The Myth of Pluralism, Diversity, and Vigor"; Cromwell, "Cultural Discrimination."

11 Joshi, *New Roots in America's Sacred Ground*, 123–26; Joshi, "Christian Privilege in Schools and Society."

12 Schlosser, "Christian Privilege"; Killerman, "30+ Examples of Christian Privilege."

13 The following examples of Christian privilege draw upon both primary and secondary sources of data to show what everyday Christian privilege looks like. The primary source data include interviews conducted with White Christian public school educators, from which I also quoted above; and interviews conducted with second generation Indian American Sikhs, Muslims, Hindus and Christians in the 1990s, 2000s and 2010s. Secondary sources include published studies and news sources. I also draw from over twenty years of interaction with undergraduate and graduate students, faculty colleagues, and workshop participants, including teachers, lawyers, and judges in the US.

14 Mitra, "Merchandizing the Sacred."

15 There are exceptions to the respectful presentation of Christian imagery, of course—from Madonna's *Like a Prayer* video to artist Andres Serrano's photograph *Immersion (Piss Christ)*—but it seems fair to say that the exceptions more often fall into the category of art as social commentary rather than art for commercial consumption at retail.

16 Cannon, "Cutting Edge."

17 2014 N.J. LEXIS 1391 (2014).

18 Dewan, "All Her Life, Nikki Haley Was the Different One."

19 Interview with research participant 010 in Summer 2007 as part of the study: "Examing the Religious Identity of Public School Teachers." This project was funded by the Wabash Center for Teaching and Learning about Religion and Theology.

20 For a discussion on the connection of the Protestant influence on the beginning of the Common Schools movement, the precursor to today's public schools, see Fraser, *Between Church and State*.

21 Clark et al., "Diversity Initiatives in Higher Education."

22 Moffitt, "Sikh Comedian Forced to Remove Turban at SFO"; Schrader, "Long Island Bar Turns Away Stony Brook Graduate Wearing Turban"; Sikh American

Legal Defense and Education Fund, "Virginia Restaurant Apologizes to Sikh American for Wrongfully Denying Entry to Restaurant Because of Turban."

23 Liptak, "Muslim Woman Denied Job over Head Scarf Wins in Supreme Court."

24 Of course, it is not always the majority that wields legal and social power and defines norms. We know this is true from apartheid South Africa and from the fact that women are a majority everywhere while men wield society's power. But in the present context, Christians' legal and social power and their status as the American religious majority are mutually reinforcing.

5. Voices of Christian Privilege

1 Mamta Accapadi, "Christmas in a Cultural Center," 126.

2 Stewart and Lozano, "Difficult Dialogues at the Intersections of Race, Culture, and Religion."

3 Sue, *Race Talk and the Conspiracy of Silence*; Sue, *Microaggressions in Everyday Life*.

4 Kishi, "Key Findings on the Global Rise in Religious Restrictions."

5 Yancey, "Yes Academic Bias Is a Problem and We Need to Address It."

6 This bias is not directly only against Christians. As a Hindu, I have felt alienation from my colleagues, including Hindus and others, for observing certain holidays or participating in temple worship. Before even receiving my doctoral degree, I attended a retreat for graduate students and junior faculty in Asian American Studies. One of the days of the retreat was Shivratri, a holiday I observe by fasting. The bias against being a practicing Hindu that I felt from my peers in that space was palpable. As a young scholar working on religion, and looking for a tenure-track position, I was so concerned that my religiosity would work against me, in terms of my scholarship and job prospects, that I decided to hide my fast at the retreat.

7 Miller v. Davis, 2015 WL 10692640 (6th. Cir. Aug. 26, 2015) (County Clerk); Masterpiece Cakeshop v. Colorado Civil Rights Commission, 584 US ___, 138 S. Ct. 1719 (2018).

8 International Mission Board, *Diwali*.

9 See Pharr, *Homophobia*; Frankenberg, *The Social Construction of Whiteness*; Jost, Banaji, and Nosek, "A Decade of System Justification Theory."

10 Bell, Funk, Joshi, and Valdivia, "Racism and White Privilege," 137.

11 There is always going be an inherent tension around Christianity's social power and the American right of free exercise. If a Christian is practicing freely, then among other things they are probably following the Bible's instruction to spread the "Good News" by encouraging others to acknowledge Jesus as the Messiah—the "way, and the truth, and the light," whom Christians believe to be the only path to God and salvation. The power of Christian normativity aids and abets this activity, which many Christians see as a spiritual obligation but which many members of religious minorities and atheists perceive as aggression and discrimination.

12 Black, "What White Nationalism Gets Right About American History."

13 Kelleher, "Millburn School Board Approves Diwali, Lunar New Year as Days Off for Students."

14 Freire, *Pedagogy of the Oppressed*; hooks, *Teaching to Transgress*.

15 Adams et al., *Teaching for Diversity and Social Justice*.

16 Purkayastha, *Negotiating Ethnicity*; Kurien, "Being Young, Brown, and Hindu"; Joshi, *New Roots in America's Sacred Ground*.

17 Joshi, *New Roots in America's Sacred Ground*.

18 Kamran, "The American Muslim Dilemma," 82.

19   Kamran, "The American Muslim Dilemma," 81.

20 Joshi, *New Roots in America's Sacred Ground*, 27.

21 As it turned out, the puppet show presented the *Ramayana* as told by Malaysian Hindus, and presented a completely different set of visual images than I expected. It was the first time I learned that there were Hindu communities outside of India and its diaspora.

22 Adams, "My Grandmother and the Snake," 108.

23 Adams, "My Grandmother and the Snake," 108–109.

24 Clark et al., "Diversity Initiatives in Higher Education."

25 Dhillon, "Covering Turbans and Beards."

26 Singh Gohil and Sidhu, "The Sikh Turban."

27 Singh Gohil and Sidhu, "The Sikh Turban."

28 Until 1981, Sikhs serving in the Army were allowed to wear turbans and keep their unshorn hair. Since 1981, however, stricter grooming regulations have required recruits to request religious accommodations on an individual basis.

29 Dickstein, "Army Allows Sikhs Permanent Exemptions to Wear Beards and Turbans, Muslims to Wear Hijab."

30 Carey, "I Dance for Me."

31 The author points out the inaccuracies of the college lore: the tradition was supposedly started by three Native American students who graduated together in 1850. However, no three natives graduated together from Dartmouth until 1970. Also, as the author asserts, no Native American would break a sacred pipe.

32 Carey, "I Dance for Me," 127.

33   Carey, "I Dance for Me," 128–129.

34 Gupta-Carlson, *Muncie, India*; Purkayastha, *Negotiating Ethnicity*; Adur and Purkayastha, "On the Edges of Belonging."

35 Joshi, *New Roots in America's Sacred Ground*, 136.

36 Thank you to Jonathan Zur, Executive Director at Virgina Center for Inclusive Communities for connecting me to Rev. Dennis Roberts. A special thanks to Dr. James Wright and his family for their gracious hospitality.

6. Making Meaning and Making Change

1 Auburn Seminary, "America's Leading Religious Leaders Condemn SCOTUS Muslim Ban Ruling."

2 Auburn Seminary, "America's Leading Religious Leaders Condemn SCOTUS Muslim Ban Ruling."

3 The Center is named for Fred Korematsu, a Japanese American who was arrested for refusing to be interned with other Japanese Americans during World War II. Korematsu's case reached the Supreme Court in Korematsu v. United States, 323 U.S. 214(1944), which affirmed Korematsu's criminal conviction.

4 Love, "Developing a Liberatory Consciousness," 599.

5 Love, "Developing a Liberatory Consciousness," 599.

6 This rejecting of the "messenger" as well as the message is especially common in courses taught by racial and religious minorities, particularly female faculty.

7 Note TK.

8 Love, "Roots, Routes and Race."

9 Kruse, *One Nation under God*.

10 Perhaps not surprisingly, one of the most consistent findings in the literature on religion and civil liberties has been the unwillingness of those who affiliate with conservative Protestant denominations to grant civil liberties to unpopular groups. (Mainline Protestant and Catholics are relatively more willing to do so.) For poll and data analysis, see Reimer and Park, "Tolerant (in) Civility?"

11 Personal correspondence with James Wright, May 8, 2018. The guidelines for public events were written by Rev. Nathan Brooks to address the issue of public prayer for participants in annual MLK Breakfast in Lynchburg, Virginia. James Wright, May 18, 2018.

12 Jeung, *Faithful Generations*.

13 Patel, *Intersectionality in Action*.

14 Allam and Ansari, "State and Local Republican Officials Have Been Bashing Muslims."

15 Robertson, Mele, and Tavernise, "11 Killed in Synagogue Massacre."

16 See the work of Putnam and Campbell, *American Grace* and Allport, *The Nature of Prejudice*.

17 And by the way, if it's pie, it's a pie you stole in the first place. But it's not pie.

Bibliography

Accapadi, Mamta. "Christmas in a Cultural Center." In *Investigating Christian Privilege and Religion Oppression in the United States,* edited by Warren Blumenfeld, Khyati Y. Joshi, and Ellen Fairchild. Rotterdam, Netherlands: Sense Publishers, 2009.

Adams, Maurianne and Khyati Joshi. "Religious Oppression." In *Readings for Diversity and Social Justice,* edited by Maurianne Adams, Warren Blumenfeld, Rosie Castaneda, Heather W. Hackman, Madeline Peters, L. and Ximena Zuniga, 227–33. New York: Routledge, 2010.

Adams, Maurianne, Lee Anne Bell, Diane J. Goodman, and Khyati Y. Joshi, eds. *Teaching for Diversity and Social Justice: A Sourcebook.* 3rd ed. New York: Routledge, 2016.

Adams, Nicole. "My Grandmother and the Snake." In *First Person, First Peoples: Native American College Graduates Tell Their Life Stories,* edited by Andrew Garrod and Colleen Larimore, 93–114. Cornell University Press, 1997.

Adur, Shweta Majumdar and Bandana Purkayastha. "On the Edges of Belonging: Indian American Dalits, Queers, Guest Workers and Questions of Ethnic Belonging." *Journal of Intercultural Studies* 34, no. 4 (2013): 418–30.

Allam, Hannah and Talal Ansari. "State and Local Republican Officials Have Been Bashing Muslims. We Counted." *Buzzfeed News, April 10,* 2018. www.buzzfeednews.com.

Allen, Ricky Lee. "The Globalization of White Supremacy: Toward a Critical Discourse on the Racialization of the World." *Educational Theory* 51, no. 4 (2001): 467–85.

Allport, Gordon W. *The Nature of Prejudice.* Cambridge, MA: Perseus, 1979 [1954].

Alsultany, Evelyn. "The Prime Time Plight of the Arab Muslim American after 9/11." In Jamal and Naber, *Race and Arab Americans before and after 9/11,* 204–28.

Asiatic Exclusion League. "Proceedings of the Asiatic Exclusion League." 1908.

Auburn Seminary. "America's Leading Religious Leaders Condemn SCOTUS Muslim Ban Ruling." Accessed October 7, 2019. https://auburnseminary.org.

Banton, Michael P. *The Idea of Race.* London: Tavistock Publications, 1977.

Barton, David. "Church in the US Capitol." December 6, 2017, https://wallbuilders.com.

Baum, Bruce. *The Rise and Fall of the Caucasian Race: A Political History of Racial Identity.* New York: New York University Press, 2006.

Bayoumi, Moustafa. *This Muslim American Life: Dispatches from the War on Terror.* New York: New York University Press, 2015.

BBC. "Trump's Executive Order: Who Does Travel Ban Affect?" *BBC,* February 10, 2017. www.bbc.com.

Beaman, Lori G. "The Myth of Pluralism, Diversity, and Vigor: The Constitutional Privilege of Protestantism in the United States and Canada." *Journal for the Scientific Study of Religion* 42, no. 3 (2003): 311–25.

Bell, Lee Anne, Mike Funk, Khyati Joshi, and Marjorie Valdivia. "Racism and White Privilege." In Adams, Bell, Goodman, and Joshi, *Teaching for Diversity and Social Justice*, 133–182.

Bellah, R. N. "Civil Religion in America." *Daedalus, Journal of the Academy of Arts and Sciences* 96, no. 1 (1967): 1–21.

Berry, Damon T. *Blood and Faith: Christianity in American White Nationalism*. Syracuse, NY: Syracuse University Press, 2017.

Bialik, Carl. "Elusive Numbers: US Population by Religion." *Wall Street Journal*, August 13, 2010, https://blogs.wsj.com.

Black, Derek "What White Nationalism Gets Right About American History." *New York Times*, January 20, 2018. www.nytimes.com.

Blumenfeld, W. J. "Christian Privilege, the Public Schools, and the Promotion of 'Secular' and Not-So 'Secular' Mainline Christianity." *Equity and Excellence in Education* 39, no. 3 (2006): 195–210.

Blumenfeld, Warren J., Khyati Y. Joshi, and Ellen E. Fairchild. "Introduction." In *Investigating Christian Privilege and Religious Oppression in the US*, edited by Blumenfeld, Joshi and Fairchild, vii-xix. Amsterdam, Netherlands: Sense Publishers, 2009.

Brown, David. "Gingrich Denounces Ground Zero Mosque." *Atlantic*, July 22, 2010. www.theatlantic.com.

Brown, Joel A. "Dylann Roof, the Radicalization of the Alt-Right, and Ritualized Racial Violence." *Sightings*, January 12, 2017, https://divinity.uchicago.edu.

Bryant, Edwin. *The Quest for the Origins of Vedic Culture: The Indo-Aryan Migration Debate*. Oxford University Press, 2001.

Cannon, Katie Geneva. "Cutting Edge: Christian Imperialism and the Transatlantic Slave Trade." *Journal of Feminist Studies in Religion* 24, no. 1 (Spring 2008): 127–34.

Carey, Elizabeth. "I Dance for Me." In *First Person, First Peoples: Native American College Graduates Tell Their Life Stories*, edited by Andrew Garrod and Colleen Larimore, 115–35. Ithaca, NY: Cornell University Press, 1997.

Carr, Matthew. "Spain's Moriscos: A 400-Year-Old Muslim Tragedy Is a Story for Today." *Guardian*, March 14, 2017, www.theguardian.com.

Chang, Iris. *The Chinese in America: A Narrative History*. Penguin, 2004.

Cheah, Joseph. *Race and Religion in American Buddhism: White Supremacy and Immigrant Adaptation*. Aar Academy Series. New York: Oxford University Press, 2011.

Clark, Christine, Mark Brimhall Vargas, Lewis Scholsser, and Craig Alimo. "Diversity Initiatives in Higher Education: It's Not Just 'Secret Santa' in December; Addressing Educational and Workplace Climate Issues Linked to Christian Privilege." *Multicultural Education* 10, no. 2 (2002): 52–57.

Clark, Emily Suzanne. "Religion and Race in America." In Oxford Research Encyclopedia of American History, edited by Jon Butler. Oxford Research Encyclopedias, 2017. http://oxfordre.com.

Collier's Weekly, "What the World Is Doing." March 26, 1910. Reproduced in South Asian American Digital Archive. Accessed October 9, 2019. www.saada.org/item/20101217-157.

Conason, Joe. "Coalition of Fear: Tea Party, the Religious Right and Islamophobia." Salon, September 19, 2010. www.salon.com.

Corbin, Caroline Mala. "Terrorists Are Always Muslim but Never White: At the Intersection of Critical Race Theory and Propaganda." Fordham Law Review 86 (2017): 455–85.

Costello, Maureen. "The Trump Effect: The Impact of the 2016 Election on the Nation's Schools." Southern Poverty Law Center. November 28, 2016. www.splcenter.org.

Cox, Daniel and Robert P. Jones. "America's Changing Religious Identity." PRRI. September 6, 2017. www.prri.org.

Cromwell, J. B. "Cultural Discrimination: The Reasonable Accommodation of Religion in the Workplace." Employee Responsibilities and Rights Journal 10, no. 2 (1997): 155–72.

Daniels, Roger. Coming to America. 2nd ed. New York: Harper Perennial, 2002.

Delgado, Jessica and Kelsey Moss. "Religion and Race in the Early Modern Iberian Atlantic." In The Oxford Handbook of Religion and Race in American History, edited by Kathryn Gin Lum and Paul Harvey, 40–60. New York: Oxford University Press, 2018.

Deloria, Vine. God Is Red: A Native View of Religion. Golden, CO: Fulcrum Publishing, 2003.

Dewan, Shaila "All Her Life, Nikki Haley Was the Different One." New York Times, June 13, 2010, A11.

Dhillon, Kiran Preet. "Covering Turbans and Beards: Title VII's Role in Legitimizing Religious Discrimination against Sikhs." Southern California Interdisciplinary Law Journal 21 (2011): 213–52.

Dickstein, Cory. "Army Allows Sikhs Permanent Exemptions to Wear Beards and Turbans, Muslims to Wear Hijab." Stars and Stripes, January 7, 2017, www.stripes.com.

Dinnerstein, Leonard, Roger L. Nichols, and David M. Reimers. Natives and Strangers: A Multicultural History of Americans. 4th ed. New York: Oxford University Press, 2003.

Dinnerstein, Leonard. Antisemitism in America. Oxford University Press, 1995.

Dunbar-Ortiz, Roxanne. An Indigenous Peoples' History of the United States. Beacon Press, 2014.

Edwards, Kirsten T. "Perceptions of Power and Faith among Black Women Faculty: Re-Thinking Institutional Diversity." Journal of Innovative Higher Education 40, no. 3 (2015): 263–78.

Emerson, Michael and Christian Smith. Divided by Faith: Evangelical Religion and the Problem of Race in America. New York: Oxford University Press, 2000.

Feldman, Stephen M. "A Christian America and the Separation of Church and State." In *Law and Religion: A Critical Anthology*, edited by Stephen M. Feldman, 261–78. New York: New York University Press, 2000.

Feldman, Stephen M. "Religious Minorities and the First Amendment: The History, the Doctrine, and the Future." *University of Pennsylvania Journal of Constitutional Law* 6 (2003): 222–77.

Feldman, Stephen M. *Please Don't Wish Me a Merry Christmas: A Critical History of the Separation of Church and State*. Critical America. New York: New York University Press, 1997.

Fletcher Hill, Jeannine. *The Sin of White Supremacy: Christianity, Racism, and Religious Diversity in America*. Maryknoll, NY: Orbis Books, 2017.

Foner, Nancy. *In a New Land: A Comparative View of Immigration*. New York: New York University Press, 2005.

Fong, Seanan, Russell Jeung, Brett Esaki, and Alice Liu. "The Roots of Chinese American Religious Nones: Continuities with the Liyi Tradition." In *Envisioning Religion, Race, and Asian Americans*, edited by David Yoo and Khyati Y. Joshi. Honolulu: University of Hawai'i Press, 2019.

Foucault, Michel and Colin Gordon. *Power/Knowledge: Selected Interviews and Other Writings, 1972–1977*. New York: Pantheon Books, 1980.

Foucault, Michel. *Discipline and Punish: The Birth of the Prison*. New York: Vintage, 2012.

Fox News. "Fox News Poll: 64 Percent Think It's Wrong to Build Mosque near Ground Zero." www.foxnews.com.

Fox, Cybelle and Irene Bloemraad. "Beyond "White by Law": Explaining the Gulf in Citizenship Acquisition between Mexican and European Immigrants, 1930." *Journal of Social Forces* 94, no. 1 (2015): 181–207.

Frankenberg, Ruth. *The Social Construction of Whiteness: White Women, Race Matters*. London: Routledge, 1993.

Fraser, James. *Between Church and State: Religion and Public Education in a Multicultural America*. New York: Palgrave, 1999.

Fredrickson, George M. *Racism: A Short History*. Princeton, NJ: Princeton University Press, 2002.

Freedman, Samuel "Muslims and Islam Were Part of Twin Towers' Life." *New York Times*, September 11, 2010, A12.

Freire, Paulo. *Pedagogy of the Oppressed*. 3rd ed. New York: Continuum, 1996.

Frichner, Tonya Gonnella. "The Preliminary Study on the Doctrine of Discovery." *Pace Environmental Law Review* 28 (2010): 339–45.

Frontline. "Documenting Hate: Charlottesville." *PBS*. August 7, 2018. www.pbs.org.

Gerbner, Katharine. *Christian Slavery: Conversion and Race in the Protestant Atlantic World*. Philadelphia: University of Pennsylvania Press, 2018.

GhaneaBassiri, Kambiz. *A History of Islam in America: From the New World to the New World Order*. New York: Cambridge University Press, 2010.

Gilder Lehrman Institute of American History. "The Doctrine of Discovery, 1493: A Spotlight on a Primary Source by Pope Alexander VI." Accessed October 9, 2019. www.gilderlehrman.org/content/doctrine-discovery-1493

Gohil, Necha Singh and Dawinder S. Sidhu. "The Sikh Turban: Post-911 Challenges to This Article of Faith." *Rutgers Journal of Law & Religion* 9 (2007): 1.

Goldberg, Susan "For Decades, Our Coverage Was Racist. To Rise above Our Past, We Must Acknowledge It." Accessed October 9, 2019. www.nationalgeographic.com.

Goldschmidt, Henry and Elizabeth A. McAlister, eds. *Race, Nation, and Religion in the Americas*. New York: Oxford University Press, 2004.

Gotanda, Neil. "A Critique of 'Our Constitution Is Color-Blind.'" In *Critical Race Theory: The Cutting Edge*, edited by Richard Delgado and Jean Stefancic, 35–38. Philadelphia: Temple University Press, 2000.

Gotanda, Neil. "The Racialization of Islam in American Law." *The ANNALS of the American Academy of Political and Social Science* 637, no. 1 (2011): 184–95.

Graber, Jennifer. "Religion and Racial Violence in the Nineteenth Century." In *The Oxford Handbook of Religion and Race in American History*, edited by Kathryn Gin Lum and Paul Harvey, 387–402. Oxford: Oxford University Press, 2018.

Grant, Madison. *The Passing of the Great Race*. New York: Charles Scribner's Sons, 1916.

Greenawalt, Kent. *Does God Belong in Public Schools?* Princeton, NJ: Princeton University Press, 2005.

Grewal, Zareena. *Islam Is a Foreign Country: American Muslims and the Global Crisis of Authority*. New York: New York University Press, 2014.

Gross, Ariela Julie. *What Blood Won't Tell a History of Race on Trial in America*. Cambridge, MA: Harvard University Press, 2008.

Gualtieri, Sarah. "Becoming 'White': Race, Religion and the Foundations of Syrian/Lebanese Ethnicity." *Journal of American Ethnic History* 20, no. 4 (2001): 29–58.

Gualtieri, Sarah. "Strange Fruit? Syrian Immigrants, Extralegal Violence and Racial Formation in the Jim Crow South." *Arab Studies Quarterly* 26, no. 3 (2004): 63–85.

Gualtieri, Sarah. *Between Arab and White: Race and Ethnicity in the Early Syrian American Diaspora*. Berkeley: University of California Press, 2009.

Guglielmo, Thomas A. *White on Arrival: Italians, Race, Color, and Power in Chicago, 1890–1945*. New York: Oxford University Press, 2003.

Gupta-Carlson, Himanee. *Muncie, India (Na): Middletown and Asian America*. Champaign: University of Illinois Press, 2018.

Hafiz, Sameera and Suman Raghunathan. "Under Suspicion, under Attack: Xenophobic Political Rhetoric and Hate Violence against South Asian, Muslim, Sikh, Hindu, Middle Eastern, and Arab Communities in the United States." Washington DC: South Asian Americans Leading Together, 2014. www.saalt.org

Haney-López, Ian. *White by Law: The Legal Construction of Race*. 2nd ed. New York: New York University Press, 2006.

Harpalani, Vinay. "*Desi*crit: Theorizing the Racial Ambiguity of South Asian Americans." *NYU Annual Survey of American Law* 69, no. 1 (2013): 77–183.

Harvey, Leonard Patrick. *Muslims in Spain, 1500 to 1614*. University of Chicago Press, 2005.

Harvey, Paul. "'A Servant of Servants Shall He Be': The Construction of Race in American Religious Mythologies." In *Religion and the Creation of Race and Ethnicity: An Introduction*, edited by Craig R. Prentiss, 13–27. New York: New York University Press, 2003.

Haynes, Charles and Oliver Thomas. *Finding Common Ground: A Guide to Religious Liberty in Public Schools*. Nashville, TN: First Amendment Center, 2007.

Herberg, Will. *Protestant, Catholic, Jew : An Essay in American Religious Sociology*. Chicago: University of Chicago Press, 1983.

hooks, bell. *Teaching to Transgress: Education as the Practice of Freedom*. New York: Routledge, 1994.

Ignatiev, Noel. *How the Irish Became White*. New York: Routledge, 1995.

International Mission Board. *Diwali: Festival of Lights Prayer for Hindus*. Richmond, VA: Southern Baptist Convention, 1999.

Iwamura, Jane Naomi, Khyati Joshi, Sharon Suh, and Janelle Wong. "Reflections on the Pew Forum on Religion and Public Life's Asian Americans: A Mosaic of Faiths Data and Report." *Amerasia Journal* 40, no. 1 (2014): 1–16.

Iwamura, Jane Naomi. *Virtual Orientalism: Asian Religions and American Popular Culture*. New York: Oxford University Press, 2011.

Jackson, Joe and Bill Hutchinson. "Plan for Mosque near World Trade Center Site Moves Ahead." *Daily News,* May 11, 2010. www.nydailynews.com.

Jacobson, Matthew Frye. *Whiteness of a Different Color: European Immigrants and the Alchemy of Race*. Cambridge, MA: Harvard University Press, 1998.

Jamal, Amaney A. and Nadine Christine Naber. *Race and Arab Americans before and after 9/11: From Invisible Citizens to Visible Subjects*. Syracuse, NY: Syracuse University Press, 2008.

Jensen, Joan M. *Passage from India: Asian Indian Immigrants in North America*. New Haven: Yale University Press, 1988.

Jeung, Russell. *Faithful Generations: Race and New Asian American Churches*. New Brunswick, NJ: Rutgers University Press, 2005.

Johnson, Jenna. "Donald Trump Calls for Total and Complete Shutdown of Muslims Entering the United States." *Washington Post*, December 7, 2015, www.washington-post.com.

Johnson, Lauri. "'My Eyes Have Been Opened': White Teachers and Racial Awareness." *Journal of Teacher Education* 53, no. 2 (2002): 153–67.

Johnson, Sylvester A. *African American Religions, 1500–2000*. New York: Cambridge University Press, 2015.

Jones, Robert P. *The End of White Christian America*. New York: Simon and Schuster, 2016.

Joshi, Khyati Y. "Because I Had a Turban." *Teaching Tolerance* 32 (2007), n.p. www.tolerance.org

Joshi, Khyati Y. "Brick by Brick: The Struggles for Religious Freedom." *Reflections.* 2016. http://reflections.yale.edu.

Joshi, Khyati Y. "Christian Privilege in Schools and Society." In *Encyclopedia of Diversity in Education* edited by James A. Banks. Thousand Oaks, CA: Sage Publications 2012.

Joshi, Khyati Y. "Patterns and Paths: Ethnic Identity Development in Second Generation Indian Americans" (PhD diss., University of Massachusetts, 2001).

Joshi, Khyati Y. "South Asian Religions in Contemporary America." In *The Oxford Handbook of Religion and Race in American History,* edited by Kathryn Gin Lum and Paul Harvey, 457–73. Oxford: Oxford University Press, 2018.

Joshi, Khyati Y. *New Roots in America's Sacred Ground: Religion, Race, and Ethnicity in Indian America.* New Brunswick: Rutgers University Press, 2006.

Jost, John T., Mahzarin R. Banaji, and Brian A. Nosek. "A Decade of System Justification Theory: Accumulated Evidence of Conscious and Unconscious Bolstering of the Status Quo." *Political Psychology* 25, no. 6 (2004): 881–919.

Jung, Moon-Ho. *Coolies and Cane: Race, Labor, and Sugar in the Age of Emancipation.* Baltimore, MD: Johns Hopkins University Press, 2006.

Kaiwar, Vasant and Sucheta Mazumdar. *Antinomies of Modernity: Essays on Race, Orient, Nation.* Durham: Duke University Press, 2003.

Kamran, Omar. "The American Muslim Dilemma: Christian Normativity, Racialization, and Anti-Muslim Backlash." Master's thesis, Texas A & M University, 2012. http://hdl.handle.net/1969.1/ETD-TAMU-2012-08-11531

Kane, Nazneen. "Frantz Fanon's Theory of Racialization: Implications for Globalization." *Human Architecture* 5 (2007): 353–61.

Kayyali, Randa A. *The Arab Americans.* Boulder, CO: Greenwood Publishing Group, 2006.

Kelleher, Lindsey. "Millburn School Board Approves Diwali, Lunar New Year as Days Off for Students." November 7, 2017. www.northjersey.com.

Kenoyer, Jonathan M. "Cultures and Societies of the Indus Tradition." In *Historical Roots in the Making of "the Aryan,"* edited by R. Thapar, 21–49. New Delhi: National Book Trust, 2006.

Kenoyer, Jonathan M. *Ancient Cities of the Indus Valley Civilization.* New York: Oxford University Press, 1998.

Killerman, Sam. "30+ Examples of Christian Privilege." *It's Pronounced Metrosexual.* Accessed October 7, 2019. https://itspronouncedmetrosexual.com/2012/05/list-of-examples-of-christian-privileg/.

Kim, Nami. "Engaging Afro/black-Orientalism: A Proposal." *Journal of Race, Ethnicity, and Religion* 1, no. 77 (2010): 1–22.

Kishi, Katayaoun. "Key Findings on the Global Rise in Religious Restrictions." Pew Research Center. June 21, 2018. www.pewresearch.org.

Kruse, Kevin. *One Nation under God: How Corporate America Invented Christian America.* New York Basic Books, 2015.

Kurien, Prema. "Being Young, Brown, and Hindu: The Identity Struggles of Second-Generation Indian Americans." *Journal of Contemporary Ethnography* 34 (2005): 434–69.

Lal, Vinay. "Sikh Kirpans in California Schools: The Social Construction of Symbols, Legal Plurism, and the Politics of Diversity." In *New Spiritual Homes: Religion and Asian Americans*, edited by David Yoo, 87–133. Honolulu: University of Hawaii and UCLA Asian American Studies Center, 1999.

Lee, Daniel B. "A Great Racial Commission: Religion and the Construction of White America." In Goldschmidt and McAlister, *Race, Nation, and Religion in the Americas*, 85–110. New York: Oxford, 2004.

Lee, Erika. *The Making of Asian America: A History*. New York: Simon and Schuster, 2015.

Lincoln, C. Eric and Lawrence H. Mamiya. *The Black Church in the African American Experience*. Durham, NC: Duke University Press, 1990.

Lincoln, C. Eric. *Race, Religion, and the Continuing American Dilemma*. New York: Hill and Wang, 1999.

Lipstadt, Deborah E. *Antisemitism: Here and Now*. New York: Schocken, 2019.

Liptak, Adam. "Court Orders Removal of Monument to Ten Commandments." *New York Times, July 2*, 2003. www.nytimes.com.

Liptak, Adam. "Muslim Woman Denied Job over Head Scarf Wins in Supreme Court." *New York Times*, June 1, 2015. www.nytimes.com.

Little India Desk. "Indian American Becomes First Turbaned Sikh to Be Inducted in Trump's Security Team." *Little India, September 14*, 2018. www.littleindia.com.

Love, Barbara J. "Developing a Liberatory Consciousness." *Readings for Diversity and Social Justice* 2 (2000): 470–74.

Love, Barbara J. "Roots, Routes and Race: Enacting Liberatory Consciousness in Schools." MSAN Student Conference, Brookline MA Minority Student Achievement Network, 2018.

Lum, Kathryn Gin and Paul Harvey. "Introduction." In *The Oxford Handbook of Religion and Race in American History*, edited by Kathryn Gin Lum and Paul Harvey, 1–24. Oxford: Oxford University Press, 2018.

Martin Luther King, Jr. Research and Education Institute. "Communism." In *King Encyclopedia*. Accessed October 7, 2019. https://kinginstitute.stanford.edu/encyclopedia/communism

Martinot, Steve. *The Machinery of Whiteness: Studies in the Structure of Racialization*. Philadelphia: Temple University Press, 2010.

Mazur, Eric. *The Americanization of Religious Minorities: Confronting the Constitutional Order*. Baltimore, MD: Johns Hopkins University Press, 1999.

McCoy, Terrance. "'Saviors of the White Race': Perpetrators of Hate Crimes See Themselves as Heroes, Researchers Say." *Washington Post*. October 31, 2018. www.washingtonpost.com.

Mehta, Gita. *Karma Cola: Marketing the Mystic East*. New York: Random House, 2012.

Menand, Louis "Morton, Agassiz, and the Origins of Scientific Racism in the United States." *The Journal of Blacks in Higher Education*, no. 34 (2001): 110–13.

Menchaca, Martha. *Recovering History, Constructing Race: The Indian, Black, and White Roots of Mexican Americans.* Joe R. and Teresa Lozano Long Series in Latin American and Latino Art and Culture. Austin: University of Texas Press, 2001.

Miller, Batya. "Enforcement of the Sunday Closing Laws on the Lower East Side, 1882–1903." *Journal of American Jewish History* 91, no. 2 (2003): 269–86.

Miller, Robert J. and Elizabeth Furse. *Native America, Discovered and Conquered: Thomas Jefferson, Lewis & Clark, and Manifest Destiny.* Boulder, CO: Greenwood Publishing Group, 2006.

Mitra, Semontee. "Merchandizing the Sacred: Commodifying Hindu Religion, Gods/Goddesses, and Festivals in the United States." *Journal of Media and Religion* 15, no. 2 (2016): 113–21.

Model, Suzanne and Lang Lin. "The Cost of Not Being Christian: Hindus, Sikhs and Muslims in Britain and Canada." *International Migration Review* 36, no. 4 (2002): 1061–92.

Moffitt, Mike. "Sikh Comedian Forced to Remove Turban at SFO, Feels 'Humiliated.'" *SF Gate*, February 24, 2016. www.sfgate.com.

Molina, Natalia. *How Race Is Made in America.* Berkeley: University of California Press, 2014.

Mueller, Max Perry. "An Evolving Mormon Church Finally Addresses a Racist Past." Religion and Politics. December 12, 2013. https://religionandpolitics.org/.

Munshi, Sherally. "Beyond the Muslim Ban." South Asian American Digital Archive. October 10, 2018. www.saada.org.

Murji, Karim and John Solomos. *Racialization: Studies in Theory and Practice.* New York: Oxford University Press, 2005.

Narayanan, Vasudha. "Sacred Land, Sacred Service: Hindu Adaptations to the American Landscape." In *A Nation of Religions: The Politics of Pluralism in Multireligious America,* edited by Stephen R. Prothero, 139–59. Chapel Hill: University of North Carolina Press, 2006.

Ng, Jennifer C., Sharon S. Lee, and Yoon K. Pak. "Contesting the Model Minority and Perpetual Foreigner Stereotypes: A Critical Review of Literature on Asian Americans in Education." *Review of Educational Research* 31, no. 1 (2007): 95–130.

Ngai, Mae M. *Impossible Subjects: Illegal Aliens and the Making of Modern America.* Politics and Society in Twentieth-Century America. Princeton, NJ: Princeton University Press, 2004.

Omi, Michael and Howard Winant. *Racial Formation in the United States: From the 1960s to the 1990s.* 2nd ed. New York: Routledge, 1994.

Paddison, Joshua. *American Heathens: Religion, Race, and Reconstruction in California.* Western Histories. Berkeley: University of California Press, 2012.

Page, Jeremy. "Sikhs Head for the Barber and Turn Their Backs on Tradition: Western Intolerance of Religious Symbols and a Series of Street Attacks Are Prompting Young Men to Shed Their Hair and Turbans." Times Online. November 24, 2006. www.timesonline.co.uk

Painter, Nell Irvin. *The History of White People*. New York: Norton, 2010.

Parekh, Parthiv N. "A Faith Driven Governor in a Secular Society." *Khabar* magazine. *January* 2004. www.khabar.com.

Park, Jerry Z., and James C. Davidson. "Rendered Invisible: Decentering the White American Religious Experience." In *Religion Is Raced: Understanding American Religion in the Twenty-First Century*, edited by Grace Yukich and Penny Edgell. New York: NYU Press. Forthcoming 2020.

Patel, Eboo. *Intersectionality in Action: A Guide for Faculty and Campus Leaders for Creating Inclusive Classrooms and Institutions*. Sterling, VA: Stylus Publishing, 2016.

Pew Research Center. "America's Changing Religious Landscape." Pew Research Center: Religion and Public Life. May 12, 2015. www.pewforum.org.

Pew Research Center. "In U.S., Decline of Christianity Continues at Rapid Pace: An Update on America's Changing Religious Landscape" October 17, 2019. www.pewforum.org.

Pew Research Center. "Modern Immigration Wave Brings 59 Million to US, Driving Population Growth and Change through 2065." September 28, 2015. www.pewresearch.org.

Pew Research Center. "Origins of the US Immigrant Population, 1960–2017." Pew Research Center Hispanic Trends. June 3, 2019. www.pewhispanic.org.

Pew Research Center. "Political Polarization in the American Public." Pew Research Center: US Politics & Policy. June 12, 2014. www.people-press.org.

Pharr, Suzanne. *Homophobia: A Weapon of Sexism*. Inverness, CA: Chardon Press, 1988.

Prashad, Vijay. *The Karma of Brown Folk*. Minneapolis: University of Minnesota, 2000.

Prewitt, Kenneth. "The Census Counts, the Census Classifies." In *Not Just Black and White: Historical and Contemporary Perspectives on Immigration, Race, and Ethnicity in the United States*, edited by Nancy Foner and George M. Fredrickson, 145–64. New York: Russell Sage Foundation, 2004.

Public Religion Research Institute. "PRRI Releases Largest Survey of American Religious and Denominational Identity Ever Conducted." Cision PR Newswire. September 6, 2017. www.prnewswire.com.

Purkayastha, Bandana. *Negotiating Ethnicity: Second-Generation South Asian Americans Traverse a Transnational World*. New Brunswick, NJ: Rutgers University Press, 2005.

Putnam, Robert D., and David E. Campbell. *American Grace: How Religion Divides and Unites Us*. New York: Simon and Schuster, 2012.

Raboteau, Albert J. *Slave Religion: The "Invisible Institution" in the Antebellum South*. New York: Oxford University Press, 2004.

Rajghatta, Chidanand. "Christian Activists Disrupt Hindu Prayer in US Senate." *Times of India*, July 13, 2007. https://timesofindia.indiatimes.com.

Rana, Junaid. *Terrifying Muslims: Race and Labor in the South Asian Diaspora*. Durham, NC: Duke University Press, 2011.

Ravitch, Frank S. *School Prayer and Discrimination: The Civil Rights of Religious Minorities and Dissenters*. Boston: Northeastern University Press, 2001.

Reeve, W. Paul. *Religion of a Different Color: Race and the Mormon Struggle for Whiteness*. New York: Oxford University Press, 2017.

Reimer, Sam and Jerry Z. Park. "Tolerant (in) Civility? A Longitudinal Analysis of White Conservative Protestants' Willingness to Grant Civil Liberties." *Journal for the Scientific Study of Religion* 40, no. 4 (2001): 735–45.

Resnick, Brian "White Fear of Demographic Change Is a Powerful Psychological Force." *Vox*, January 28, 2017. www.vox.com.

Resnick, Brian. "All Muslims Are Often Blamed for Single Acts Of Terror; Psychology Explains How Stop It." *Vox*, November 30, 2017. www.vox.com.

Robertson, Campbell, Christopher Mele, and Sabrina Tavernise. "11 Killed in Synagogue Massacre; Suspect Charged with 29 Counts." *New York Times*, October 27, 2018. www.nytimes.com.

Roediger, David R. *Colored White: Transcending the Racial Past*. Berkeley: University of California Press, 2002.

Roediger, David R. *The Wages of Whiteness: Race and the Making of the American Working Class*. The Haymarket Series. Rev. ed. New York: Verso, 1999.

Rogoff, Leonard. "Is the Jew White? The Racial Place of the Southern Jew," *American Jewish History* 85, no. 3 (1997): 195–230.

Rosentiel, Tom. "How many Sikhs in the US." August 6, 2012. www.pewforum.org.

Said, Edward. *Orientalism*. New York: Vintage Books, 1978.

Sandhu, Sabeen. "Instant Karma: The Commercialization of Asian Indian Culture." In *Asian American Youth: Culture, Identity, and Ethnicity*, edited by Jennifer Lee and Min Zhou, 131–41. New York: Routledge, 2004.

Sands, Kathleen. "Territory, Wilderness, Property, and Reservation: Land and Religion in Native American Supreme Court Cases." *American Indian Law Review* (2011): 253–320.

Scaminaci, James. "PRRI Survey: Religion and Race Underlie Tea Party Movement Beliefs." October 14, 2010. http://politicalchili.com.

Schlosser, L. Z. "Christian Privilege: Breaking a Sacred Taboo." *Journal of Multicultural Counseling and Development* 31, no. 1 (2003): 44–51.

Schrader, Adam. "Long Island Bar Turns Away Stony Brook Graduate Wearing Turban." *New York Post*, May 15, 2019. www.nypost.com

Selod, Saher. "Citizenship Denied: The Racialization of Muslim American Men and Women Post-9/11." *Critical Sociology* 41, no. 1 (2014): 77–95.

Sensoy, Özlem and Robin DiAngelo. *Is Everyone Really Equal?: An Introduction to Key Concepts in Social Justice Education*. New York: Teachers College Press, 2015.

Serwer, Adam. "The Terrorism That Doesn't Spark a Panic." *Atlantic*, January 28, 2019. www.theatlantic.com.

Shaheen, Jack G. *Reel Bad Arabs: How Hollywood Vilifies a People*. New York: Olive Branch Press, 2001.

Shaheen, Jack G. *The TV Arab*. Bowling Green, OH: Bowling Green State University Popular Press, 1984.

Sian, Katy Pal. "Gurdwaras, Guns and Grudge in 'Post-Racial' America." *Sikh Formations* 8, no. 3 (2012): 293–97.

Sikh American Legal Defense and Education Fund. "Virginia Restaurant Apologizes to Sikh American for Wrongfully Denying Entry to Restaurant Because of Turban." *SALDEF*, December 4, 2006. www.saldef.org.

Singh, Jaideep. "A New American Apartheid: Racialized, Religious Minorities in the Post-9/11 Era." *Sikh Formations* 9, no. 2 (2013): 115–44.

Singh, Jaideep. "American Apartheid for the New Millennium: The Racialization and Repression of Asian American Religious Minorities." In *Envisioning Religion, Race and Asian Americans*, edited by David Yoo and Khyati Y. Joshi. Honolulu University of Hawai'l Press, 2020.

Singh, Jaideep. "The Racialization of Minoritized Religious Identity: Constructing Sacred Sites at the Intersection of White and Christian Supremacy." In *Revealing the Sacred in Asian and Pacific America*, edited by Jane Naomi Iwamura and Paul Spickard, 87–106. New York: Routledge, 2003.

Smith, Andrea. "Heteropatriarchy and the Three Pillars of White Supremacy: Rethinking Women of Color Organizing." *Transformations: Feminist Pathways to Global Change* 264 (2015): 66–73.

Smith, Andrea. "Indigeneity, Settler Colonialism, White Supremacy." In *Racial Formation in the Twenty-First Century*, edited by Daniel Martinez HoSang, 66–90: Berkeley: University of California Press, 2012.

Snow, Jennifer. "The Civilization of White Men: The Race of the Hindu in *United States v. Bhagat Singh Thind*." In Goldschmidt and McAlister, *Race, Nation, and Religion in the Americas*, 259–81.

Snow, Jennifer. *Protestant Missionaries, Asian Immigrants, and Ideologies of Race in America, 1850–1924*. New York: Routledge, 2006.

Spencer, Hawes and Sheryl Gay Stolberg. "White Nationalists March on University of Virginia." *New York Times,* August 11, 2017, www.nytimes.com.

Spring, Joel. *Deculturalization and the Struggle for Equality: A Brief History of the Education of Dominated Cultures in the United States*. 4th ed. Boston: McGraw Hill, 2006.

Stewart, Dafina Lazarus and Adele Lozano. "Difficult Dialogues at the Intersections of Race, Culture, and Religion." *New Directions for Student Services*, no. 125 (Spring 2009): 23–31.

Stone, Michael. "Pittsburgh Synagogue Shooter Identified as Christian Nationalist Robert Bowers." Progressive Secular Humanist. October 27, 2018. www.patheos.com

Sue, Derald Wing. *Microaggressions in Everyday Life: Race, Gender, and Sexual Orientation*. New York: John Wiley & Sons, 2010.

Sue, Derald Wing. *Race Talk and the Conspiracy of Silence: Understanding and Facilitating Difficult Dialogues on Race*. New York: John Wiley & Sons, 2016.

Suh, Sharon A. *Silver Screen Buddha: Buddhism in Asian and Western Film*. New York: Bloomsbury Publishing, 2015.

Takaki, Ronald. *A Different Mirror: A History of Multicultural America.* Rev. ed. Boston: Little, Brown, 2011.

Takaki, Ronald. *Strangers from a Different Shore: A History of Asians in America.* Rev. ed. Boston: Little Brown, 1998.

Talking Points Memo. "Poll: 68% of Americans Oppose 'Ground Zero Mosque'." https://talkingpointsmemo.com.

Tochluk, Shelly. "'But I Just Don't See It!': Making White Superiority Visible." *Understanding and Dismantling Privilege* 3, no. 1 (2013): 1–21.

Trautmann, Thomas R. "Does India Have History? Does History Have India?" *Comparative Studies in Society and History* 54, no. 1 (2012): 174–205.

Trautmann, Thomas R. *Aryans and British India.* Berkeley University of California Press, 1997.

Tuan, Mia. *Forever Foreigners or Honorary Whites?: The Asian Ethnic Experience Today.* New Brunswick, NJ: Rutgers University Press, 2001.

US Census Bureau. "Quickfacts: United States, Population Estimate July 1, 2018." www.census.gov.

Vogel, Kenneth P. "Mosque Debate Strains Tea Party, GOP." Politico, August 18, 2010. www.politico.com.

Volpp, Leti. "The Citizen and the Terrorist." *UCLA Law Review* 49 (2002): 1575–99.

Wenger, Tisa. *Religious Freedom: The Contested History of an American Ideal.* Chapel Hill: University of North Carolina Press, 2017.

Williams, Duncan Ryûken *American Sutra: Buddhist and the Japanese American Fight for Religious Freedom in World War II.* Cambridge, MA: Harvard University Press, 2019.

Wills, David W. *Christianity in the United States: A Historical Survey and Interpretation.* Notre Dame, IN: University of Notre Dame Press, 2005.

Wishon, Jennifer. "A Shifting America with a New Minority." CBN News. August 30, 2016. www1.cbn.com.

Wong, Janelle S. *Immigrants, Evangelicals, and Politics in an Era of Demographic Change.* New York: Russell Sage Foundation, 2018.

Yancey, George. "Yes Academic Bias Is a Problem and We Need to Address It: A Response to Larregue." *The American Sociologist* 49, no. 2 (2018): 336–43.

Yen, Hope. "Rise of Latino Population Blurs US Racial Lines." Associated Press. March 17, 2013. www.apnews.com.

Yoo, David, ed. "Racial Spirits: Religion and Race in Asian American Communities." Special issue, *Amerasia Journal* 22, no. 1 (1996).

Yoo, David. "For Those Who Have Eyes to See: Religious Sightings in Asian America." *Amerasia* 22, no. 1 (1996): xiii–xxii.

Yoo, David. *New Spiritual Homes: Religion and Asian Americans.* Honolulu: University of Hawaii and UCLA Asian American Studies Center, 1999.

Zauzmer, Julie. "The Alleged Synagogue Shooter was a Churchgoer Who Talked Christian Theology, Raising Tough Questions for Evangelical Pastors." Washington Post, May 1, 2019. www.washingtonpost.com.

Index

About the Author

Khyati Y. Joshi is Professor in the School of Education at Fairleigh Dickenson University. She is the author of *New Roots in America's Sacred Ground: Religion, Race and Ethnicity* in Indian America (Rutgers, 2006) and a co-editor of *Teaching for Diversity and Social Justice*, 3rd edition (Routledge, 2016). She can be reached at www .Khyatijoshi.com and on Twitter @ProfKJozhi.